C000201847

The Last Roman

Also by Mark Peel and published by André Deutsch

Cricketing Falstaff: A Biography of Colin Milburn

The Last Roman

a biography of Colin Cowdrey

MARK PEEL

André Deutsch

First published in Great Britain in 1999 by
André Deutsch Limited
76 Dean Street
London W1V 5HA

www.vci.co.uk

Copyright © Mark Peel 1999

The right of Mark Peel to be identified as author of this book
has been asserted by him in accordance with the Copyright,
Designs and Patents Act 1988

A catalogue record for this book is available from the British Library

ISBN 0 233 99461 0

All rights reserved. This book is sold subject to the condition that it may not be
reproduced, stored in a retrieval system or transmitted in any form or by any
means, electronic, mechanical, photocopying, recording or otherwise, without
the publisher's prior consent

Typeset by Derek Doyle & Associates
Mold, Flintshire
Printed and bound in Great Britain by
MPG Books Ltd, Bodmin, Cornwall

Contents

Acknowledgements

Although this isn't an authorized biography, I am most grateful for the help that I have received from Lord Cowdrey and his son Christopher. They were able to provide me with a number of insights, which otherwise would not have come my way. I would also like to thank the following, who have put their recollections of Lord Cowdrey at my disposal:

Keith Andrew, Alex Bannister, Jack Bannister, F. C. Bernardes, Brian Booth, Ben Brocklehurst, Michael Bushby, David Clark, Greg Chappell, Giles Cheatle, Ian Craig, Alan Davidson, Ted Dexter, Hubert Doggart, John Dye, Tom Graveney, Tony Greig, Robin Hobbs, Dr Gerald Howat, Colin Ingleby-Mackenzie, Doug Insole, Richard Jefferson, Simon Langdale, David Larter, Alan Lee, The Rt Hon John Major MP, Robin Marlar, Christopher Martin-Jenkins, Michael Melluish, Arthur Morris, John Murray, Paul Normand, Peter Parfitt, Pat Pocock, Tony Pocock, Peter Richardson, Fred Rumsey, The Rt Rev Lord Runcie, The Lord Sheppard of Liverpool, Dennis Silk, Jack Simmons, Billy Slayter, Jonathan Smith, M. J. K. Smith, Philip Snow, Chris Stone, E. W. Swanton, Fred Titmus, Alan Turner, Derek Ufton, Derek Underwood, Bob White, Ian Wooldridge, Bob Woolmer, John Woodcock and Jim Woodhouse.

I should also like to extend my thanks to the Curator of the MCC Library at Lord's, Stephen Green, and his assistants for their help, to Jeff Hancock, the Surrey CCC librarian, to David Studham, Alf Batchelder, Ray Webster and the staff at the Melbourne Cricket Club Library, the staff at the National Library of Scotland in Edinburgh and to *The Times* for the use of their newspaper library.

In addition, I am greatly indebted to Mike Denness, David Kemp, Patrick Shervington, Colonel John Stephenson and Ivo Tennant for all their advice and reminiscences on particular parts of Cowdrey's career, to Paul Dyson for the statistical appendix and to Sandra Edwards for typing the whole text with immaculate care. Finally, a special word of gratitude to Tim Forrester, managing director of André Deutsch Ltd and to Louise Dixon, editorial director, for all their help and support throughout this project.

Mark Peel
Edinburgh, 1999

INTRODUCTION

From the moment he was endowed with the game's most famous initials, Colin Cowdrey almost seemed destined to lead a charmed life at the heart of English cricket. Born into a sports-loving family, the young Cowdrey's skills were so fervently nurtured by his father in India, and his prep school headmaster in Surrey, that by the time he entered Tonbridge school he was the boy David ready to tame the Philistines.

Walking straight into the school XI, he crowned a phenomenal first term not only by reputedly becoming the youngest cricketer ever to appear at Lord's, but also by winning the annual tussle against Clifton with a towering all-round performance. After five years of sporting excellence, Cowdrey left Tonbridge with every honour to travel a similar road at Oxford. He acquitted himself so assuredly in the first-class game that, even in his leaner moments, his star always shone through. In 1954 the selectors, ignoring his youthful inexperience, picked him for Australia, and he repaid their faith with several match-winning innings, the pick of which was an acclaimed maiden century in Melbourne. So well did he play that even the most trenchant critic searched his dictionary for superlatives.

Fresh from an Ashes triumph at twenty-two, Cowdrey had catapulted to fame, and now, for the next two decades, he was rarely out of the public eye as one of England's leading batsmen. In 1957 he featured in a record-breaking partnership with Peter May at Edgbaston, and in the Caribbean nearly three years later his inspired batting against extreme pace helped his country to victory. Technically close to perfection, Cowdrey's classical elegance on the field won as much admiration as his gracious deportment off it. 'I

1

enjoyed Lord's,' wrote George Lyttleton to Rupert Hart-Davis on 27 June 1957. 'Weekes was good, so was Cowdrey. I passed him and Bailey as they went in on Friday morning. I murmured Good Luck! Cowdrey said "Thank you Sir", Bailey said nothing. In five balls Bailey was out and in five hours Cowdrey had made 152. The god of cricket likes good manners.'

In 1967 it was this image which helped him to regain the England captaincy after Brian Close, his predecessor, had fallen out with the game's authorities for unacceptable gamesmanship in a crucial county match. For their trip to West Indies, England travelled very much as underdogs, but Cowdrey triumphed against all expectation, and he gained further laurels the following summer with a century in his hundredth Test – appropriately against Australia. In 1970 he led Kent to the championship in their centenary year, and in 1973 he reached another personal milestone when he joined the select few to score a hundred centuries. Not yet finished, he became the pride of the nation in December 1974 as he gamely left his fireside to answer an emergency summons from Australia to take on the might of Dennis Lillee and Jeff Thomson in his forty-second year. There, within days of his arrival, he was thrust into the heat of battle and performed heroically in a dying cause. Months later he bowed out with a sublime century for Kent against the 'old enemy', before seeing his legacy live on in the form of his sons Christopher and Graham.

In time, he was back establishing for himself a new career in cricketing administration. So alluring was the Cowdrey name, and so accommodating was his support for the prevailing ethos, that his rise through the corridors of power was nearly as effortless as anything he had accomplished on the field. In 1986 he was accorded the supreme honour of being elected MCC president in the club's bicentenary year, and in 1989 the first elected chairman of the newly reconstituted International Cricket Council. During his four-year tenure, substantial achievements were registered, prominent among which was the return of the new South Africa from cricketing exile. In recognition of his contribution to the game he was awarded a knighthood in 1991 from a cricket-loving Prime Minister whose outlook broadly resembled his own. When that same Prime Minister nominated him for a life peerage in the Queen's Birthday Honours List in 1997, the wheel had come full circle.

From a distance, this brief trawl through Cowdrey's life looks like one long flowing stream of tranquillity. On closer assessment, however, there were a number of swirls and rapids to negotiate, particularly with regard to the England captaincy. Given Cowdrey's background as the gentleman amateur, and his reputation as one of England's finest cricketers, it might readily be assumed that the mantle of leadership would fall easily onto his shoulders. He enjoyed it as an intellectual challenge and for the prestige which went with it, but not for its hard, unpopular choices.

Cowdrey's sensitivity to criticism can be traced back to his formative years when, as an only child separated from his parents for long periods, he always lived in the debt of others. At school he was subjected to the mercy of a series of authoritarian masters whose word was indisputably law, in particular his prep school headmaster, Charles Walford, whom Cowdrey described as the most ruthless man he ever met. Starved of affection and encouragement at this school, he entered Tonbridge a diffident, retiring youth, uneasy with the great expectations soon to be placed upon him. Despite continuing his meteoric rise Cowdrey never acquired the accruing confidence, so that when the captaincy of Kent and England came his way he was *primus inter pares* as opposed to *optimus maximus*. Thrust into the national spotlight in 1959 as Peter May's deputy, while his close friend recovered from illness, his tenure extended on and off for two years without any suggested stay of permanence.

Living continuously in May's shadow inhibited him from following Polonius's advice to Laertes of being true to himself, and after a disappointing defeat against Australia at Lord's in 1961 he was quietly relieved of his duties. With May's retirement from Test cricket at the end of that summer Cowdrey could still have expected to be his successor. Family commitments, however, ruled him out of the tour to India and Pakistan and Ted Dexter took over instead. The results were not spectacular, leaving Cowdrey a serious contender for the top position on the tour to Australia the following winter, until he contracted kidney trouble at a vital moment. Once again, he had to be content with the vice-captaincy.

Six months later his chance to lead England on tour seemed finally to have arrived when Dexter declared his unavailability for India. Cowdrey was appointed, but then was forced to withdraw because of a serious fracture to his elbow. His replacement, M. J. K. Smith, rose to the challenge and subsequently led England in South Africa and Australia. By the time he gave way to Cowdrey in 1966, the opponents were the all-conquering West Indians with Gary Sobers in full cry. Exposed to this explosive force, Cowdrey's response was considered to be too tepid, and he was unceremoniously ditched after three matches. Bruised by the experience, he retired to the shadows only to be called back in dramatic circumstances the next year. Following his Caribbean triumph, when his leadership had assumed an unprecedented authority, he seemed destined to crown a distinguished career with a lengthy run as captain, culminating with the tour to Australia in 1970-71. Alas, what the gods give they as soon take away. A ruptured Achilles tendon in May 1969 not only ruled him out for the summer, it enabled Ray Illingworth, his replacement, to display his aptitude for leadership and the selectors stuck with him for Australia. Devastated by this rebuff, Cowdrey found little consolation in the vice-captaincy and, now under a leader with whom he had little in common, he endured the unhappiest few months of his career.

To be always the bridesmaid and never the bride in Australia suggests that fate dealt him a particularly rough hand, as injury or illness conspired to prevent him from attaining his ultimate ambition. Some critics remained unconvinced. Surveying this litany of setbacks in his book on the England captains, Alan Gibson wondered whether there were not too many to be mere coincidence and that 'the fault, dear Brutus, lies not in our stars but in ourselves that we are underlings'.

Certainly the charge of indecisiveness continued to be laid at Cowdrey's door as he wrestled with the contentious issues in the combustible world of cricketing politics, where not every administrator seemed to share his passion for the game. Yet alongside his good-natured tolerance and careworn sensitivity there lurked a streak of dogged resolution which emanated from his childhood and was rigorously reinforced by his great hero, Len Hutton, a

Yorkshireman to his bootlaces. It has enabled him to withstand the vicissitudes of leadership, a testing family life and serious ill health as much as lethal bouncers from the world's best. It has also enabled him, as the last great amateur, to drift with the professional tide in order to cope with the massive changes in the game during his life-time. What it has failed to do is satisfy that craving for peace which, according to his son Christopher, he needs but has never found, the consequence doubtless of being a very private man performing on a very public stage.

1

'He Shall Be Great'

Colin Cowdrey was born on 24 December 1932 into a family with cricket in its blood. On the small ground behind his grandfather's house at Sanderstead in Surrey, they fielded their own eleven, down to Aunt Mildred as scorer, to take on allcomers. Grandfather Cowdrey was first and foremost a tennis player, but his love of cricket was great enough to instil similar sentiments into his son, Ernest. He followed his father to Whitgift School in Croydon, winning a place in the first XI, aged fourteen, and his considerable promise as an all-rounder encouraged him to contemplate a career in the game. But although Ernest played for Surrey second XI, and Berkshire in the Minor Counties championship, his father saw that he lacked the necessary class to fulfil his great ambition. He persuaded him to work in the City instead, as a prelude to entering the reputable family paper-manufacturing firm of John Dickinson. Ernest went along with this advice at first, but the monotony of it all soon frustrated him and, in search of something more adventurous, he resolved to head for India, where he had spent some of his child- hood, to become a tea-planter. There he found his niche and, entranced by the colonial life, he had five contented years before returning in 1929 to marry his sweetheart, Molly Taylor. Her father had looked after a farm in Beddington Park in Surrey, several miles from the centre of Croydon, and it was here on this enchanting ground that she had met Ernest when he had played for Beddington. Her prowess at hockey and tennis, coupled with a more than passing interest in cricket, made her a suitable addition to the Cowdrey clan. After their wedding in Beddington Church, she accompanied Ernest back to India and three years later their only child, Colin, was born at Ootacamund, high up in the Nilgiri Hills one hundred miles to the north of Bangalore. Ernest, with his wife's blessing, promptly celebrated by investing him with the initials of the world's most famous cricket club and putting his name down for membership.

Surrounded by a breathtaking vista of rolling tea estates, and blessed with long hours of sunshine, the Cowdrey lifestyle in the hills had all the trappings of a simple colonial existence. While Colin's mother, with her old-fashioned sense of duty, devoted her time to looking after the family, Ernest inculcated in his son a love of sport. On the lawn next to their bungalow home he built a miniature golf course, where he and Colin practised in the morning before he went to work. When he returned in the evening, attention switched to the tennis court where cricket was the overriding priority. Still a good enough player to get 48 for a European XI against MCC at Madras during their 1926–27 tour to India, Ernest was determined that Colin should learn the rudiments of the game from his earliest years. Consequently, an exacting coaching schedule was devised. While his father was managing the 2,000-acre estate during the day, Colin was entrusted to the care of the servants, one of whom, Krishnan, a genial teenager who always referred to him as 'Dear Little Master', played with him for hours.

Then, amidst the lengthening shadows, Ernest took over, coaching him with a precision and intensity which left no detail untouched. The stance was adjusted, the grip corrected and the bat would be kept in good shape. When Colin used to remonstrate about the need to oil his bat, saying he would rather be riding his bicycle, he was told that a real cricketer would always do this. By the age of five his education had taken another step forward when the automatic swipe to leg was outlawed from his repertoire of strokes. To diminish the temptation of playing in this vicinity, a rule was devised whereby he immediately had to forfeit his innings and endure a long bowl to his father as an act of contrition. Many an evening he would go to bed thinking how he could stay in at all costs.

Already, Colin's life in sport was being shaped. Sheltered from the cares of the outside world and closeted in a warm, caring home, he spent an idyllic first five years before England beckoned. On the journey home in April 1938, Colin vividly recalled the night at Port Said when his excited father hauled him out of his cabin and rushed him up to the deck. There they watched the ship carrying Don Bradman's Australian team to England glide gently past them in the dusk. That this rather remote encounter with cricket's greatest maestro filled the young Cowdrey with as real a sense of awe as his father helps to illustrate the deep bond the game had created between them. While England that summer fretted about Hitler's intentions in Europe as war loomed ever closer, Ernest found solace watching the Tests, including Len Hutton's historic 364 at The Oval, whenever he wasn't playing himself.

Before leaving India he and Molly had wrestled with the dilemma of where to educate Colin. The sacrifice of being separated from their only child for an interminable length of time was balanced by Ernest's desire to give him both a thorough all-round education and the best possible environment for his sport to flourish. In the end the latter held sway and Homefield House, Sutton, a prep school with a proud cricketing tradition, and close to his grandmother's house, was chosen. Colin spent some time there in the summer term of 1938 to play cricket before beginning there officially as a day boy in September. His parents saw him settle in and then one day, as Cowdrey recalls in his autobiography, MCC, *The Autobiography of a Cricketer*, they were gone. 'They took me to school one morning and left me there. They never made the ceremony of saying "Goodbye", but when I came out it was my grandmother who returned. She said nothing. When I eventually asked where my mother and father were she said, 'Oh, they've gone to work'. This was September 1938 and I next saw them in December 1945.'

The war prolonged what was to have been a four-year separation to over seven years. Brought up in a sober middle-class household where emotions were rarely displayed, Cowdrey gave little thought to their parting. It was only many years later, when they were reunited, that he harboured a sense of resentment for their neglect of him. He later recalled his sense of surprise at how small they were when they returned, strangers to a boy who had become immersed in his own company. It needed a period of painful readjustment, aided by trips to the Chelsea football ground with his father to imbibe the post-war euphoria of mass gatherings, before the former rapport was re-established. Thereafter he continued to see his parents intermittently through his teenage years, but despite long periods of separation, Cowdrey knew they always had his interests at heart. Many years later he reflected on how he owed them everything.

While his parents were in India, Cowdrey had been looked after by his maternal grandmother and his unmarried uncle, John Taylor, himself a keen cricketer. Among her many acts of devotional care, his grandmother read to him in bed and taught him how to work. Alas she became seriously ill in May 1942, forcing him to become a weekly boarder at Homefield, an experience he didn't enjoy. When he returned for the weekends, she talked endlessly to him about heroes such as Scott of the Antarctic, implanting in him an admiration for great men and women which has never receded. Unaware of how gravely ill she was, he was devastated when he was informed by John Taylor in December 1942 on a pre-Christmas shopping trip that 'Granny's gone to heaven'. He now divided his time between John Taylor and another uncle, Newton Thirlby, on his farm in the Leicestershire countryside, where he revelled in his own company, particularly when in possession of a ball. All these relations did their best to help the young Colin compensate for the years without his parents. Their influence on his development was secondary, however, in comparison to the gargantuan figure of Charles Walford, the headmaster of Homefield.

As befitted so many Victorian-style headmasters, this intimidating bachelor and accomplished sportsman was a Spartan autocrat who answered to no one in the way he ran his school, considered one of the best in the area. An addict of cold showers and early morning runs, Walford was a stern disciplinarian who constantly resorted to the cane to root out the flaws of childhood. Idleness, bad manners and disobedience were considered particularly heinous offences in a moral code which, however rigid it might appear today, left boys with a clear sense of right and wrong. Apart from his insistence on rigorous standards in the classroom, Walford expected something similar in sport. Taking charge of all football and cricket practice himself, to the extent of supervising the preparation of the wicket by the pupils, he was a hard taskmaster, quick to find fault. The better boys in particular felt the full force of his tongue, but it was under his tyrannical tuition, as Cowdrey put it, that he began to make giant strides.

Originally a wicket-keeper who could bat, Cowdrey, aged seven in an under-eleven game, boosted his standing in the school with a carefully compiled century. The animated cheers which greeted this landmark caused him to raise his bat in appreciation, before gamely giving his wicket away. He returned a conquering hero, only to be cast into deep gloom a few minutes later when a double check on his score revealed that it was in fact only 94. Amidst the tears of frustration, the more human side of Walford's character shone through. Not present to witness the innings, he wrote, unknown to Cowdrey, to Jack Hobbs, the doyen of English cricket who then owned a sports business in Fleet Street, relating the turn of events. Three weeks later a charming letter in the great man's handwriting arrived out of the blue with a size four bat, then worth twenty-five shillings. The letter read:

July 19th 1940

Dear Master Cowdrey,
I have just heard about your wonderful performance of scoring 94 not out out of a total of 135. Please accept my heartiest congratulations.

It is a pity you could get nobody to stay long enough to get your hundred, but I hear you are very keen on the game and feel sure you will score many centuries in the years to come.

I shall watch your career with interest and I wish you the very best of health and fortune.

Yours sincerely,
J. B. Hobbs

The letter, which was read out at the school's Speech Day and became a prized possession of Cowdrey's thereafter, was yet another little landmark in his utter fixation with the game.

Shortly after this episode, Cowdrey's education was interrupted by the onset of war. As Britain prepared herself to face the full might of the German Luftwaffe alone in September 1940, his grandmother, in the interests of safety, decided to remove him from Sutton and Homefield, with their close proximity to London, to the safer climes of Bognor. Her understandable caution found no sympathy from Walford, who saw it as a slur on his professionalism. When Cowdrey returned in May 1942 after eighteen months of gentle nurturing in the hands of the Rev. M. P. Gale, the headmaster, and his wife at their school, Holyrood House, his Homefield homecoming was less than charitable. After an embarrassing work-out in the nets he was met by Walford's frosty response: 'What have they been doing to your cricket down at Bognor?' This humiliating put-down, and his inability to praise, all helped douse the individual sparkle of his protégé, leaving Cowdrey desperately short of confidence. It was an impediment which stalked him thereafter. Only twice did Walford express any enthusiasm towards Cowdrey, who was his favourite pupil. First, when he discovered him bowling a googly in the nets, and, secondly, when some deft on-side shots in a game he was umpiring led him to remark to a colleague, supposedly out of earshot, 'You're watching an England batsman in the making.'

By Cowdrey's last summer term at Homefield, which brought him two centuries and two hat-tricks, there wasn't one shot in the coaching manual which was beyond his understanding. In addition, the basic technical attributes of a side-on stance, a straight bat and the top hand in control had all been learnt and assimilated. His bowling was even better, given his mastery of the googly as well as the leg-break, skills which had been learnt under the tuition of Ken Harman, the groundsman at the Sutton club, where Cowdrey would spend the better part of his leisure time. When he visited the celebrated Sandham-Gover Cricket School in south London in the holiday before going to Tonbridge, he captivated his coaches with an uninhibited demonstration of his talent. So impressed were they that Gover wrote to Ewart Astill, the coach at Tonbridge, advising him to keep an eye on 'that young Cowdrey'.

But for a small quirk of fate the cricketing feats of the Cowdrey family would have been the preserve of Marlborough rather than Tonbridge. A friend of Ernest's in India, John Maples, had been a schoolmaster there, and the prospect of Colin playing for Marlborough against Rugby at Lord's had excited him. He travelled down to Wiltshire one cheerless day in February 1946 full of expectation but the headmaster's refusal to take Colin for the summer term because of lack of vacancies, before he and his wife returned to India, left him feeling depressed when he arrived home that evening. His wife then raised the possibility of Tonbridge and persuaded him to telephone the school. The reaction was positive, and before he knew what had hit him he was down there the next day. The interview went well, and once Colin had passed the common entrance examination he was to become part of a new house of twenty-one in a school with 400 years of history behind it.

Founded in 1553 by Sir Andrew Judd, a member of the Skinners Company, Tonbridge expanded during the nineteenth century to become one of the nation's leading schools, with a strong local following and close links with the City. In an era where sport still played a vital part in shaping the ethos of the place, Cowdrey found a quick way to ascend the school's cricket hierarchy without incurring the jealousy of his peers. Unknown to him, Ewart Astill, the ex-Leicestershire cricketer, who ironically had bowled his father at Madras in 1926-7, had been well acquainted with his potential and sought him out on his first day to join the XI at net practice. The unfamiliar sight of a young-looking thirteen-year-old in his grey flannels, bowling to the bloods in all their finery, was too much for one master, unaware of Astill's initiative. He berated the young Cowdrey for breaching the strict dress code, and, even though Astill intervened on his behalf, Cowdrey sneaked away in embarrassment.

Cowdrey's anxiety continued two days later, on the Monday morning, when he could not find his name in any of the cricket teams placed on the school notice board. Because of Gover's letter he had leapfrogged the junior teams and won a place in the Colts. The fact that the other boys began to discuss his spectacular promotion added to the pressure on him to succeed. He duly responded with a duck and no wickets, but won a reprieve with four wickets against Judd School in a Colts match. His next break was a two-innings trial game to sort out the best twenty-two players in the entire school. At the end of it he had taken seventeen wickets, dismissing most of the likely XI twice. A conference involving the headmaster and Cowdrey's housemaster was necessary to authorise a thirteen-year-old playing in the first XI. He was reminded of the need to keep a level head but, given his natural diffidence, there was little problem on this score. David Kemp, a fellow member of the XI, has recollections of him almost apologising to his seniors as he bamboozled them in the nets with his leg-breaks, and in any case a team not suffused with talent could hardly afford to spurn such riches.

His selection nevertheless was big news and a large crowd turned up at the Head, the Tonbridge first XI ground, to see how he fared against the Free Foresters, whose side included G.O.B. (Gubby) Allen, the former England captain and later a leading selector. Batting at no. 10, Cowdrey disappointed his following by getting out second ball, and ended up without taking a wicket. His luck, however, was to change three days later against Malvern when he looked the part, reaching double figures and taking four for 36. Further profitable returns of five for 36 against Bedford and four for 25 against Lancing cemented his place in the team, and for the rest of the season he took a hatful of wickets. The incongruous sight of a small, roly-poly figure with a cherubic face and small hands luring his elders to their doom with his flighted leg-breaks became increasingly commonplace. Michael Bushby, then a fourteen-year-old in the Dulwich team, recalls his captain's instructions to get either right forward or right back to Cowdrey. The first ball he went back and was flummoxed. The second he went forward and was stumped by several yards, one of four Dulwich men among the fifteen to be dismissed by Cowdrey in this fashion that season. He finished his first summer term with thirty-six wickets at 14 apiece, his best performance being nine for 38 against Cranbrook, which included a hat-trick.

His batting, although less spectacular at this stage, was also beginning to win him admirers. 'Cowdrey alone seemed to treat good bowling as it should be by hitting it properly', reported the school magazine after his 31 against MCC at no. 9. His reward was a gradual promotion up the order to no. 3, and a solid 49 against the Old Tonbridgians ensured that he made this position his own for the two-day match against Clifton at Lord's. The importance of the occasion rested heavily upon Cowdrey and he recalls feeling sick as he walked

13

out to bat on the first morning, a mere single the summit of his ambitions. His horizons remained limited during the early stages when he surprised himself by staying in, but gradually those years of dedicated practice under his father's and Walford's tutelage began to pay off handsomely. He finished with the top score of 75. 'Youthful fantasies are often uncertain quantities', wrote R. B. Vincent in *The Times*, 'but it would surely seem that in Colin Cowdrey Tonbridge have produced a boy now only thirteen-and-a-half years old of quite exceptional promise. Already he has the footwork and wrists of a gifted batsman.' He followed this up with three wickets for 58, and 44 in the second innings, before Clifton were set 118 to win. Much would depend on whether their opening batsman, T. S. Penny, would be back at Lord's in time after having been summoned north by his mother to attend his dying father, only to discover that the SOS had been a false alarm. Clifton started steadily until Cowdrey got to work, having the first three batsmen all stumped and finishing with five for 59, but it was Tonbridge's quick bowler, Kirch, who was their saviour in the final stages as the game hung on a knife edge. With Clifton needing just 3 to win, he took their ninth wicket, and with still no sign of Penny – he arrived five minutes later – Tonbridge had won in the most dramatic fashion by two runs.

The next day a quietly elated Cowdrey was *en route* from Paddington to Cornwall for a holiday with his aunt when he espied his fellow passengers in the compartment reading about his exploits in the newspaper. 'Little Colin Cowdrey, thirteen-year-old Tonbridge schoolboy', enthused the *Daily Mail* correspondent, 'is claimed by cricketing experts as the boy wonder of the century, and a certain Test player before he is eighteen. He is the youngest player ever to play at Lord's, the youngest ever to play for a public school first XI and the youngest ever to be invited for a county's young amateurs.' The piece went on to quote Astill saying that Cowdrey bowled leg-breaks and googlies like Tich Freeman, the great Kent and England bowler, and batted like Hobbs. It was, as Cowdrey recalled in *MCC*, a curious experience.

Having holidayed in Cornwall, Cowdrey travelled to Leicestershire to play some club cricket through contacts of Astill who hailed from those parts. A particular highlight was appearing in

Les Berry's benefit match for the county against the local village, Blaby. He was most taken with the kindness of his seniors, not least a deliberate missed catch early in his innings so as to give him an extended bat. In contrast, the two matches he played for the Surrey Young Amateurs against Middlesex and Essex at The Oval afforded him little satisfaction. For, apart from some expensive bowling figures, he felt like a fish out of water in this unknown company.

Familiarity was always very important to Cowdrey, and this is what Tonbridge, with its sense of continuity and interlocking relationships, could provide. A conformist by nature, he went in awe of his masters, ready to work hard and to be guided by them, but three in particular were central to his development. First, there was his housemaster, James McNeill, who besides being head of English was an Irish rugby trialist with some interest in other sports. As a housemaster he ruled the roost in a direct, no nonsense way, whilst catering for the welfare of all those under his care. In Cowdrey's case this meant cautioning him about undue conceit, but also helping him to combat inflated expectations, particularly during his disappointing second season, and to cope with his hectic schedule. It was not uncommon for McNeill, on seeing Cowdrey overcome by fatigue, to send him off to bed and arrange for supper to be brought up to him. He and his wife, Jean, were also good enough to look after him throughout the Easter holiday of 1949 when he was recovering from a serious operation to his foot, as well as acting *in loco parentis*. Years later, Cowdrey referred to McNeill as a remarkable man who possessed that priceless pedagogic gift of being able to establish a great rapport with his charges without losing his authority or dignity.

A second figure to loom large in Cowdrey's life was C. H. (John) Knott, an Old Tonbridgian and like McNeill an alumnus of Brasenose College, Oxford. The son of a clerical headmaster, Knott contemplated taking holy orders himself before opting to return to Tonbridge. A top-flight ball player himself, good enough to have captained Oxford and play for Kent, Knott ran the cricket throughout Cowdrey's time there. A gruff, austere bachelor of few words, Knott, like Walford before him, was a martinet of the old school who had strong views about how the game should be played.

15

Immaculately turned out in his Harlequin cap and blazer, he gave no quarter to those whose standards fell short of expectation. In *MCC*, Cowdrey recalled how the mildest show of dissent during his first year in the XI after receiving a debatable decision was met with an indignant homily from Knott on his return to the pavilion. Simultaneously, a loose shot, a dropped catch or general bad play could induce a disapproving frown or an acerbic aside, so telling that any miscreant thought twice about reoffending. Once, when captain at an away match, Cowdrey was dashing to the bus to return to Tonbridge when Knott snapped at him, 'Groundsman'. In his eyes everyone from groundsmen and tea ladies to umpires and scorers had to be thanked for their efforts. Such was his reputation for unbending rectitude that even to this day Cowdrey and David Kemp, his close friend, often remark to each other with a chuckle, 'What would John Knott have said?', when they come across some minor breach of etiquette. But for all his forbidding exterior, there lurked within a warm and sensitive soul whose whole being was dedicated to the school he so proudly served, and his pupils gave him their all in return.

With his assortment of leg-breaks and googlies, Knott wheeled away in the nets year in, year out, becoming a role model for the young Cowdrey as he plied a similar trade. He was also ideal to bat against since he helped his protégés to master the art of playing slow bowling by getting them to watch his hand and use their feet. When Cowdrey became captain, Knott would issue some instructions at the pre-match practice which he expected to be followed, but otherwise he gave Cowdrey his head, a gesture which he found distinctly liberating. As he grew into a position of seniority, his relationship with Knott became closer, to the point that he became an ardent disciple of his mentor's approach to cricket, tempered only slightly by the pressures of the professional game, while Knott in turn looked on him as an honorary son. Years later when Knott died, it was Cowdrey who gave the most moving of addresses at his memorial service in the Tonbridge chapel.

Helping Knott with the coaching was the school professional, a traditionally revered figure among the cricketing fraternity. Ewart Astill, 'a marvellously encouraging coach' according to Cowdrey, conformed to this image before his untimely retirement in 1947 because of illness. Then, after two years with George Mobey, who briefly kept wicket for Surrey, Cowdrey had Maurice Tate, the former Sussex and England fast bowler, as coach during his time as captain. Tate was no technician, but his sunny personality, combined with his passion for the game, did much to compensate. Immediately he took the boys to his heart, none more so than Cowdrey, who could do nothing wrong. In his book *Time for Reflection*, Cowdrey recalled how many a game in which Tate was umpiring would be held up while he revelled in some exquisite stroke flowing from his bat. 'Jack [Hobbs] used to play that one,' he would chortle to anyone in earshot; or 'Maurice [Leyland] couldn't have played it better.'

The final father figure was the headmaster himself. When Cowdrey arrived at Tonbridge the incumbent was E. E. A. Whitworth, who, although no cricketer himself, took great pride in Cowdrey's accomplishments and counted his two days at the Clifton match each year as his happiest in the school calendar. Cowdrey, in turn, was fond of him, but developed a much closer relationship with his successor, Lawrence Waddy, a charismatic young cleric who hailed from an eminent Australian sporting family. Not only was the Marlborough-educated Waddy an inspirational preacher who helped lead Cowdrey into spiritual awareness, and a brilliant classicist, he was a gifted all-round games player who loved to pit his wits against the boys. A former squash blue, he beat the captain of squash, and during his earlier duels with Cowdrey on the racquets court he invariably emerged the victor. What struck Cowdrey as he got to know Waddy in these exchanges, and then later as head of school, was that, however busy his schedule, he still made time for people. It was a lesson which rubbed off on him, a point later acknowledged by Knott who recalled Cowdrey's willingness as captain to go out of his way to help coach the smaller boys.

Of course, it was not just on the cricket field that Cowdrey cut his teeth. His natural ball-playing skills gave him an automatic entry into most other teams, and he recalls exhausting half-holiday afternoons during the winter when he would shuttle between racquets court, rugby field and squash court, pausing only for a quick snack at the tuck shop. Benefiting once again from Knott's instruction at racquets, he became a good enough performer to play for the school for four years and to win the under-sixteen Public Schools Amateur Championship at Queen's. He was also a redoubtable performer at squash, and after leading the Colts rugby team to an unbeaten season in 1949 he went on to captain the XV in his final year. Michael Bushby, from the Dulwich perspective, recalls a gifted fly-half, quick over ten yards, who kicked with shrewd precision into the open spaces, and David Kemp has memories of a superb pair of hands and an instinctive ability to get a line going. Because of its physical roughness, rugby never appealed to Cowdrey quite as much as other sports, but the fact that he played the game to a decent standard helps explain how the portly figure of later years could display such athleticism on the cricket field.

After his great triumphs in 1946, the next year was something of an anti-climax with his batting even regressing. 1948 brought better things as he topped both the batting and bowling averages, with 86 against Lancing his best score. His term ended disappointingly, however, since 37 runs in two innings and four wickets was all he could manage at Lord's, when Clifton had the measure of Tonbridge for the second consecutive year. During that term, Cowdrey recalls, Bryan Valentine, the Kent captain, came down to Tonbridge to play against the school and was browbeaten by Knott, his good friend, for the county's failure to take an interest in him. With David Clark, Valentine's successor as Kent captain, expressing similar sentiments about Cowdrey's potential, it was not long before the message sank home. A few days later Cowdrey was accosted by Knott on his bicycle and told that he had been invited to play several matches for Kent Young Amateurs during the holidays. He was instructed to accept the invitation. When he played, he repaid Kent's faith in him by making 157, 87 and 79 against Sussex, Middlesex and Surrey respectively. His future with the county was now assured.

In 1949 Cowdrey was captain of Tonbridge and keen to dispel any fears that the recent operation on his toes to cure a stiffening of the joints would hamper his progress. With a special type of cricketing size 11 shoe to take the weight off his toes, he soon showed that he meant business, with 119 and five for 28 in the school's second match, against Lancing. He followed this with 181 not out against the

Buccaneers, the highest school innings for forty years, 123 against Haileybury, 88 against the Free Foresters, 140 against the Old Tonbridgians, and six for 46 against Dulwich. Sadly he was unable to repeat such heroics at Lord's and a mediocre Tonbridge side went down to Clifton by an innings.

With 893 runs at an average of 55.8, and forty-nine wickets at 13.8, Cowdrey had not let the cares of captaincy affect his performances. Indeed, his batting had made real advances, helping him to gain selection for the Southern Schools against the Rest. His 85 in that match ensured him a place in the Public Schools XI against the Combined Services. He failed with the bat, but compensated with the ball, numbering Peter May, for the only time, among his five victims. He made his debut for the Kent second XI against Norfolk at Norwich with a solid 35, followed by games against Wiltshire and Devon. His fondest memory of the summer, however, came when he was summoned from class to play for Denis Compton's XI in one of his benefit games at Horsmonden in the Kent weald. 'What a thrill,' Cowdrey later recalled. 'We had a partnership of about 120, and although I got very few, I did manage to play one rather good cover-drive. Walking off later Compo said, "One day you must teach me that shot." '

In his final year at Tonbridge, Cowdrey did not allow the onerous burden of being head of school on top of his captaincy to curb his insatiable appetite for runs. He began with 63 against Tonbridge Town in a side which contained the headmaster, then made 145 against Lancing, a school which he repeatedly ground into the dust during his five years in the team. Next came a chanceless 175 out of 228 for nine against Christ's Hospital, 108 against the Old Tonbridgians, 95 and six for 66 against Dulwich, and finally 116 and six for 75 against the Band of Brothers. To Dennis Silk, the mainstay of the Christ's Hospital side during the Cowdrey era, and later a Somerset player it was the superb eye, the beautiful footwork and brilliant coaching of Knott that distinguished his batting. 'If you got Cowdrey out early you beat Tonbridge,' he recalled. In 1949, when he was bowled in the first over of the match, Silk saw the Tonbridge heads drop. Despite a tantalising spell of leg-break bowling from Cowdrey, they lost, and so the following year there was unfinished business to settle. Silk, who took six for 96, recalls the glint of steel in Cowdrey's eye as he elegantly despatched him to all parts of the ground during his 175. The next highest score was 19.

With a goodish record behind them, Tonbridge went to Lord's intent on erasing the memory of three successive defeats. Clifton, boasting seven old colours, batted first and made 200, with Cowdrey taking four for 59. Their lead of 74 on the first innings was frittered away so that Tonbridge were left 176 to win. They lost a wicket in the opening over before Cowdrey entered and took control. A massive roar from the Tonbridge supporters when he had reached 63 celebrated his 1,000 runs for the year, and although he was disappointed to be bowled for 96 when the end was in sight, victory by four wickets was sweet.

And so ended five glorious years which had brought Cowdrey 2,894 runs at an average of 40.34 and 216 wickets at 10.05, breaking the previous school record in both departments. His batting continued to come on leaps and bounds, with an average of 79 for his final year, while his bowling (forty-seven wickets at 14), although exceptional at schoolboy level, no longer troubled very good players. There was an obvious explanation. The older he had become and the more he had grown, the more he lost his natural curving flight and the suppleness of his fingers. They were skills which did not return. Despite occasional glimpses of his former art, his first-class record of 65 wickets at an average of 51, taken in the main during his early years, make very modest reading.

After a summer holiday getting a feel for the professional game, Cowdrey returned to Tonbridge for two more terms, a leader decorated with honours as the profusion of blazers, scarves and ties amply demonstrated. He had intended to stay until the end of the 1951 summer term, but, accepting his father's advice that a full season of first-class cricket before going to Oxford would be in his best interests, Cowdrey bowed out at the end of the Easter term. In *Time for Reflection*, he recalled the sad journey home on the train to Croydon as he looked back on the previous five years with unmitigated pleasure and wondered whether he would ever experience such happiness again. He had, of course, taken full advantage of the sporting opportunities which had come his way, not least the wonderfully hard wickets on the Head, but, more than this, Tonbridge had been his home at a time when half the globe separated him from his parents. The camaraderie of the teams and his house, the close relationships he formed with a number of the staff, and the time-honoured rituals of boarding school life, had given him a much needed security during these formative years. From then on his life would revolve around a plethora of male institutions in which tradition, hierarchy and etiquette would predominate.

Tonbridge had also given him a valuable grounding in leadership at an early age. In common with the traditions of the time, he used his powers as head of school to the full, beating other boys with the headmaster's permission when necessary. The general tenor of his regime, however, was an enlightened one as he tended to the needs of the majority. Simon Langdale, later headmaster of Shrewsbury, recalls his first term watching Cowdrey, the head of school, practising racquets. To his amazement – for he wasn't in his house – Cowdrey addressed him by his surname, and asked him to go and fetch his sweater from some other part of the school. The fact that Cowdrey knew who he was greatly impressed Langdale, who attributed his great respect as head boy not only to his being a Kent cricketer, but also to his lack of conceit.

Already, then, the down-to-earth philosophy of his various mentors had seeped into his consciousness, and the courteous self-effacement which quickly became his trademark had won its first admirers.

2

Hammond's Disciple

By Cowdrey's last summer at Tonbridge his reputation was such that Kent, with a paucity of talent, were only too keen to blood him. Tonbridge had already turned down one overture during term time (recalling the even more striking refusal of the Fettes headmaster Dr Heard to allow one of his star pupils, K. G. Macleod, to play rugby for Scotland in 1905), but once Cowdrey was free of representative commitments in the holidays David Clark decided to take the plunge. He invited the young eighteen-year-old to play in Kent's final four matches of the season. It was with some trepidation that Cowdrey travelled up to Derby for the first of these matches, having met few of the team before. His anxieties were not alleviated when he was ushered into the amateurs' dressing-room, until Les Ames, the former England wicket-keeper/batsman and captain in place of Clark, came to join him. After Derbyshire had run up an imposing total on the first day, Kent were forced to bat in unpleasant conditions against Cliff Gladwin and Les Jackson, one of the most fearsome opening attacks in the country. Cowdrey later recalled turning to Derek Ufton, his team-mate, as he waited to go in to bat and asking about their respective identities. Despite an innings defeat and Ames's first ever pair in his forty-fourth year, Cowdrey acquitted himself quite competently, scoring 15 and 26, although he was rather disconcerted by receiving his first ever bouncer from Jackson.

After playing in both games during the traditional week at Dover, and forming a good impression in the second against Nottinghamshire, his year concluded at Canterbury against John Goddard's victorious West Indians. On a turning wicket Kent were outclassed, but a two-hour vigil against their renowned spinner, Alf

Valentine, won Cowdrey a warm hand from the crowd and gave him hope for the future. His overall return of 104 runs from seven innings was not anything special at first glance, but given the nature of the conditions and the quality of the bowling it was a useful start. *Wisden* marked him out as easily the most promising of all Kent's debutants, while for Cowdrey himself the experience had only hardened his ambition to play for England. It was to that end that he now directed all his energy.

Although preoccupied by cricket enough to while away Saturday morning periods in the summer term setting out his field positions for the impending match, Cowdrey had not neglected his academic studies at Tonbridge. The reward for his diligence was a place at Brasenose College, Oxford to read Geography on a Heath Harrison Exhibition worth £60 per year. With his immediate future safe-guarded, the summer of 1951 now promised to be a leisurely inter-lude until he was attracted by Clark's suggestion of playing for Kent for a season. Not only would the opportunity broaden his experi-ence, Kent's scant resources would facilitate his chances of holding down a regular place.

For a team devoid of great ability, Kent's start could not have been more depressing when icy conditions at Gillingham in their first match helped put paid to the career of Les Ames, who after having contracted back trouble should not even have been playing. They continued to struggle thereafter, which placed additional pressure on a promising youngster trying to make his way in the game. Unable to advance into double figures in his first three innings and nonplussed by the swing of Derek Shackleton and Vic Cannings at Southampton, Cowdrey felt his confidence draining away. He asked to be omitted from the first team, but Tom Crawford, captain of the second XI and fellow Old Tonbridgian, who was deputising for Clark, would have none of it. He assured him that his time would come. Crawford's faith in Cowdrey was immediately justified when his astute 47 helped Kent to victory against Northamptonshire. After scores of 19 and 34 against Lancashire his fortunes fluctuated widely, with five ducks in as many games being matched by his first two half-centuries and a maiden century when playing for the Free Foresters against Oxford University.

During a three-week break to rest his feet – the stiffening of the joints in his big toes which was to trouble him throughout his career – Cowdrey was able to give some thought to his uneven progress so far, in particular his vulnerability to late swing because of a tendency to play from the crease and thus a fraction early. With the help of Arthur Fagg, Kent's prolific opening batsman, he began to learn the art of moving early into position and the value of playing late. The coaching had its desired effect. He marked his return with 84 against Sussex at Hastings and then celebrated his first Canterbury Week with a skilfully played 90 against Hampshire, facing the same attack which had caused him such trouble previously. He continued to show greater consistency, with 87 against Leicestershire and 71 against the South Africans at Canterbury – an innings which won him his county cap, the youngest in the club's history to be accorded this honour. He then signed off in style for the Gentlemen against the Players at Scarborough when before a crowd of 20,000 he overcame early difficulties against Alec Bedser and Tom Pritchard to make 106. 'I had expected to see a schoolboy in action and was amazed by the maturity of this knock,' recalled Trevor Bailey, the England all-rounder. Others also took note, not least Len Hutton, who, although the opposition captain, gave him some useful advice during his innings and sought him out afterwards to compliment him on his achievement. He departed for Oxford in a better frame of mind than he could have dared hope for earlier in the summer.

With its natural beauty and sense of history Oxford has acted as the stepping stone for thousands of thrusting young tyros as they aimed to turn dreams into reality. But whereas they would gravitate towards the Union or the undergraduate societies, Cowdrey gained little stimulus from matters academic and political or the world of high living. His chosen path was the more obvious one of sporting endeavour, beginning with college squash and football. He also played golf, won a racquets blue and was runner-up in 1953 to Geoffrey Atkins in the Amateur Racquets Championship. Enjoyable though all this was, it was secondary to the main purpose of his university life. Once liberated from Preliminary Examinations in March 1952 Cowdrey's life took on a new meaning as the rigours of the lecture hall gave way to the pleasures of the Parks, the university's cricket ground.

In this enchanting setting Cowdrey's education continued apace as he established himself as the outstanding player in the university team and arguably the most promising Oxford freshman since Douglas Jardine in 1920. After scoring 80 against Lancashire in his third match, Cowdrey went one better against the Indians with 92 and 54. With his other successes including 82 against the Free Foresters, 56 against Kent and 79 and 92 against Somerset, Cowdrey carried the hopes of his side on his shoulders for the university match at Lord's. Whereas Oxford had not won all summer Cambridge, boasting a vintage team with names such as David Sheppard, Peter May and Raman Subba Row gracing their line-up, started as overwhelming favourites. Oxford, however, with Cowdrey leading the way with 55 in the first innings, played above themselves and although they were in deep trouble on the final afternoon a spirited 46 from fast bowler Alan Coxon spared them a loser's medal.

His university year now behind him, Cowdrey returned to Kent but initially he could offer little comfort to a team still struggling in the nether regions of the table. His first fifteen innings produced only two half-centuries before he raised his game during the closing weeks. He fed off the Indian attack with relish, with a century against them at Canterbury, his first for the county, and then was Kent's sole saving grace in their innings defeat by Yorkshire. His immaculate technique employed to good effect in an undefeated 85, again left a favourable impression on Hutton. No music could be sweeter to his ears. As England's premier batsman for well over a decade, with a record-breaking 364 against Australia at The Oval in 1938, Hutton stood next to none in Cowdrey's pantheon of heroes. Now, he had the opportunity to travel up to Yorkshire by car with him for the Scarborough Festival and listen to him in conversation with Godfrey Evans, the Kent and England wicket-keeper. At Scarborough, Hutton's influence continued to cast its spell over Cowdrey as the great player carved out two centuries for Yorkshire against MCC and then 99 for the Players against the Gentlemen until being expertly run out from cover by his most devoted admirer.

Elected as Secretary of the university cricket club in his second year, Cowdrey was a magnet which drew old and young alike to the Parks to watch the runs flow from his bat. He followed his 127 against Hampshire, his maiden century for Oxford, with 69 and 47 against Middlesex, 94 against Hampshire, 53 and 72 against Derbyshire, and 51 against Warwickshire. On tour he continued to dominate, with 88 against Worcestershire and 154 and 31 against the formidable Surrey spinners Tony Lock and Jim Laker on a turning wicket at The Oval, when Oxford were shot out for 63 in their second innings. So assuredly did Cowdrey cope with this top-flight attack that Laker felt that he played him better than any young batsman at any time in his career. Once again Cowdrey remained by some way Oxford's best hope of getting the better of Cambridge at Lord's.

In common with many great players, Cowdrey found the big stage brought the best out in him, and his 116 on the opening day gave E. W. Swanton much to applaud in the *Daily Telegraph*.

Cowdrey's century was the bright jewel of the day, the best piece of batsmanship perhaps in the university match since H. E. Webb's 145 not out put Oxford on the road to victory five years ago. Cowdrey had just one major piece of luck and it was a very vital piece. Before he reached double figures slip missed a low catch off Marlar. When he was in the 60s Marlar failed to take what would have been a wonderfully good catch off his own bowling. Early in his innings Cowdrey once or twice was in trouble against Marlar, apparently playing for the off-break to balls that came straight on. But while these items are mentioned in justice to Marlar, the general impression was of a fine, mature piece of batsmanship in which two strokes predominated, the off-drive and the forcing hit wide of mid-on.

There is a picture taken of Cowdrey at the age of eighteen making a stroke that was the very image of Hammond. Extravagant predictions seldom help anyone and more often than not they recoil on the heads of their authors. All I will say then is this, that Cowdrey, who is now only twenty, has two important points of resemblance with that of the great batsman: poise and balance.

When he is hitting the ball he is usually steady as a rock,

head still and the feet firmly planted. Some of his off-driving was a joy to see, and to at least one distinguished old player added pleasure was given by the sight of Lumsden and Hayward, one from West Indies, one from Australia, standing at short-leg, applauding the stroke.

With Cowdrey's 116 the cornerstone, Oxford's 312 had somewhat surprisingly gained them a first innings lead of 121 and although they were dismissed cheaply second time around their attack made Cambridge struggle as they chased 238 to win. With thirty-seven minutes remaining, 52 were still needed with only two wickets left, but the arrival of the Cambridge captain, Robin Marlar, seemed to galvanise Dennis Silk, the hitherto sedate opener. Such was the quality of his stroke play that the score swiftly mounted, and with three minutes to go Cambridge celebrated a famous victory.

For the second year running Cowdrey's form for Kent paled in comparison with his Oxford record, although it was still good enough for him to head the county's averages and win the Cricket Writers' Young Player of the Year Award. He also had a taste of his future destiny when a set of extraordinary circumstances led to a brief encounter with the Kent captaincy. In 1951 the county had appointed Bill Murray-Wood, a well-meaning amateur, to take over from David Clark but, try as he might, he was unable to lift their fortunes. In 1952 they finished in fifteenth place, two above bottom, and in 1953 they had a run of fifteen games without a win. Against this depressing backdrop confidence in the captain diminished fast and the crisis came to a head during Canterbury Week when the team rose up to a man against his leadership. The committee felt obliged to act, and Murray-Wood was immediately relieved of his duties. Doug Wright, the long-serving leg-spinner, was nominated as his successor, and when injury prevented him from playing in the next match against Leicestershire at Loughborough, Cowdrey took over the captaincy. Any misgivings he had soon evaporated as the team rallied behind him, and although they lost again he was well pleased with a fighting 81 on a turning wicket.

Two weeks later Cowdrey again showed his worth when he appeared for the Gentlemen of England against Australia at Lord's.

27

His team was well beaten, but not before he had risen to the occasion with two quality half-centuries against Lindwall and Miller which in *Wisden*'s words 'emphasised his exceptional ability'. Alan Davidson, one of Australia's finest all-rounders, has recollections of watching the match from the balcony and thinking to himself after one sumptuous Cowdrey cover drive, 'This bloke's going to be a thorn in our flesh in 1954–5.'

Cowdrey once again bowed out at Scarborough with élan when, after a double-century from Hutton for the Players, in a long partnership with May he showed that the Gentlemen would be no pushover. By shining in such illustrious company he ensured that he continued to attract notice. When the editor of *Wisden* in 1954 speculated on candidates for the forthcoming Australian tour, Cowdrey was one of the hopefuls he had in his sights. 'Last summer at the age of twenty,' he wrote, 'Cowdrey made 1917 runs in such impressive style that his admirers have much confidence that he will reach great heights.' His words turned out to be prophetic. Although Cowdrey's captaincy of Oxford in 1954 brought no change in the university's fortunes – they were not able to manage one first-class win throughout his three years in the team – he was, according to M. J. K. Smith, held in the highest esteem since he had already been noted as a player out of the ordinary. Smith, then a freshman, recalls the pleasure of batting with him on a number of occasions that year since he was always very helpful and his advice was of more value than any number of nets or coaching sessions. Although not quite touching the heights of the previous year, Cowdrey's batting again displayed a striking maturity. An innings of 78 in the first match against Gloucestershire was the prelude to 112 and 51 against Kent, 94 against Lancashire and 140 against Sussex. What struck Hubert Doggart, the Sussex captain, about his opposite number was his admirable timing off both the front and the back foot. 'It took a cursory glance only to see that he had both style and class,' Doggart later recalled, describing him as a 'master not least of that marvellous shot, the straight-drive.'

At Lord's, Cowdrey featured in an entertaining 180-run partnership with M. J. K. Smith on the opening day of a convivial varsity match fondly remembered by Cambridge captain Michael Bushby.

Smith, a gifted enough sportsman subsequently to win an England rugby cap as well as captaining the national cricket team, made 201, Cowdrey 66 and they scored at 90 runs per hour while together. Cowdrey declared Oxford's first innings at 401 for three but despite having the better of the game they were unable to capture the final two Cambridge wickets. Unknown to him at the time, Cowdrey had played his last game for Oxford. His three years there had had a less enduring effect on his character than Tonbridge, but there is no doubting the close affinity he developed for its tranquil surroundings or the lasting place it has in his affections.

Again in 1954, as in the two previous years, the transition from university to county cricket was not an easy one, and with the team to tour Australia about to be picked a barren run seemed to have put paid to his chances. Cowdrey was certainly not hopeful when the party was announced during the closing stages of Kent's match against Surrey at Blackheath. In *Time for Reflection* he recalls crossing to his car during the six o'clock news when suddenly horns began to blow and some members shouted out to him, 'You're on the boat, Colin.' With a number of Surrey men, most notably Lock and Laker, missing out, Cowdrey, sensing the hostile atmosphere, disappeared off to Northampton as quickly as possible.

Although very young by English standards to be chosen for an overseas tour, Cowdrey had been around long enough in the first-class game to make a strong case for his inclusion. Scarborough 1951 was certainly an important turning point because from that moment on he could count the England captain Hutton as one of his most fervent admirers. 'At Oxford,' Hutton later recalled, 'I had seen how straight was his bat and how much time he had for his shots and told him he was a disciple of my methods.' But for all his support the one who really ensured Cowdrey's passage to Australia was Gubby Allen. He had seen enough of him (as with Frank Tyson) to convince himself that here was a player with real class. He particularly liked Cowdrey's classical method and thought his exceptional facility of timing would serve him well on Australian pitches. Always a respecter of Allen's judgement, Hutton needed little persuasion, although when Yorkshire's Vic Wilson was added to the party as an insurance against a recurrence of Compton's knee problem, the captain was rash enough to bet Allen £1 that Wilson would average more than Cowdrey. Never a man to part with money lightly, Hutton paid up in Adelaide.

Given the competition for batting places, Cowdrey's selection caused some surprise, but in general the news was widely welcomed. 'The vote has gone to Cowdrey', declared *The Times*, and 'anyone who has seen him play as he was doing until a few weeks ago will be delighted. Together with May he is potentially one of the greatest of the young batsmen and now that he no longer has the worries of inclusion hanging over him one feels that he will repay the selectors for the faith in him. He should be suited by Australian conditions and may well return as an established England player for years to come.' 'Cowdrey was perhaps fortunate on 1954 form to get a place', Alan Ross later wrote in *Australia 1955*, 'but anyone who saw him in 1953 could hardly doubt that he is a vintage player, mature beyond his years. He is heavily built, not unlike Hutton in his follow through with an economic bat and brush forward defence method modelled on Fagg and he scores in the bountiful arc between cover and mid-wicket. Jim Parks was the probable alternative, but Cowdrey is to him as burgundy to a sparkling hock and on a tour of this kind body is preferable to fizz.'

Now more than ever in the public eye, Cowdrey's first match after his inclusion was ironically against Tyson at Northampton. The press were out in force to watch the duel, won indisputably by the latter since he bowled Cowdrey for 18 in the first innings and had him caught at the wicket for 0 in the second. Thereafter his form began to perk up and he celebrated another turn at the Kent captaincy with 85 and 43 against Nottinghamshire at Dover. In preparation for Australia, Cowdrey was made twelfth man for the final Test against Pakistan at The Oval. The experience left him cold. Not knowing many of the England team, Cowdrey felt so unsure of himself at net practice that he found communicating with his team-mates a real trial. He felt no better when called upon to field during the match, so that when a chance high temperature prevented him from continuing his duties he fled The Oval in relief. In this frame of mind it seemed vital that one of the established players should take him under his wing in Australia. Hutton had already earmarked himself for that responsibility. What neither of them knew at the time was how close that bond would become during the months ahead.

3

Finest Hour

It was like being back at school for the first time as the twenty-one-year-old Cowdrey travelled to Tilbury with his parents on 15 September 1954 for the farewell ceremonies which accompanied the departure of the MCC party to Australia on the SS *Orsova*. Amidst his many other duties as captain, Hutton made a point of drawing Ernest Cowdrey aside and assuring him that he would keep an eye on Colin. Unlike in these days of jet travel, a tour to Australia then was a more lengthy, leisurely affair, with a three-week voyage giving the players a real opportunity to relax after the rigours of an English season and to establish a close rapport with their fellow tourists. With his shy, sensitive personality, and aware of his humble status in the party, Cowdrey deliberately kept a low profile during the first few days, spending much of his time closeted in his cabin with his room-mate, Peter May. Two weeks later the team docked briefly in Colombo, allowing them a gentle work-out against Ceylon in front of a vast crowd. After such a long period at sea the transition to playing in the tropics proved quite taxing, and the scoreboard read 38 for four when Cowdrey nervously walked out to join Vic Wilson. To his relief he found his timing at once and scored at little less than a run a minute in a fluent 66 not out before May's declaration. The outing had been a valuable one, not only because it had boosted Cowdrey's sagging confidence but because it also impressed the non-playing Hutton, who had watched proceedings with keen interest. Now, for the rest of the voyage, Hutton deliberately sought out the youngster, joined him in deck games, and tried to prepare him for the challenge of playing in Australia. He stressed in particular the roar of the large crowds and the uncompromising nature of the opposition. 'You're a young player. They're going to try to rough you up a bit,' he cautioned. This developing friendship between master and pupil was given added meaning following the shattering news which awaited Cowdrey on arrival at Fremantle.

On the evening of his son's innings in Colombo, Ernest Cowdrey was sitting listening to the radio and on hearing of his success hurried upstairs to fetch a pen to make a note of the scores. Within a few minutes of returning he had died of a massive heart attack, aged only 54, his early death cruelly depriving him of watching his pride and joy cross the final frontier. At first a cable was sent to Cowdrey by John Taylor, which read, 'Congratulations on your innings. Happy landings tomorrow. Regret father not too well. All at home.' Cowdrey later recalled that instinctively the words did not ring true and next day, at Fremantle, another telegram awaited him at the team's hotel informing him of his father's death. Soon realising that it would be impractical to return home for the funeral, Cowdrey went to his room and stayed there for the rest of the afternoon. He was comforted by a number of telegrams, including one from Sir Robert Menzies, the Australian prime minister, which read, 'You have the heartfelt sympathy of everyone in Australia.' When he came down to dinner most of his team-mates approached him to express their sympathy, but Hutton said nothing and it was only afterwards over coffee in the lounge that he came up to commiserate. 'I'm sorry,' he said with tears in his eyes, a gesture which greatly touched Cowdrey, sensitive to the emotional effort this would have necessitated on his captain's part. Hutton never mentioned Cowdrey's father again, but from that moment onwards he and the team manager, Geoffrey Howard, went to great lengths to ensure that their young protégé was kept fully occupied.

Hutton's kindness made a deep impression on Cowdrey throughout the tour. Not only did he find riveting his post-dinner vignettes about the game in quiet corners of hotel lounges, he studied him at net practice, bowled to him for hours and went knocking at his door in search of further advice. His influence on the young Cowdrey and his approach to the game was to be quite inestimable. Another important ally was Freddie Brown, the former England captain, covering the tour from the press box. He had already endeared himself to Cowdrey when, during the middle of a match against Northamptonshire in Cowdrey's first full season, he had suddenly invited him out to dinner and given him ample encouragement. Now, keen to keep himself involved, Brown volunteered his services to a young enthusiast desperate to improve, and Cowdrey, always a good listener, recalls these additional post-prandial sessions in the nets as both enjoyable and instructive. 'It was a kind game then,' he said.

After an encouraging start up country at Bunbury with 48 not out and four for 35, Cowdrey for the first time batted with Hutton in the opening first-class game against Western Australia in Perth. Joining him at 70 for four, Cowdrey's main priority through their substantial partnership was to avoid running out his captain. With Hutton in sublime form the partnership proved an invaluable tutorial for Cowdrey as his mentor frequently sauntered down the wicket to proffer advice and encouragement in equal measure.

After accomplishing little against South Australia, Cowdrey entertained few hopes of making the Test team as MCC continued to wend their way around this vast continent. All this was to change, however, by the time they played New South Wales in Sydney. On a lively pitch they were soon in trouble at 38 for four when Cowdrey came to the wicket. He began with a lovely straight drive for four off Keith Miller and kept pace with Hutton throughout their fifth-wicket partnership of 163, scoring at a run a minute. Hutton finished with 102, Cowdrey with 110 and the rest scored 40 between them. 'It was an innings to remember,' wrote Lindsay Hassett, the former Australian captain, in the Sydney *Herald Sun*. 'Although this young player is bound to make many centuries against Australia in the future it is doubtful whether he will ever delight the crowd more than he did during this glorious display.' Cowdrey's driving in particular had impressed Hutton. When the players left the field at the end of the New South Wales innings, he asked him to open in the second innings. Reluctantly Cowdrey agreed. On 38 not out overnight, he remembered being handed an unsigned cable on the way to the ground. It said, 'See 1 Kings 18:34.' He stuffed it in his pocket and didn't give it another thought. That morning he made his second century of the match, sharing in another large partnership with Hutton. It was only a few days later, when preparing his laundry, that he came across his cable again and on doing some biblical research discovered the mystery of the content. The appropriate passage read, 'The Lord said to Elijah, "Do it a second time".'

Despite 4 and 0 against Queensland as an opener, Cowdrey's bravura performance against New South Wales had guaranteed him a place in the first Test, especially with Tom Graveney out through influenza and Wilson short of runs. England held the Ashes, and with a talented team behind him which nicely blended youth with experience Hutton was quietly confident of emulating Douglas Jardine's feat of winning in Australia in 1932–33, but at Brisbane he was guilty of a serious error. Assuming that the wicket would be as green as it had been for the game against Queensland, he sent the opposition in to bat, overlooking the fact that there had been no rain in the week before the Test, unlike during the week before the state game. Finding themselves batting on a perfect pitch, Australia, with centuries from Arthur Morris and Neil Harvey, took full advantage of some shoddy English outcricket to pile on the runs. They declared at 601 for eight, then set Lindwall and Miller to work, and in no time Cowdrey found himself entering at 11 for three. 'Rough time for a young fellow to come in. Good luck to you,' said Miller, who promptly gave him the treatment.

Undeterred, Cowdrey batted with admirable composure and was unlucky to be given out caught at slip off the boot for 40. After a first innings total of 190, England initially put up a better fight when following on. Thereafter, with Cowdrey retreating into what Alan Ross called monklike abstinence in mustering 10 in over an hour, they fell away, going down by an innings and 154 runs. Losing by such a hefty margin left Hutton close to despair. His mood could barely have been lightened by the panning he received from the critics, and Cowdrey has vivid memories of his tortured countenance on the flight from Brisbane to Rockhampton for a fixture against Queensland Country XI.

Despite his unflattering figures of one for 160 Hutton still felt that Tyson was his main weapon to tame the Australians. Alf Gover, the former Surrey and England fast bowler turned journalist, helped him experiment with a shorter run and his efforts bore immediate fruit against Victoria. Cowdrey made runs in both innings of this game and morale began to pick up as England travelled to Sydney for the second Test. For Hutton, however, the agonising continued as he pondered his final eleven. Under pressure to play Johnny Wardle and Bob Appleyard, his two spinners, he wrestled with the question of whether to leave out the faithful Bedser, who had not fully recovered from an attack of shingles. Confronted with a heavy atmosphere on the morning of the match and a well-grassed pitch, conditions ideal for Bedser, Hutton's dilemma intensified right up to the toss. When finally forced to choose he not only omitted Bedser, but failed to notify him of his decision. The responsibility of having to prepare himself for the task of opening the innings was Hutton's only defence. His nerves were once again in pieces as England's batting, without the injured Compton, failed for the third time in succession. Their bowlers fought back doggedly, restricting Australia's lead to 74, but once again their top order failed. Minutes before lunch on the third day they had slumped to 55 for three.

'As we watched Cowdrey walking out to join May at the wicket,' recalled Denis Compton, 'I was nagged by the old familiar misgivings. Another wicket then, and the game was as good as Australia's.' 'If I had the chance to play the innings of my life I would like to do it this afternoon,' May remarked to Cowdrey as they returned to the middle after the interval. Eschewing all risk, England's most gifted young amateurs proved equal to everything that Australia could throw at them and very gradually their fortunes began to mount. Not many loose balls were bowled but there were enough to bring out the Cowdrey cover-drive, as broad and gracious as Hammond's according to Denys Rowbotham of the *Manchester Guardian*. 'For three hours in their contrasting styles,' observed Alan Ross, 'they batted with unforced authority, one upright flowing and lithe, the other powerful with the gentleness of strength. May split the air with the noise of his strokes, Cowdrey the field with the ease of his timing. There was little to choose between them in the correctness of their technique, the natural assertion of their breeding.' Together they battled it out for over three hours until with the close in sight a weary Cowdrey gave Benaud, the leg-spinner, the charge and was caught at deep mid-off for his pains. Well aware that he had meekly surrendered at a crucial stage of the match, he hurried off in a terrible state. 'I have never seen a man so disappointed with himself as Cowdrey was when he got out,' Brian Statham later recalled. 'He felt he had thrown his wicket away and let the side down.' ('Been to confession?' was George Duckworth, the engaging baggage master's comment when seeing him return to his hotel room the next day.)

Thanks to a splendid 104 from May and a spirited rearguard action by the tail, England closed on 296, setting Australia 223 to win. 72 for two at the close, they collapsed the next day in the face of immensely fast bowling from Tyson and Statham. A magnificent 92 not out from Harvey, in partnership with last man Bill Johnston, kept their chances alive, but when the latter gloved Tyson to Evans, England emerged victors by 38 runs. The series had come alive. Christmas was spent in high spirits in Sydney, and now all roads led to Melbourne for the crucial third Test. Compton was fit again, but Hutton, afflicted by fibrositis and nervous exhaustion, had to be coaxed from his room on the morning of the match by his senior team-mates. In front of more than 60,000, England, on winning the toss, suffered their usual dismal start as they encountered one of the finest ever opening spells in a Test match. Miller had missed the previous Test because of a serious knee injury and had not reckoned on being fit to bowl at Melbourne. However, on the morning of the match he decided to give it a try, and on a lively pitch his late movement made him close to unplayable. Only two scoring shots were scored off him in 71 balls during the entire opening session in an extraordinary pre-lunch spell of 9 overs, 8 maidens, 5 runs, 3 wickets. With Lindwall proving a menace at the other end, dismissing May for a duck, Cowdrey entered at 21 for two to join his tense-looking captain. He was greeted by an umbrella field of slips and short-legs. At 29, Hutton was out to Miller and retired to the dressing-room, where for the next hour he sat motionless, head in his hands without even bothering to take off his pads. May recalled that his mood only changed when he realised from the excitement on the balcony that Cowdrey was playing so effortlessly. Before long he joined the others to share their enthusiasm.

Having survived to lunch through his immaculate defence,

Cowdrey increasingly dominated thereafter, once the pitch had dried out and Miller had taken his jersey. It was only when Bill Johnston and Ian Johnson, the off-spinner, operated together that Cowdrey temporarily lost his way as he was unable to pierce the cover field, keenly patrolled as ever by Harvey. He was becalmed for forty minutes on 56 before lashing out at Johnson with an on-drive that just cleared Ron Archer at mid-on. Thereafter, regaining his fluency, he fought a lone hand until on 97 he clipped Archer wide of mid-on and ran for his life. Around him he heard clapping as he ran one, a rising cheer as he scampered a second and a veritable roar as he turned for a third. Les Favell, then fielding on the boundary, later recalled the feeling that went up and down his spine as the spontaneous wave of applause thundered round the ground to greet Cowdrey's hundred, the youngest Englishman to have made one against Australia for forty years. It had taken him four hours and he had scored it out of 158. When he was bowled minutes later to a freak ball from Johnson which pitched outside his off stump and clipped leg, the crowd stood to him a second time. The next day the critics were ecstatic in their accolades. 'England's youngest player, Colin Cowdrey, made a glorious fighting century,' wrote Tom Goodman in the *Sydney Morning Herald*. 'He saved his team from complete collapse and in hitting 15 fours gave a display of classical stroke play.' 'No player in the game', declared Bill O'Reilly, one of the game's most waspish critics, 'compares with Cowdrey for effective offside play. I have no hesitation in placing him number one batsman in the game today.' His innings left a similarly unforgettable mark on his team-mates. Hutton doubted if Cowdrey ever played better again, Bedser felt it was so brilliant 'that I fear we consequently expected too much of him', while Graveney called it 'unbridled genius unsurpassed for both merit and technique'. It was, indeed, his finest hour.

England made 191 and the Australians replied with 181 for eight by the Saturday evening. On Monday morning, a monumental row erupted as the colour of the pitch had radically changed, giving rise to allegations of illegal watering to benefit the home team. As it turned out, the artificial refreshment suited England, for it gave them the truest surface of the match for their second innings. For once they began soundly, and although Cowdrey was unable to repeat his earlier heroics, an invaluable 91 from May enabled England to reach 279. A sharp catch by Cowdrey at short-leg off Tyson sent back Morris, and Australia, chasing 240, closed an eventful day at 75 for two. With everything to play for, Melbourne again turned out in force on the morrow but Tyson, with six for 16 in eighty minutes of sustained ferocity, destroyed the remainder of the Australian batting. He was the fastest bowler Morris, their veteran opener, ever faced, a view endorsed to this day by Cowdrey, who throughout his life never saw anything quite like Tyson on this tour.

While the home team retreated to regroup, England were buoyed by an innings defeat of South Australia, and began the vital fourth Test as clear favourites. In the sweltering Adelaide heat, a taut, tight contest ensued, with the result in the balance until the game's dying stages. Replying to Australia's first innings total of 323, Cowdrey recalled in *MCC* how he was unnerved by periodic bouts of barracking during a painstaking partnership with Compton. The upshot was that Hutton sent the twelfth man, Wilson, on to the field in his blazer, replete with a couple of bananas in his pocket which he proceeded to give Cowdrey. 'I said, "What the hell are these for?" Wilson replied, "Well, skipper thought you might be hungry. He watched you play a couple of wild shots just now. It rather suggested that he is keen for you to stay out here batting a little longer. Get your head down." The crowd and the Australian players must have been intrigued by it all. From that moment I batted properly and scored 79.'

Beginning their second innings with a deficit of 18, Australia collapsed to Tyson, Statham and Appleyard and were all out for 111, leaving England a mere 94 to win. But this proved no formality. Rising to the challenge, Miller shot out Edrich, Hutton and Cowdrey for 18, eliciting from the captain his immortal line, 'The boogers have done us', as he gloomily surveyed the wreckage from the pavilion. Fortunately Compton, along with May and Bailey, stood firm and eventually England coasted home by five wickets. The Ashes had been retained for the first time in Australia since 1928–29 and Hutton paid tribute to his younger players – May, Cowdrey, Tyson and Statham – before retreating to the team hotel for extensive celebrations.

The final Test, again in Sydney, was an anti-climax. Monsoon conditions not seen in half a century, prevented a start until the fourth day. In the remaining time available, England totally dominated and were unlucky not to win yet again. A combination of shock from a broken nose caused by a blow from Morris at Adelaide and a chill had put Cowdrey in hospital for five days. He was barely fit to play, but Hutton insisted and he was out without scoring.

After Australia, Cowdrey enjoyed the month in New Zealand which in those days was the traditional epilogue to this long campaign. Huge crowds flocked to see Hutton's victorious team, but after the enthralling encounters of Sydney, Melbourne and Adelaide the cricket was disappointingly one-sided. England won the first Test in Dunedin and the second by an innings in Auckland when New Zealand were sensationally dismissed for 26, the lowest ever Test score.

It was while they were sightseeing in Rotorura that Cowdrey received news that his mother had suffered heart trouble. With the blessing of the management, Cowdrey returned home early via America, with Graveney as company. Happily, his mother soon recovered, leaving him to look back on a momentous six months which had irrevocably changed his life. His inspirational selection had been fully vindicated, but the sheer brilliance of his batting had given rise to great expectations which would be something of a millstone round his neck in the years to come.

Having returned from Australia a hero, Cowdrey decided that no real purpose would be served by returning to Oxford, especially given the financial pressures it placed on his widowed mother at a time when money was scarce. There was also lurking in his mind the rather irksome commitment of two years' National Service which he decided to get out of the way as soon as possible. He wrote to the RAF and within two weeks in early May he was reporting to their base at Cardington, Bedfordshire. By the end of the month he had been discharged, enabling him to return to his true priorities. No sooner had he arrived at Cardington, than he was examined by two orthopaedic specialists – one services, the other civil – who had at their disposal a letter from Cowdrey's own doctor outlining his previous trouble with stiff toe joints. Both specialists advised that the disability would likely be aggravated by service life, thereby precipitating an operation. Not wanting to accept responsibility for such people in peacetime and having to end up paying Cowdrey a disability pension, the RAF decided on 31 May 1955 to discharge him. The decision caused an outcry as politicians and members of the public rounded on him for a dereliction of duty and dubious tactics to secure his release. 'If he is fit to undertake a tour of that nature [referring to Australia], surely he is fit to peel spuds in the RAF?' ranted Willie Hamilton, the Labour MP for West Fife and later scourge of the monarchy. 'What I find most hurtful', retorted Cowdrey, 'is the implication that I could ever be a party to the pulling of strings. The word "wangle" was actually used in the House last week (June 12th). This is an unwarranted reflection on me personally.' He did derive some satisfaction from the retraction from Sir Gerald Nabarro, the fiery Conservative MP for South Worcestershire and one of his main accusers, who, after meeting him accepted that Cowdrey had no case to answer; but in a sense the damage had been done. The letters poured in from service families and others, many of them containing poisonous barbs, leading Cowdrey to complain that 'to be the target for this volume of censure, utterly beyond my control, seemed an unkind burden to have to bear at the age of 21'.

Ironically his cause was not helped by his prodigious form when he returned to the cricket field. Having warmed up nicely against Oxford for MCC with 47 and 107, he marked his first match for Kent with a brilliant 139 against Northamptonshire. Then, after 48 and 44 against Sussex, he made 115 and 113 not out against Essex at Gillingham, a feat emulated by Doug Insole for the opposition, and 3 and 67 against Surrey. After this run glut it was no surprise that he should be back in national colours for the third Test against South Africa at Old Trafford. England were already two up in the series but an opposition attack containing the likes of Peter Heine, Neil Adcock, Hugh Tayfield and Trevor Goddard offered little in the way of profligacy and Cowdrey, out for 1 in the first innings, was given a thorough examination in the second. He eventually reached 50 but it took him over four hours and exposed severe deficiencies in his technique. The main threat came from Heine and Adcock, two huge, hostile quick bowlers who, discerning his propensity to go forward, peppered him with short balls causing untold damage to his fingers. He doggedly tried to brazen it out by playing for the Gentlemen against the Players the next day, but twenty minutes of discomfort at the wicket convinced him that he was unable to continue. It was to be nearly three weeks before he played again, by which time South Africa had squared the series at two all. With England struggling to find a reliable opening pair, Cowdrey was asked to help fill the breach. Thus, on 30 July, he returned to Kent in a position which brought him minimal fulfilment over the years. He did make 45 and 67 in the first match against Hampshire but, as *Wisden* remarked, 'by methods far removed from his usual freedom and certainty'. He was less successful thereafter and when his finger was damaged yet again, this time by Trevor Bailey, the injury was serious enough not only to pull him out of the final Test but for the remainder of the season. Fragmented and frustrating though it had been, Cowdrey could at least take comfort from a healthy average of well over 50 and *Wisden*'s decision to make him one of their Five Cricketers of the Year. He had also learnt from his mauling at the hands of Heine and Adcock that technical flexibility was called for when facing quick bowling of this type, with its bounce. From now on, therefore, he would play such bowling off the back foot and discover in the process that great batsmen could play off either foot with equal ease.

4

Taming the Sorcerer

After a winter in civvy street working for Stuart Chiesman, an influential member of the Kent committee, at the family department store in Lewisham, Cowdrey looked forward to returning to his true vocation as winter gave way to spring. A pre-season tonic was a five-week tour to the West Indies as captain of E. W. Swanton's XI, a goodwill trip designed to eradicate the legacy of bitterness – caused by the riot in the Georgetown Test and generally poor umpiring – from the MCC tour two years earlier. Although he was not at his most prolific, Cowdrey loved the relaxed informality of the Caribbean and the opportunity to get himself in trim for the forthcoming season. He began with two half-centuries against Glamorgan at Canterbury, and then saved Kent much embarrassment at Fenners with an undefeated double-century after Cambridge University had forced them to follow on. From there it was to Dartford and a belligerent 80 against Essex on a fiery pitch, all in a lost cause.

Such nonchalance was not to last, because by the end of May England's inability to find a ready successor to Hutton to open the innings meant that Cowdrey was again considered for a role he always disliked. As he went out to open at Gravesend, Cowdrey later recalled, he could see Les Ames, Doug Wright and Godfrey Evans sitting behind the bowler's arm and having a heated discussion about his suitability for this position. In his favour was his supreme skill against the moving ball and fast bowling in general. Against was his extreme reluctance to perform a specialist role which, with its exacting responsibilities, he felt took the edge off his game and limited his opportunity to dominate.

A week later all this seemed rather immaterial when Cowdrey, casting aside his reservations, teamed up with debutant Peter Richardson to open for England against Australia at Trent Bridge. The 1956 Australians were a shadow of the great 1948 side but under Ian Johnson they still contained a number of extremely fine cricketers, not least the still revered combination of Lindwall and Miller. In conditions unhelpful to batting, Cowdrey and Richardson were equal to the challenge and put on 53 for the first wicket before Cowdrey was caught at slip off the glove. Their one major piece of luck, prior to this, concerned their running between the wickets. Cowdrey drove Miller towards Davidson at deep cover, ran a single and turned for a second, but seeing Davidson pounce, he quickly shouted 'Wait'. Richardson, turning, hastily checked his run, slipped, fell on to his knees and lost his bat at the wicket-keeper's end. Feeling that Richardson had no chance of recovering, Cowdrey set off on what seemed a wasted journey. Davidson returned rather wide and Langley, the wicket-keeper, faced with one stump to aim at from four yards, threw the ball instead to Miller. His throw was a wild one, and with Richardson yards out, the excitable Miller slipped in his effort to reach it. By the time he had broken the stumps with both body and ball, Richardson had – much to the crowd's amazement – regained his ground.

With bad weather eating into playing time, England – having dismissed Australia cheaply – needed quick runs in their second innings. The openers obliged with a stand of 151, their country's first century partnership for the first wicket since Hutton and Cyril Washbrook at Headingley in 1948. Richardson made 73, Cowdrey 81. Their efforts, however, were wasted as more rain consigned the match to a draw.

Before the second Test Cowdrey continued in a rich vein with 197 for Kent against Worcestershire at Stourbridge, one of his best ever championship innings. His dismissal three short of another double-century disappointed his colleagues, since they had hoped to sample for the second time that year a crate of ale offered by a brewing firm for every 200 made. At Lord's, in the second Test, Australia won convincingly with Miller taking five wickets in each innings. In a match in which a number of stupendous catches were taken, including a splendid effort by Cowdrey to get rid of Australian opener, Colin McDonald, nothing surpassed the one by Richie Benaud to dismiss Cowdrey off Ken Mackay. Mackay recalls being livid that an lbw appeal had been turned down the previous ball and gave the next one everything he had. Driving what he thought to be a half-volley, Cowdrey, then on 23, hit it extremely hard only to see Benaud throw up his hands in the gully and pull off an astonishing reflex catch.

After Australia had set England an imposing fourth innings target, Benaud was again Cowdrey's bogeyman by virtue of some clever psychology which exposed his inhibitions. During the previous match against Kent, the Australians had noticed that Cowdrey was uncomfortable when left-armer Jack Wilson pitched the ball up on his toes as he thrust his left leg forward. Now, in order to combat Cowdrey effectively stonewalling him with his pad while May attacked at the other end, Benaud asked Peter Burge to go in very close at silly mid-on, hoping that Cowdrey would be forced on to the back foot. The ploy clearly unsettled Cowdrey, who walked down the wicket to May and informed his captain that 'It will kill this bloke if I happen to hit him'. Johnson approached May to enquire whether it was all right for Burge to stay there. 'Yes, if you don't mind his being killed,' May replied tartly. In the event Johnson moved Burge a couple of inches squarer and soon afterwards Cowdrey, falling victim to Benaud's plan, was palpably lbw on the back foot to a quicker top-spinner. He returned to the pavilion bitterly regretting his diffidence and resolved not to be so deterred in future, even if this meant hitting one of the close-in fielders.

One down after Lord's and in some trouble, the English selectors caused something of a sensation by recalling for the third Test one of their own panel, the forty-one-year-old Cyril Washbrook, five years after he had last played for his country. Many reacted sceptically but their hunch was more than vindicated after Ron Archer, in a fiery opening spell, dismissed Cowdrey, Richardson and Oakman for 17. In company with May, who scored 100, Washbrook put on 187 for the fourth wicket and was unfortunate to miss a century by two runs. England made 305, and on a deteriorating pitch Australia were no match for Laker and Lock as they careered to an innings defeat.

With the series now delicately balanced, the selectors sprang another surprise by bringing back David Sheppard after a mere handful of innings that summer because of his clerical commitments. His return helped to create an interesting anomaly: the top five positions in the batting order were all filled by amateurs. Faced with another arid wicket unlikely to last, the decisive moment came when May won the toss and chose to bat. On this slow, dead strip the Australian bowlers simply seemed to go through the motions and Cowdrey and Richardson were soon into top gear. By the time Cowdrey was caught by wicket-keeper Len Maddocks off Lindwall for 80, their partnership was worth 174, the highest opening stand against Australia since Hutton and Charles Barnett made 219 together at Trent Bridge in 1938. With Richardson and Sheppard both making centuries, England scored an imposing 459.

Between the innings, the dust brushed off the wicket resembled a desert storm and now, on a wearing surface, the Australians floundered badly against Laker. In front of 30,000 excited spectators they lost their last eight wickets for 36 runs to finish 84 all out, with Laker claiming nine for 37. They followed on but with wildly unseasonal weather confining play to a minimum over the next two days, they looked as if they might survive when the final day began. On a wicket now made sluggish by the rain the third-wicket pair survived to lunch. Afterwards the appearance of the sun caused another calamitous collapse to Laker and, resolutely though McDonald played for his 89, he could not stop the deluge. When Laker claimed Maddocks lbw with an hour to go he not only ensured that England retained the Ashes, he wrote his name into cricket history by capturing all ten wickets in the innings and nineteen in the match. This later statistic is one record which surely will stand the test of time.

Like a prisoner on parole, Cowdrey was released from the shackles of opening to make a brief return to his favoured no. 4 position for Kent and promptly celebrated with a hundred in Canterbury Week. His freedom lasted all but two matches before he once again assumed the poisoned chalice in preparation for the final Test. An unbeaten 65 against Gloucestershire in a lost cause was his only significant contribution and *Wisden*, reviewing his mediocre season for Kent, observed that he rarely did himself justice when going in first. He fared no better in the final Test at The Oval, with 0 and 8, when the weather saved Australia more humiliation after they again experienced problems with the turning ball. In a summer when Gubby Allen and his colleagues could congratulate themselves on a number of inspired selections, their experiment with Cowdrey as an opener had met with only mixed success. He had played two sparkling innings, it is true, but he barely averaged 30 for the series. Rather greater consistency would be expected of him on the winter tour to South Africa.

Before that there was the small matter of Cowdrey's wedding. Because of a life led in male-orientated institutions, he had rarely come across girls, let alone known them at all intimately, until he befriended Penny Chiesman, the daughter of Stuart Chiesman, his employer, during the winter of 1955–6. A forceful personality, a generous patron of charities and, above all, a benevolent supporter of Kent cricket, Chiesman's commitment to high standards generated respect wherever he went.

He and his brother, Russell, had inherited the family's draper's shop in Lewisham, south-east London and, by virtue of hard work, built up a chain of departmental stores in Kent. His success brought him a sizeable home in Chislehurst and social prominence, in time becoming High Sheriff of Kent and Chairman of the county cricket club from 1956–69. But behind this life of unostentatious affluence there lay a more tragic side, as Chiesman's wife had died prematurely of septicaemia, leaving him, at twenty-seven, to bring up three small children, the youngest of whom, Graham, was to be killed in a plane crash at the age of thirteen.

Reared in these difficult circumstances, Penny, the younger of the two girls, was educated at Ravenscroft School in Eastbourne and Farringtons in Chislehurst, where she excelled on the running track. Later, her love of horses led her to become a qualified instructor, and she held a genuine interest in cricket.

It was through her visits to Canterbury with her father that she first met Cowdrey in August 1951 and they became engaged in the spring of 1956. They were married, days after the end of the season, on 15 September at St Nicholas Church, Chislehurst, by the late Lord Bishop of Rochester, Dr Christopher Chavasse, abetted by David

Sheppard. Peter May was best man, and in a reception suffused with cricketing symbols, the 400 guests included Ian Craig and Len Maddocks from the Australian party that summer.

There was just time for a two-week honeymoon in Cornwall before Cowdrey left for South Africa. His regrets were to some degree tempered by the appetising feast in front of him, for the South African tour, with its combination of climate, scenery and hospitality, ranked with the very best. In contrast to the opulent life off the field which endeared itself to the whole team, the cricket, while never lacking in intensity, was of a rather soulless nature as batsmen struggled to come to terms with sluggish pitches and a defensive approach.

During the voyage out, the thorny question of opening once again reared its head. Cowdrey had no wish to continue in the role but, well aware that there were only two other specialists in the party, he wavered when May broached the subject. His accommodating attitude resulted in his partnering either Richardson or Alan Oakman during the first four matches. Against some fairly gentle opposition his record paled in comparison with May, who began the tour with four centuries, but neither was it negligible. His 173 against Orange Free State was part of a second-wicket partnership of 318 with Oakman, and his 84 against Transvaal was top score in either innings. It took him six hours, though, and afterwards he reckoned that Heine and Adcock were more formidable than Lindwall and Miller the previous summer because of their extra speed and bounce. Against such hostility the selectors decided that a player of Cowdrey's class would be better served down the order. He was only too happy to oblige.

Although England were unbeaten in a series for six years they took nothing for granted against a South African team reckoned by their leading cricket-writer, Louis Duffus, to be their strongest since 1905–06. The first Test in Johannesburg, watched by a crowd of 100,000, offered little in the way of entertainment, with a scoring rate of only 28 runs per hour which set the tone for the series. England, thanks to the batting of Richardson and Cowdrey in the first innings and the bowling of Bailey in the second, won comfortably. They retained their ascendancy at Cape Town days later in the second Test. Again, they batted first on another slow pitch and, led by a six-hour century from Cowdrey, ground out 369. Despite enjoying a lead of

164, May chose not to enforce the follow-on. The decision seemed to backfire as his batsmen dithered until Cowdrey showed them a route out of the maze. May recalled emerging from the shower after his innings when he was summoned to watch the cricket. 'I went to the window and there was the Colin of Australia two years before stroking the ball through the gaps as if it was the easiest thing in the world. Cowdrey the great enigma made 61 out of a stand of 87, with Denis Compton, a proportion which few can have achieved.' Set 385 to win, South Africa had no answer to Wardle's googlies and chinamen and crashed to defeat by 312 runs.

After this enterprising little gem, Cowdrey – much to everyone's frustration – retreated once again into his shell at Durban, particularly against Tayfield, whose 38 wickets during the series made him a force to be reckoned with. With May unable to get going in the Tests both he and the manager, Freddie Brown, spent some time trying to persuade Cowdrey to lead the assault on the off-spinner. He took some convincing. Brown recalled that in the second innings, with the match evenly poised, Cowdrey went in with their instructions ringing in his ears. Soon he hit Tayfield for an effortless six over long-on. The next ball he hit him for three to long-off. 'After that Cowdrey hardly played a shot at Tayfield for the next 10 overs and eventually got out. I said, "What happened? You had him." He replied, "I was dropped and felt I had to stay in."' Tayfield, who could not bowl at him, was allowed to get back on top. He finished with eight for 69 and South Africa were even money to score 190 to win. They were once again toiling against Wardle until May surprisingly took him off and they escaped with a draw.

Drawing fresh hope from this reprieve, South Africa, urged on by their enthusiastic supporters, played with such frenzied determination thereafter that they clawed their way back into contention. At Johannesburg in the fourth Test England, needing 232 to win, were 65 for two when Cowdrey joined Insole and together they motored along at nearly a run a minute. Victory seemed almost assured until Insole was out at 147 followed shortly afterwards by May and Compton. Cowdrey continued to play freely as others came and went. Then, with 35 wanted from the last three wickets, he drove Tayfield back like a bullet only to see the bowler clutch the ball into his stomach. Minutes later Tayfield had added two more scalps to finish with nine for 113, and he was chaired from the field as South Africa ran out worthy winners by 17 runs. They won again on a terrible wicket in Port Elizabeth, to square the series, leaving England to rue missed opportunities. For Cowdrey, a Test average of 33.1 gave some credence to Alan Ross's view in his book *Cape Summer* that he was disappointing largely because after Australia the ultimate was expected of him. Ross acknowledged several important innings, notably his second at Cape Town, 'but in between [he] had moments of looking quite terrible. When the bowlers were on top he appeared incapable of asserting his own personality; it was as if sensing himself a victim he had already connived with destiny. . . There were moments when one wanted to send him out a double Scotch and instruct him to take the cotton wool off his bat and really hit it. He played always *andante*: more often it should have been *con brio*.'

Ross's opinion reflected Cowdrey's own disillusionment with his batting on the tour. Apart from a propensity still to play Heine and Adcock off the front foot he was all at sea against the accuracy of Tayfield. To combat the threat from the off-spinner, who dismissed him four times in the series, Cowdrey felt he must learn to hit the ball in the air. Consequently, he used net sessions to practise the lofted on-drive, which in time became a useful weapon in his already formidable armoury.

It was while Cowdrey was in South Africa that he was surprised to receive a cable from Kent asking if he would succeed the increasingly injury-prone Doug Wright as captain. Daunted by the thought of leading such senior players as Arthur Fagg, Fred Ridgeway, Godfrey Evans and Wright himself, and guessing correctly that much of the team took their lead from Evans, Cowdrey sought out his wicket-keeper to discover their likely reaction. Evans was typically fulsome and, duly encouraged, Cowdrey accepted. He began with a duck against Middlesex at Lord's, but Kent won handsomely and although they had to wait two more months before they triumphed again, four more victories thereafter gave some modest cause for optimism and the Kent report was glowing about the new captain's impact. Cowdrey certainly brought great enthusiasm to his new responsibilities, but once again he was absent for nearly half the matches because of his England commitments.

The summer's visitors were John Goddard's West Indians, hoping to repeat their great triumph of seven years earlier. The three W's – Worrell, Walcott and Weekes – were still in attendance to lend a touch of class to their batting, along with their exciting new youngsters, Collie Smith, Gary Sobers and Rohan Kanhai, but their bowling looked rather less well-endowed. Much would depend on their celebrated spinners, Sonny Ramadhin and Alf Valentine, who had wrought so much damage on the 1950 tour. As things turned out, Valentine was so innocuous that he did not even make the side for the first Test, but Ramadhin, the little Indian magician, still exercised a continuing mystique over his opponents as they struggled to fathom the secrets of his genius. Encouraged by tales from Australia of how Ramadhin had wilted under sustained bombardment, the English batsmen tried something similar, ignoring the fact that a sluggish Edgbaston pitch was not the ideal surface for such tactics. The result was a minor humiliation as England, on the opening day of the series, were shot out for 186 by Ramadhin, who finished with seven for 49 from 31 overs.

The scale of England's humiliation was merely underlined by their opponents who, on the same wicket, made 474, a lead of 288. By close of play on Saturday, Ramadhin had added two more to his tally, and when Brian Close was out early on Monday morning at 113 for three, there was an expectation that the match would be over by teatime. However, the doom merchants had reckoned without May and Cowdrey. Having spent much of the weekend discussing the best way to combat Ramadhin, they resolved to get onto the front foot as much as possible and play him as an off-spinner. This would enable them to protect their stumps and allow the leg-spinner to pass harmlessly across the bat. Once out in the middle, both batsmen kept rigidly to their game plan as Ramadhin ran through his whole bag of tricks against them. Cowdrey in particular struggled to pick the leg-break and there were plenty of moral victories for the little Trinidadian as he induced any number of false shots, but the luck was not running his way. He also had to contend with some unresponsive umpiring, as Cowdrey repeatedly stretched his pads down the wicket to anything pitched on or outside the off stump on a length just too short to drive. Ramadhin appealed repeatedly, but Cowdrey placed great faith in the umpires, rightly assuming that his distance down the wicket would create an element of doubt as to whether the ball would actually hit the stumps.

Cowdrey, 25 not out at lunch when England had reached 176, kept May company during a tense afternoon as Gilchrist, the erratic quick bowler, and Ramadhin gave no quarter. Then as bowlers began to tire, daylight gradually appeared. May, now past his century, went on to the offensive, and England 279 for three at tea had advanced to 378 for three at the close with the captain on 193, and Cowdrey on 78. Commenting on their epic tussle with Ramadhin, John Woodcock in *The Times* declared that it had been a battle royal and the two batsmen, in winning it, had displayed rare character and skill.

On the final morning they continued where they had left off the previous evening, scoring 40 in the first hour and slightly more in the second as Ramadhin sleep-walked into history with his marathon bowling stint. It was just after one o'clock when Cowdrey reached his first Test century in England, after 7½ hours of disciplined resistance. He promptly celebrated by hitting four classic boundaries. By lunch England were 467 for three, 179 ahead and all but safe. Afterwards, both batsmen, now free of their chains, were able to play according to their lights, and the West Indies, according to Woodcock, 'looked increasingly disconsolate as Surrey and Kent, Charterhouse and Tonbridge, Cambridge and Oxford splayed the field with the loveliest of strokes'. When Cowdrey was finally caught at mid-on for 154, his partnership with May had amassed 411, a record English stand, the highest for the fourth wicket in the history of Test cricket, and the third highest overall. 'They had been in together eight hours twenty minutes, wherein supreme concentration, good judgement and strength of purpose had never wavered,' declared E. W. Swanton. Evans was now promoted, and he and May did what they liked with the bowling until the captain finally signalled an end to the slaughter. His unbeaten 285 was his highest score in first-class cricket, and the highest by an England captain, surpassing Hammond's 240 against Australia at Lord's in 1938. Ramadhin, in contrast, 'with the spring long vanished from his step and the poison from his fingers', to use Woodcock's colourful description, had finished with two for 179 off 98 overs, the most balls every delivered in a Test innings (He bowled 129 overs in the match, also a Test record.) Embittered by his treatment from Cowdrey and the umpires, he was never the same bowler again.

Owing to May's delayed declaration, West Indies managed to escape from Edgbaston with a draw at 72 for seven. They were not so fortunate in the next Test at Lord's. Following up from his previous triumph, Cowdrey again shaped the outcome of the match. Entering at 34 for three in reply to the West Indies first innings total of 127, he first saw off Gilchrist in a spectacular stand with Richardson of 95 in eighty-five minutes. Next day, with England still in some trouble at 134 for five, in company with Evans he added 174 for the seventh wicket. The contrast in style between the two could not have been starker. Evans recalls Cowdrey's concern at the way his rustic belligerence upset the temperamental Gilchrist. Eventually he said, 'Godfrey, if you are going to lash at this bloke and keep getting tickles, for heaven's sake don't let's take a single. I keep getting these bouncers. They're very dangerous indeed.'

Gilchrist aside, the rest of the attack were his minions, as Cowdrey lorded it over the sacred turf. Evans paid tribute to the perfect ease and timing which sent the ball rocketing to the boundary. 'I wanted to start running and as Colin watched the ball he said, "My boy, there's no need to run". He was always right. It was four all the way.'

With Cowdrey scoring 152 and Evans 82, England finished on 419 and despite an acclaimed 90 from Weekes, West Indies were well beaten. They did not recover, getting the worst of a draw at Trent Bridge and suffering heavy defeats at Headingley and The Oval. Cowdrey continued to cash in with consecutive half-centuries in the third and fourth Tests, failing only in the last one. His average of 72.50 for the series was one of the best he ever achieved at home. Contrasting these figures with less impressive ones for Kent, *Wisden* was unduly carping in its comments. Apart from having the captaincy to think about, there could be little to quibble about, a county average of 44.50 and an August which produced one century and five fifties in nine innings. There were times when Cowdrey rightly felt that the burden of expectation sat too heavily upon him, and this was one such instance.

5

An Athenian in Sparta

However great the enjoyment Cowdrey derived from the game, the need for constant success, as with all top players, was a fundamental priority to which he devoted much time and effort. Nothing was left to chance. His kit would always be tenderly cared for, appearance absolutely immaculate, opponents rigorously analysed and wickets closely inspected before play commenced. Most days would begin with a net or at least some throw-downs. Then, if his side was batting, he would watch quietly from the dressing-room or the pavilion balcony, battling to contain his nerves before making an entry as stately as a Roman emperor, such was the scale of reception accorded him. After sedately walking to the middle, shoulders sloping and slightly hunched, to adapt to the light he would take guard (invariably leg stump unless facing genuinely quick bowling), look round the field and touch the peak of his cap before facing up to his first ball. Learning from the greats such as Hobbs, Cowdrey would look to get off the mark with a single, then quietly accumulate during the first few overs, employing to good effect the flick off his legs, the gentle run down to third-man or the push into the off side. A fierce concentrator, Cowdrey frequently talked to himself at the crease to ensure that his attention did not wander, particularly when weighed down with worry. If beaten by a good ball he would try to fathom the cause and make the necessary adjustment next time round, sometimes by taking a fresh guard. Fascinated by the art of batting and constantly analysing its finer points, he might share some thought with his partner at the end of the over as they discussed the state of the game or the way to play a particular bowler. He would also use these conferences as the chance to relieve the tension by engaging in some lighthearted banter. Peter Richardson recalls the occasion when, facing the Australian tearaway Gordon Rorke, Cowdrey came down the wicket and suggested he hit him back over his head. Ken Barrington, one of Cowdrey's most prolific partners for England, greatly appreciated his ability to settle him either through his mimicking of famous cricketers or by drawing his attention to some attractive woman in the crowd.

Because of his technical help, an uncommon ability which forced bowlers to change their length, and his unselfish encouragement, Cowdrey was an ideal person to bat with. Always an excellent judge of a run himself, and surprisingly nimble for a big man, he invariably responded to his partner's call, never trying like some great batsmen, to monopolise the strike. As befitted his unostentatious character, he showed little emotion in the middle, quietly acknowledging a good ball with a smile or a word of commendation and ignoring any deliberate act of provocation. When hitting a four, he looked almost apologetic as he watched the ball speed to the boundary. When reaching 50 or 100 he would respond to the acclaim with a modest raising of the bat, as he would when returning to the pavilion at the end of a fine innings. Contentious decisions might induce some wry comment in the dressing-room, but otherwise there would be no bitter recrimination about dismissals; just a reflective post-mortem, a determination to learn from the experience, and forty winks in the corner, a habit which earned him the sobriquet of 'Kipper'.

In the field his cheerful demeanour was rather more apparent when the pressure was slightly less intense. Trevor Bailey recalls Cowdrey's splendid company in the slips with his genial asides or pithy comments, while a wicket would be greeted with a hearty handclap or a boyish skip of delight. When he himself was the catcher he would celebrate by throwing the ball up in the air or nonchalantly pouching it in his pocket, often to the bafflement of the crowd who were slow to see what had happened. Keen as mustard to win, Cowdrey never allowed his partisanship to deter him from paying obeisance to traditional courtesies such as congratulating a member of the opposition when he reached a notable landmark.

As for his profile at the crease, there was no better model for a spectator to admire or a youngster to emulate. Equipped with a correct stance, grip and back-lift, Cowdrey, by keeping his head still to the last possible second, found himself in the right position to move towards the line of the ball. This ability to get into line and play late made him an expert against swing and turn, not least the art of leaving the ball outside the off stump. Tony Greig, the Sussex and England all-rounder, recalls the time he was convinced he had found the edge of Cowdrey's bat with the perfect outswinger only to find him turning his wrists at the last moment to remove his bat from the line of danger. His natural eye and first-class defence also equipped him to cope with the fastest of bowlers. Compton, watching Cowdrey play Lindwall and Bill Johnston in his second Test, was struck by the amount of time he had at his disposal. Fifteen years later Greig recalled Cowdrey's unhurried composure compared to his Kentish team-mates when facing John Snow on a sporting wicket at Hove. On encountering the blistering pace of Wes Hall and Chester Watson in the Caribbean in 1959–60, he had to make some adjustment to his stance but his ability to withstand the rising delivery by dropping his wrists and swinging out of harm's way from a bouncer helped turn trauma into triumph. Even in Australia in 1974–75, Fred Titmus thought Cowdrey played Dennis Lillee and Jeff Thomson as capably as anyone.

Another of Cowdrey's attributes was his top-hand, soft grip which enabled him to change his shot with minimal adjustment. Jack Bannister, the Warwickshire seamer of the 1950s and 60s, recalls bowling to him on a green wicket at Coventry and being convinced that he had bowled him with an off-cutter which nipped back as he went for a drive. Suddenly Cowdrey averted the danger by closing the gap with his top hand. Bannister thought Cowdrey as good a top-hand, soft-hands player as he ever saw and it was this skill which, along with his balance, gave him his silky timing. In comparison with May and Dexter, who generated their great power from their use of the arms and shoulders, Cowdrey, relying on the pace of the ball to come on to him, leaned into it with his body weight and stroked it sweetly. A classical off-side player, he had the skill of a Compton or a Graveney to place the ball by opening and closing the face of the bat. Christopher Cowdrey's abiding memory as a youngster when watching his father bat was to see him caressing the ball through the covers with none of the fielders moving. 'When you're in form,' Cowdrey used to tell his son, 'you should be able to pick your billboard.'

His range of options for shot deployment was masterly. Fred Titmus, the Middlesex and England all-rounder, recalls the occasion when his team-mates John Murray and Peter Parfitt, in a game doomed to a draw, would nominate a particular shot to be played and how Cowdrey, much to their amusement, would pick him off at will regardless of the delivery. In addition to his prowess off the back foot through the off side, he was, in the eyes of Alan Davidson, as fine an exponent of the cover-drive as has ever been seen and a deft cutter, both square and late, playing with economy of movement. So effortless and unflustered was his approach that often a fielder would look up at the scoreboard and find that Cowdrey had scored 40 in no time. When in the mood, he could destroy an attack as clinically as anyone, but it was done with the subtlety of a rapier rather than with the bludgeon of an axe.

As the nature of the game changed with the demise of the leg-spinner and the onset of inswing, Cowdrey became increasingly addicted to the leg side. In his prime he was an accomplished hooker and he could always work the shorter ball on the leg stump through square leg or mid-wicket. His on-drive was exquisitely balanced and to the off-spinner he teased the ball into the gaps by closing the bat face with an exaggerated roll of the wrist. If something more ambitious was required he could hit the off-spinner over mid-wicket or mid-on with little arm movement, as he did to Lance Gibbs in his match-winning 71 against West Indies at Port-of-Spain in 1968 or as he sometimes did later in the one-day game. He rarely swept, believing it to be a stroke fraught with danger, and employed instead the 'paddle', a drive to fine-leg to a ball outside leg stump, by pivoting with a straight bat rather than a cross one. This shot was his one departure from textbook orthodoxy but it served him well over the years, especially against the off-spinner.

Apart from his prowess against all types of bowling his faultless technique stood him in good stead on all kinds of pitches. Whilst it would be true to say that the harder surfaces of Australia or West

Indies, where the ball came on more truly, were more conducive to his style, his capacity to play late and his soft-hands approach made him the master of uncovered pitches. He was also a specialist on a turning wicket through the use of the front pad as an extra line of defence. Contrary to impression he first employed these tactics not against Ramadhin at Edgbaston in 1957, but against Johnson and Benaud in 1956, and with umpires loath to give leading players out under the existing law (particularly a captain with responsibility for marking their performances) it wasn't just Ramadhin who cried himself hoarse over the years. Many bowlers resented his methods, and when other batsmen began to do likewise an unwelcome new trend had infiltrated English cricket.

Faced with a batsman of Cowdrey's quality, constructing a strategy against him was no easy task for either bowler or captain, especially once he was into his stride. Ted Dexter had ideas about most batsmen, but for Cowdrey and Sobers he had no obvious remedies. Fred Titmus's philosophy was to bowl straight and not give him any width. Keith Andrew's tactic as captain of Northamptonshire was to give Cowdrey a single and attack his partner, while Robin Hobbs, the Essex leg-spinner, felt his best chance was to lie low and talk someone else into bowling.

Sobers found that having failed to trouble Cowdrey with his inswinger, so solid was his defence, he reverted to the outswinger in an attempt to get him to play away from the pad. A similar device was used by Alan Davidson, another left-arm quick bowler, who moved the new ball very late in the air and off the pitch in either direction. He dismissed Cowdrey nine times in Test matches, more than any other player, normally caught at the wicket or in the slip cordon, Cowdrey's most frequent mode of dismissal stemming from his ability to get a touch to the moving ball. Davidson attributed a measure of his success over Cowdrey to his increasing tendency to play with the pad, in contrast to his willingness to put bat to ball for Kent. By playing with the pad Cowdrey was committing himself to the front foot, which gave Davidson the opportunity to attack him with both the outswinger and the inswinger, knowing that if he did not give him width he would not be taken apart.

This reluctance to take the offensive was the bowler's best hope.

Jim Laker reckoned that he could bowl a maiden to Cowdrey even when he had scored 120, while Bannister remembers how he could bowl to Cowdrey on a flat wicket knowing he could avoid retribution in a way that he could not with either May or Dexter. On a slower wicket a humdrum medium pacer, bowling to a defensive field, could frustrate him because of his reluctance to improvise or hit across the line. Not only did such ungainly tactics violate the sacred principles of batting, the lack of strength in his small limbs and hands acted as a deterrent. Others exploited Cowdrey's diffidence against the slow bowler, particularly early in his innings (it was rare, even when well set, for him to advance down the wicket to them). Pat Pocock, the Surrey and England off-spinner, tried to get him caught at silly mid-off, and Ray Illingworth, the Yorkshire and England all-rounder, in tandem with Brian Close, his captain, conspired to upset his poise by crowding him with players in front of the wicket to stop him playing with his pad. Close recalls one match when he brought Illingworth on at once and crouched so close at silly mid-off that Cowdrey complained to the umpire. He was out to Illingworth shortly afterwards. Another spinner who bothered him was Richie Benaud, who used to tie him down outside the leg stump well aware that Cowdrey would be loath to hit him against the line. It was partly to break out of this siege that Cowdrey invented the 'paddle'.

All this tactical ingenuity only goes a small way to explaining the central paradox of Cowdrey's career: how such a wonderful player on so many occasions could appear in hock to bowlers decidedly his inferior. 'The word to describe Cowdrey's batting is frustrating,' recalled M. J. K. Smith. Les Ames and Doug Wright thought that he should have scored 200 centuries as opposed to just over a hundred, while their Kent colleague Godfrey Evans wished that Cowdrey, instead of trying to emulate his heroes, had just batted in his own way. 'That would have been world-class.'

The fact that such comments are typical of a wider consensus about his unfulfilled potential used to irk Cowdrey, given his achievement. His frustration is understandable, but it is difficult to think of another comparable player who could so often fall from his pedestal. Part of the explanation might be in the length of his career.

To play to the summit of one's potential year after year, six days a week, would be a huge undertaking for anyone, and although Cowdrey never lost his enthusiasm for the county game, there were times when the wear and tear of 114 Tests caught up with him. There was also the problem of deteriorating pitches and lusher outfields, particularly for a touch player like himself who relied upon the ball coming on at pace. It was no coincidence that, in common with a number of his contemporaries such as Dexter and Barrington, he reserved his best performances for overseas where the local conditions more suited his game.

And then there was the personal factor. Cowdrey was above all a man of moods who, according to John Arlott, 'could sink into pits of uncertainty when the fire ceased to burn'. He could be ruffled by the state of a wicket, an opposing bowler's reputation or an inability to pierce the field. His cricketing purity was such that once his sense of timing deserted him he felt bereft in a cruel world. The fact that he was endowed with supreme gifts seemed totally lost on him. Hubert Doggart recalls hearing Cowdrey say at Eastbourne in 1957, 'What a difficult game it is.' Tom Graveney could never understand how, after his brilliant maiden Test century in Melbourne, he could still fail to believe in himself as he continued to experiment with his technique, while John Murray recalls how before one tour Cowdrey visited Bob Wyatt, a good but not a great former England player, in the nets to discuss his grip. Titmus felt that had Cowdrey been forced to earn his money as a professional he would have been more practical and eliminated theory.

Gary Sobers has memories of batting with Cowdrey for the Commonwealth XI against an Indian XI in Calcutta in 1965 and figuring in a large partnership with him. Having watched a glorious exhibition of strokplay, Sobers said to Cowdrey as they came off, 'Colin, that's one of the best innings I've ever seen you play. Why don't you bat this way all the time?' 'Oh well,' he replied with a twinkle, 'I was watching you, at the other end.' What really struck Sobers on this occasion was Cowdrey's willingness to put bat to ball instead of using his pad. The fact that he so often reverted to more defensive methods was, according to Sobers, an awareness of his indispensability to England. He had already been compelled to shoulder an undue load when put in charge of a struggling Kent side in 1957, just at a time when he had become, with May, the vital component in England's batting line-up.

But this need to tread carefully in the interests of his team does not entirely explain the schizophrenia of Cowdrey's batting, a trait he inherited from his mentor, Hutton. E. W. Swanton recalls how even in, arguably, Cowdrey's two finest innings for England, his maiden century in Melbourne and his 97 against West Indies at Kingston in 1959–60, he suddenly became becalmed when cruising easily with the wind at his back. Walter Hammond later told Cowdrey in South Africa that he had followed his Melbourne innings with interest on the radio and was willing him to slip his moorings by looking for singles. On this particular occasion, and sometimes on others, he managed to regain his lost momentum, but the capricious nature of his mood helped only to heighten the mystery behind his genius.

Cowdrey's largesse was not confined to his batting. He was also invaluable to his team in the field. Chance dictated that he should become a specialist close fielder on his first tour of Australia when, after accepting a couple of staple offerings in the slips, he continued to be stationed there (or sometimes in the gully) from then on, which, given his lack of pace in the field and weak throw, was a logical development. Recalling Hammond's axiom to him that any slip should be so well-positioned that he never got green stains on his trousers, he tried to follow the advice of one of the world's greatest exponents of this art. Concentrating intently, he stayed crouched to the final possible moment, giving himself every opportunity to detect the flight of the ball, and moved with the knees, keeping his head absolutely still. With his keen eye, sharp reflexes and soft hands, he brought that same graceful ease to his catching as characterised his batting. Such effortless dexterity was not entirely natural. Cowdrey's commitment to improvement was such that he took no liberties with his practice. David Kemp recalls the evening Cowdrey dropped in at Tonbridge to put his left hand through a rigorous session on the slip cradle to atone for a dropped catch that day which he felt he should have held. Over the years his left hand got better and although he lacked Bobby Simpson's mobility on both sides he was, according to Peter Parfitt – a slip specialist himself – brilliant when the ball came to him; a fact borne out by Cowdrey's career tally of 638 catches, 120 of which were in Tests.

6

Dust and Ashes

The summer of 1958 was one of the wettest on record, providing the worst possible conditions for a young, inexperienced New Zealand side under John Reid. In their previous Test against England three years earlier, they had been dismissed for 26. Now, on rain-affected wickets, against Laker and Lock, they offered little opposition to a side preparing for a hard winter in Australia. Their best moments came on the opening day of the series at Edgbaston when only May, with 84, and Cowdrey, with 81, stood between them and a major upset as England slumped to 221 all out. New Zealand fared even worse and, with Cowdrey to the fore again in the second innings with 70, England ultimately won by 205 runs. He made 65 at Lord's, did not bat in a rain-interrupted match at Headingley, and was rested at Old Trafford. The decision caused some consternation, not only to Cowdrey but to all those who felt that a Test side should always comprise the best eleven available. When he returned at The Oval, England had won four out of four and only persistent rain prevented them from winning all five. By then Cowdrey's own form had deserted him. From the dizzy heights of midsummer, when he had managed three centuries in four innings, he endured the most fallow period in his career with only 115 runs in his last thirteen championship innings – an important factor in Kent's slide down the table to finish eighth.

But this mild embarrassment was soon forgotten as attention switched to Australia. Another honour came Cowdrey's way with the news that he, rather than Bailey, the previous incumbent, would be vice-captain in a side which otherwise had a predictable look to it.

Few England sides have set off on such a tide of optimism as Peter May's in 1958–59. Not only had they been unbeaten in a series for eight years and had had the better of Australia in three successive Ashes series, they had many stars of proven quality. What few people chose to recall was that sport is cyclical and that just as many of England's players were approaching veteran status, so their Australian counterparts were frisky colts champing to be put through their paces. Under Ian Craig's leadership they had restored their sagging fortunes with a convincing series win in South Africa earlier in the year. Then with Craig unavailable because of hepatitis, the selectors had raised a few eyebrows by appointing Benaud as his successor ahead of Neil Harvey, the official vice-captain and Benaud's captain at New South Wales. The choice was not instantly popular but in time was to prove amply vindicated as Benaud's tactical flair and enterprise, coupled with his concern for his players, made him one of Australia's greatest captains.

Even before MCC had docked at Fremantle problems had ominously begun to mount. First, a series of derogatory press articles by Wardle about his county, Yorkshire, had brought about his dismissal and the withdrawal of his invitation to tour. Second, a rift the previous summer between May and Laker had led to the latter vowing not to tour, and although he later had second thoughts, relations between the two men remained cool. Third, a nasty deck-chair accident on board ship deprived May of Willie Watson's services for two months. By the time he was fit again, the team had become embroiled in a bitter dispute about 'throwing' which bedevilled Anglo-Australian relations and besmirched the world of cricket.

Owing to inaction and complacency by the game's authorities, throwing had become increasingly endemic worldwide. Now, as MCC began their itinerary against Western Australia, the first mutterings about the action of Keith Slater, who bowled May for nought, were heard. When similar dubious actions appeared in the form of Hitchcox and Tretheway for South Australia and Ian Meckiff for Victoria, the mutterings turned to something stronger. The lack of rhythm, the sudden jerk and the inaccuracy of Meckiff in particular, all convinced the shocked players that he threw. Godfrey Evans, adamant that the boil should be lanced before it was too late, went to the manager, Freddie Brown, after the game against Victoria, suggesting that they contact the Australian Board of Control and apprise them of their views. Brown agreed and promised to have a word with May, but the captain, feeling that Meckiff did not pose any great threat as a bowler and not wishing to create a diplomatic incident, decided to let the matter drop. Many of his team, in retrospect, felt this to be a fatal error.

Throwing aside, the tour itself proceeded quite smoothly, with MCC unbeaten in their seven first-class matches up to the first Test and demolishing the Australian XI by 345 runs. Cowdrey felt very much at home in Perth, beginning with 28 and 65 against Western Australia and 78 and 100 not out against a Combined XI, but faltered thereafter as his batting entered one of its most introspective stages. A few nights before the first Test, Alec Bedser, covering the tour from the press box, broached this diffidence with him and arranged to bowl at him the following day in order to increase his confidence. Rain put paid to these plans but he was given something to ponder.

In conditions more appropriate to Manchester than Brisbane, May, well aware of Hutton's error four years earlier, elected to bat first on winning the toss. He soon had cause to regret this as England set an unfortunate precedent for the series with a terrible start, all out for 134. Australia, in turn, struggled to gain a lead of 52. Then England, with Bailey making 68 in nearly eight hours, scored a measly 106 runs on the fourth day – the slowest day's cricket in Anglo-Australian Tests. The situation cried out for Cowdrey at his best to shake his team out of its lethargy, and he was beginning to rise to the challenge when there occurred the game's most controversial incident. Playing back to Meckiff, Cowdrey gloved a short ball to Lindsay Kline at backward short-leg, who threw himself forward and, according to Swanton, appeared to scoop the ball, almost if not quite off the ground. There was a moment's pause before an appeal was lodged by Meckiff. Umpire Mel McInnes, at the bowler's end, looked across to his colleague Col Hoy, at square-leg, who gave the bemused Cowdrey out. As Cowdrey made to depart Peter Burge, one of the Australian close fielders, shouted, 'Hang on Kip, that's not a catch.' ''Course it's a ***** catch,' wicket-keeper Wally Grout retorted, a view echoed by Kline himself when quizzed by his captain. Meanwhile, as McInnes stood immobile at his end, Hoy finally approached him. '***** off,' McInnes hissed. 'Don't come near me. It makes it look like something's wrong.' The confusion only added to Cowdrey's disappointment as he trudged off slowly to the pavilion, frequently glancing back, amidst a chorus of boos from a crowd unhappy with the umpire's verdict. The English press corps were furious and McInnes, previously an umpire of high repute, now found himself an increasingly discredited figure. By the end of the series his stock was so low that he announced his retirement. From 153 for four, when Cowdrey was out, England subsided to 198 all out and with Australia's rising new hope, Norman O'Neill, making a mockery of the tedium hitherto, with a cultured 71 not out, Benaud's men coasted to victory by eight wickets.

As England retired to Tasmania to regroup, their mood was not lifted by the news that their request to replace McInnes had been turned down by the Australian Board of Control, which also refused to acknowledge a problem with throwing. Their reservations became ever greater after the second Test in Melbourne. On a grassy pitch May again must have regretted his decision to bat first when Davidson removed Richardson, Watson and Graveney in the third over of the day. The defeaning roar of an impassioned crowd greeting every scalp sent shudders down Cowdrey's spine as he waited anxiously in the pavilion. When he joined his captain at 92 for four, Cowdrey found batting to be an exacting business but as the afternoon wore on he began to relax. Still together at the close, at 173 for four, they started brightly the next morning until May was bowled by a thunderbolt from Meckiff which plucked out his middle stump before his bat had barely moved. His dismissal for 113 precipitated another collapse, with Cowdrey soon following for 44, and England folded for 259. Sterling fast bowling by Statham (seven for 57) restricted Australia's lead to 49, but there the contest ended. In a shade under three hours England capitulated to Meckiff, who took six for 38, and were all out for 87 en route to an eight-wicket defeat. It was a traumatic experience as Meckiff, bowling straighter than usual, numbered both May and Cowdrey amongst his victims. Tyson observed that as the best natural timers in the team these two were the most inconvenienced by the throwers, since their high back-lifts were not conducive to picking up the flight of the ball and determining its pace.

Two down after two, flummoxed by Meckiff and feeling that they were not competing on equal terms, England flew into Sydney in a dejected state. In a side which contained a number of strong-minded individuals, the troops became increasingly restless about the conduct of high command. Not only did May and Cowdrey rarely socialise with the team off the field, the captain's austere integrity, his unimaginative tactics and his aversion to accepting advice from his senior professionals presented an unfavourable contrast with his gregarious Australian counterpart. The rigid discipline, with the toning down of the antics of the popular Saturday Night Club in particular, was a further blow to morale. 'More than any other player I played with, Peter May lacked the common touch,' recalled Tyson, who also saw an amateur-professional rift developing because the former gained more in expenses compared to the latter's salary after tax. In this increasingly fractious atmosphere, Cowdrey, the loyalist of lieutenants to May, made little impact as vice-captain and later admitted that Bailey, Hutton's deputy, should have been given the job.

After their disarray in Melbourne, England faced no let-up in Sydney, trailing by 138 runs on first innings. When Arthur Milton, Bailey and Graveney were back in the pavilion with only 64 on the board, another drubbing seemed probable, until May and Cowdrey took charge. They batted with such conviction that they forced Benaud, deprived of the injured Meckiff, on to the defensive. Still together at the close and at lunch on the final day, their partnership realised 182 before May was bowled for 92 by off-spinner Burke, another Australian with a bent arm. By then the match was safe and Cowdrey plodded on to a six-hour undefeated century, then the slowest in Ashes history, to keep his team's slender hopes in the series alive.

Their respite was brief. On the morning of the fourth Test in Adelaide, Laker, to May's consternation, insisted that he was unable to play because of a finger injury and England took the field with an unbalanced attack. May felt that his best hope was to exploit any early moisture and field first when he won the toss. Statham's first ball to McDonald very nearly bowled him, but that was the nearest England came to a breakthrough as the opening pair put on 171 for the first wicket. Australia totalled 476 and once again they soon had their teeth into the English upper order. Given their repeated failure to lay any solid foundations, the case for May and Cowdrey, who had started the series at nos. 4 and 5 respectively, to bat higher in the order increasingly gained weight. Now at last, the captain bowed to his subordinates and returned to his rightful no. 3 position, while Cowdrey went in at 4. They were soon together at 11 for two and although May did not last long Cowdrey played quite beautifully, enthralling the Adelaide crowd with the artistry of his cover drives. His 84 was the one major contribution before he played on to Gordon Rorke, Australia's lofty new paceman. His dubious action and habitual tendency to drag his back foot beyond the popping crease so that he was delivering the ball from about eighteen yards' range, soon won him a prominent place in an increasingly large rogues' gallery. Laker recalls the occasion when, after Cowdrey was out in the last Test, an elderly gentleman went up to him and said, 'Excuse me, Cowdrey, do you mind if I give you a little advice?' 'Not a bit,' said Cowdrey, tactful as ever. 'This man Rorke', said the old fellow – 'all you people are playing him the wrong way. I've been watching you and him. The answer is to play forward all the time. To put your left foot right down the pitch to him.' 'Thanks for the advice,' said Cowdrey as if he meant it. He thought for a moment. 'But there's one snag. If I put my left foot down the pitch I'm scared that Rorke might tread on it.'

Following on 236 behind, England at first suggested something better than hitherto but Cowdrey's early departure to Lindwall seriously upset their chances. Despite fifties from May and Graveney, Australia won comprehensively by ten wickets and regained the Ashes amidst much jubilation.

Throughout the tour England had been plagued by injury and before the final Test in Melbourne this casualty list lengthened when Statham and Peter Loader were ruled out because of a minor car accident. Against a rampant attack England's brittleness was exposed once again, and they trailed by 146 when they began their second innings on the third evening. There now followed an hour of pure nostalgia as the great Lindwall, recalled at Adelaide, rolled back the years with a peerless exhibition of pace bowling during which he sent back Bailey for 0 and May for 4. Surviving to stumps that evening, Cowdrey came out on Monday morning, guns blazing as he tore into Davidson during a vintage little cameo, which according to Jack Fingleton, the former Australian opener turned cricket writer, showed cricket in all its glory. He sped to 46 before hesitating over a call from Richardson and was involved in a photo-finish as O'Neill's return sped in from cover. Some Australian fieldsmen claimed that Cowdrey had his bat in the air but there was no doubt in his mind that he had made his ground, for he turned and went straight back to the crease. The shrug of his shoulders on learning of his fate told of his chagrin. As English cricket writers seethed in the press box about the local umpiring, Cowdrey, according to Laker, stormed into the dressing-room, vowing never to play against Australia again.

With Cowdrey's departure went England's last hope as once more they were outclassed. For a team which had promised so much, the severity of their defeat was nearly as galling as the four-nil scoreline. Of course some allowances had to be made but, for all the hullabaloo about umpiring and throwing, the truth of the matter was that they had been outplayed in every department as seasoned warriors began to show their years. Cowdrey, with a Test average of 43.44, was one of the few players to emerge from the trip with credit. According to the respected Australian cricket writer A. G. Moyes, he often looked a better player technically than May, 'and when at his best was a sheer delight. He had the capacity to cut the Australian bowling to ribbons and perhaps was unlucky that some of his finest innings finished too soon.'

Back in England the sun shone gloriously throughout the summer of 1959 and Cowdrey, along with other batsmen, made good on some friendly-paced wickets. He began as he intended to continue with scores of 27, 89, 60, 83, 50, 198, 39 and 87. The benign conditions, unfortunately, were not enough to help the Indians under D. K. Gaekwad, so that once again a hopelessly one-sided series offered few lessons for the future. In the first Test, Cowdrey had a rare failure but warmed up nicely for Lord's with 250 (thirty-five fours and two sixes) against Essex at Blackheath, his first championship double-century and the highest first-class score ever on the ground.

At Lord's, India put up a better fight and at one time looked like inching ahead on first innings until a dogged 80 from Ken Barrington left England with a slight advantage. They disposed of the visitors for 165 in the second innings before Cowdrey, 66 not out and May, romped home with what *Wisden* called the best batting of the match. The plaudits for Cowdrey continued at Headingley where he scored 160 with effortless ease. He put on 193 with Barrington for the fourth wicket and was delighted with the evolution of his straight drive, which brought him four sixes, mainly off the leg-spinner, 'Fergie' Gupte, who underperformed all summer.

With England an unassailable three-nil up and keen to blood as much new talent as possible, the selectors decided, somewhat controversially, to rest Cowdrey from the fourth Test at Old Trafford. May, however, was seriously ill and had to undergo surgery, and Cowdrey was hastily summoned to take over the captaincy. With the opposition so supine and his own form fertile, it was a fortuitous time to inherit cricket's most prestigious position. The one-sidedness of the game, however, took the drama out of the occasion and ironically embroiled Cowdrey in an embarrassing contretemps. At the end of the second day, with India in dire straits, the captain, keen to create greater public interest in the match than hitherto, resolved not to enforce the follow-on should he be given that option. The next morning he conveyed his thoughts to Gubby Allen, the chairman of the selectors, and Geoffrey Howard, the Lancashire secretary. They raised no objections but pointed out that in order to maximise public awareness it would be necessary to make an announcement before play started. With Cowdrey's consent a statement was duly issued to the effect that owing to the settled weather and the Manchester holidays the following week, the England captain would not enforce the follow-on if the situation arose. The wording proved to be fatal, for the decision, well-meaning in its intent, seemed not only out of kilter with the ethos of Test match cricket but also rather patronising towards the Indians. The press turned its fire on the new captain and even a close friend such as Barrington thought that Cowdrey had mishandled the whole affair. As it was, India, with centuries from

Baig and Umrigar in their second innings, produced easily their most resolute cricket of the summer and gave England a few anxious moments before eventually succumbing to lose by 171 runs. With another convincing win at The Oval, Cowdrey had at least begun his captaincy on an auspicious footing, re-establishing his credentials as May's heir apparent now that his friend had been pronounced fit for the tour that winter.

7

Never Surrender

Rarely had there been such a dramatic changing of the guard as the MCC team to West Indies in 1959–60 compared to the one which sailed to Australia the previous year. Missing were stalwarts such as Tyson, Laker, Lock, Evans and Bailey and in their place was a newer, younger generation of players like Dexter, Barrington, Illingworth, Geoff Pullar and M. J. K. Smith. Some continuity was maintained through the same combination of captain and vice-captain, although an intriguing development was the choice of Walter Robins, the former Middlesex and England captain, as manager. Cowdrey's one encounter with him had been at an MCC match in Dublin a couple of months earlier and, impressed by what he had seen, he heartily approved of the appointment. As time wore on, however, he had some cause to revise his opinion as Robins, mindful perhaps of the perceived excess of player power in Australia, adopted an uncompromising hands-on approach throughout the tour. An early example of this came when, on the voyage out on the SS *Comito*, the question of Cowdrey opening the innings was once again considered. His lukewarm approach was contemptuously brushed aside and as the only other regular opener in the party was Pullar, Cowdrey did not press the matter.

Ranked outsiders in most people's estimation, MCC did little to appease their critics after an emphatic ten-wicket defeat against Barbados – the colony's first triumph over the mother country since 1926. Apart from the burgeoning genius of Sobers, West Indian hopes rested largely on their formidable new opening attack of Wes Hall and Chester Watson. When May won the toss in Bridgetown the team gathered on the balcony in nervous silence as Hall walked back to his mark, yards in from the boundary, to begin the series. Exploiting the pitch's early moisture and willed on by an excited crowd, both bowlers gave it everything as bouncers were interspersed with brutal deliveries fired in at the ribs. 'Their speed was horrifying', recalled Cowdrey in *MCC*, 'and although they bowled quite a few wide, the utter wildness of their attack added an element of shock. Batting against them was an unforgettable experience.' Cowdrey was out just before lunch for 30, caught at slip off Watson. By early afternoon, in markedly improved conditions for batting, Barrington and Dexter took charge. Both made centuries in England's total of 482, and with West Indies equally run-happy – Sobers and Worrell shared a partnership of 399 – the match ended inconclusively.

Further punishment awaited the England openers in the second Test in Trinidad when they batted first on a pitch which, according to the groundsman, had 'pace like fire'. Once again Pullar and Cowdrey had to live on their wits against the ferocity of Hall and Watson. Both bowlers, with their long arms and loose slinging actions, settled on a length, short and uppish, that kept the batsmen back on their stumps fending the ball down. Pullar's dismissal at 37 and Barrington's arrival was the signal for yet more bouncers, bringing about the downfall of Cowdrey for 18. Having been struck on the body and the boot by Hall in the space of four balls, he was unable to cope with another rearing delivery which cannonaded on to his stumps via his body. As he limped off nursing his shattered foot Cowdrey's dazed look said everything. Throughout his international career he had taken quite a pounding from the world's fastest bowlers, but compared to previous experiences this was war in its most primitive form where the normal rules did not apply. When May was caught behind without opening his account, England were in trouble at 57 for three. It needed an imperious 77 from Dexter to lift them out of the quicksands and centuries from Barrington and Smith to take them on to the high plains.

With the West Indian openers still together at the end of the second day, the match seemed evenly poised. The next day was to change all that as their batsmen, in the face of some fine fast bowling from Trueman and Statham, meekly unfurled the white flag of surrender. Their demise served only to exasperate their volatile supporters, already well inebriated and disillusioned by the number of marginal decisions which had gone against them. In these circumstances the running out of the local hero, Charran Singh, at 98 for eight, was the spark which finally lit the fuse. A hail of bottles rained from the popular corner of the ground, followed by crowds swarming on to the playing arena. With the authorities caught unprepared by the disturbances, the players had no alternative but to leave the field and wait for police reinforcements to restore law and order. When the match eventually resumed the next day in a calmer atmosphere England pressed on unremittingly towards victory. Cowdrey failed yet again in England's second innings but West Indies, set 501 to win, lost by the overwhelming margin of 256 runs.

Cowdrey's pleasure at his team's success was tempered by the battering he had taken in a position he had never wanted to occupy in the first place. He felt that, despite his experience, he had nothing in his armoury to counter the staggering pace of Hall and Watson, 'who attacked you with explosive violence on fiery wickets'. If he was to survive, Cowdrey reasoned, he had to remodel his entire approach to batting. It was a challenge that would tax even this most ardent of technicians. After much thought he decided that because he did not have time to move, he would stay put and protect his wicket. To help him prepare for this war of attrition, he went to the team masseur and got him to sew into his vest a thick layer of Dunlopillo padding which stretched from his neck to his waist. It caused great hilarity in the dressing-room in Kingston before one of the greatest challenges of his career. In *MCC* he recalls how, on the opening morning of the game, he would have given anything not to play, a feeling which intermittently haunted him throughout his career when his confidence was low. He worked desperately hard in the nets, but only felt worse, and the knowledge that his whole future was now at stake made him feel sick.

It says much for his courage and composure that he batted for seven hours, taking any number of blows on the body without demur as once again Hall and Watson threw everything at him. His 114, referred to by Swanton as 'stoical vigilance' and as 'heroic' by his captain, helped England to 277. After a typically dashing 147 from

Sobers, West Indies faltered and lost their last eight wickets for 54 runs. During the last hour Pullar and Cowdrey completed a satisfying day by reducing the deficit of 76 to 11, then the next morning, in what Swanton called 'a peerless piece of cricket', Cowdrey gave one of the finest exhibitions of his life. Particularly exhilarating was the way he turned on Hall with a succession of perfectly executed hooks and drives. During the morning session he made 76 out of the 99 runs scored, and with Pullar playing sensibly for 66 they put on 177 for the first wicket, the first time in twenty-seven Tests that an England opening pair had passed 100 unseparated. Cowdrey's dismissal to the innocuous Reg Scarlett for 97 deprived him of a richly deserved second century, but the sheer relief of returning to form proved ample compensation for missing out.

His only immediate concern was England's fragile position. Unable to follow in the steps of the openers, the rest of the batsmen struggled yet again and West Indies, wanting 230 to win in just over four hours, appeared firm favourites. It needed some superb fast bowling from Trueman to peg them back and in the end they finished at 175 for six, 55 runs short.

Now that Cowdrey had the measure of Hall and Watson he did not look back. Centuries followed in his next two innings against the Leeward Islands and British Guiana, where he and Pullar opened up with 281. 'He has played here, as in Jamaica, with the utmost ease and power,' declared Swanton. 'Hammond is the nearest parallel to him in his present form.' It was during the game against British Guiana that the private agony which had afflicted May throughout the tour finally came to light. Unable to make much of a contribution with the bat, the captain had been in much discomfort owing to the reopening of the bowel wound from his operation the previous summer. Hopeful that it would soon heal, he had not mentioned it to anyone, although he did receive medical attention as the weeks passed by. During a mid-tour break in Caracas with his wife Virginia, matters deteriorated to the extent that she decided to stay on in the Caribbean and await developments in British Guiana, where May captained the team against the colony. It was the ordeal of fielding in the heat for nearly two days that finally brought matters to a head. He let Cowdrey into his secret at the end of the first day, then after the second day his doctors finally insisted he stopped playing. His tour was over.

Now that May's private nightmare was out in the open, it was up to Cowdrey to rally a shell-shocked team for the fourth Test in Georgetown. He did his best by winning the toss on a placid pitch and making 65 in England's 295. Had the West Indies replied with greater conviction they might have built up a considerable lead. As it was, they allowed themselves to be contained by Cowdrey's defensive tactics, so that when Gerry Alexander declared 107 runs ahead only eight hours of play remained. Cowdrey began with a flourish, but this time the heroes were Dexter and Raman Subba Row. Their centuries guaranteed England a draw and at least a share of the spoils in the rubber.

Before the final Test in Port-of-Spain the tourists experienced further setbacks when Statham had to return home early because of a family illness and Subba Row was unavailable because of injury. In order to strengthen a depleted team Cowdrey and Robins had decided to send for Jim Parks, the Sussex wicket-keeper/batsman, who happened to be coaching in Trinidad. He immediately responded with 183 against Berbice. This performance presented Cowdrey with a dilemma as to who should keep wicket in the final Test. In the end Parks's superior batting won him preference over the incumbent Roy Swetman, who never represented his country again. The decision proved eminently justifiable in the light of events. Calling correctly yet again (England won the toss in all five games), Cowdrey elected to bat on another easy-paced wicket and prospered in a second-wicket partnership of 191 with Dexter. He gave two early chances but otherwise was at his flowing, elegant best. Dexter recalls walking in to bat and suggesting to Cowdrey that they should try to wrest the initiative as soon as possible. 'A lift of the eyebrow and a slight nod of the head was all the information I had to go on but once battle was joined it was soon clear that I had struck a responsive chord. I thought I played pretty well myself that morning with 40 or 50 runs on the board but all the while Cowdrey made me look like a selling-plater and he was well in the 60s or 70s by the time the interval came. Even though we had faced almost exclusively fast bowling, which was my forte, he had left me in no doubt as to who was the boss.' 'Much depended upon Cowdrey's own mood,' reported Swanton. 'Today, the cautious old owl of Georgetown fluttered his plumage and emerged as a soaring eagle. After an unusually uncertain start he played quite beautifully.'

With Cowdrey hitting 119, Dexter 76 and Barrington 69, England totalled 393. A combination of rain and slow scoring again restricted West Indies' progress, so that with time slipping away they felt obliged to declare 55 behind. Their gambit appeared to have paid off when England stumbled to 148 for six, until a record seventh-wicket Test partnership between Smith (96) and Parks (101 not out) carried them to safety. Their delight at winning a hard-fought series was soured, however, by an intemperate exchange on the final morning between manager and captain.

To many of his hosts and within the travelling press corps, Robins, with his accessible charm, was one of the best managers ever to represent MCC, but to his players he adopted a more hectoring tone which militated against close relationships. With his experience and inner resolution May had the capacity to fend off some of his manager's more extravagant ideas, something Cowdrey was less adept at doing. He did, however, prove unyielding when Robins's Corinthian values clashed with his more professional approach over what tactics to employ during the closing stages of the final Test. Seemingly oblivious to the splendid fightback orchestrated by Smith and Parks, Robins arrived late at the ground on the last morning and promptly demanded a declaration for the good of the game. To win the series by playing for a draw was, in his eyes, quite the wrong approach. Cowdrey, with the whole team behind him, stood firm. He insisted that all the toil and sweat they had expended over the previous several months shouldn't be unduly jeopardised simply to entertain a smallish crowd for an hour or two.

Recalling the altercation in his autobiography, Cowdrey clearly still regretted not only Robins's public dressing down of him but also his frosty relationship with him thereafter, with all that this entailed for his captaincy prospects, since Robins became chairman of the selectors in 1962. His feelings are easy to understand. No captain should ever be subjected to such treatment by his manager, especially when his rationale for delaying his declaration was grounded in sound tactical sense. Equally, one should not be totally dismissive of Robins's case, however tactlessly he expressed it. His priority on becoming manager was to repair the friction generated by MCC's previous trip to the Caribbean in 1953–54, and to his credit he had broadly achieved this. Not only had the players adapted themselves to local sensitivities, the Tests had been played in a good spirit. There was, however, one small eyesore and that was England's negative tactics, be it their defensive bowling or their excessively slow over rates (West Indies were not blameless either). If the former could partially be attributed to professional skill, the latter raised uncomfortable questions about gamesmanship, especially at a time when cricket around the world was becoming less of a spectacle. For all their natural desire to win, professional cricketers were entertainers too, and their failure to remember their wider responsibilities during the succeeding years cost the game much in the way of public goodwill.

8

'To be or not to be'

Behind Cowdrey's courteous, self-effacing facade there lay a keen ambition, and once it was clear that he had Evans's support for the Kent captaincy he accepted it with alacrity. From the county's perspective he was the obvious successor to Doug Wright. Not only was he already one of England's best batsmen, he was a refined amateur whose equable nature could help to heal the rifts and end the uncertainties caused by four captains in five years. His first major initiative, securing the appointment of Les Ames as manager, was probably one of the shrewdest moves he ever made. For Ames, with his vast experience and steely personality, was the ideal foil to Cowdrey, particularly in matters of discipline. 'Colin was very good tactically on the field,' recalled David Clark, 'but he hated ticking off a player.' In contrast, Ames was tough and would lay down the law in simple, uncompromising terms which left no room for misunderstanding. There would be occasional disagreements over team selection, and frustration on Ames's part when Cowdrey's indecision got the better of him, but in general it was a harmonious partnership which, along with Clark and Stuart Chiesman, launched the club on the long road back towards success. As chairman of the cricket committee, Clark was a vital intermediary between Cowdrey and the county committee, while Chiesman, who became chairman in 1958, apart from being Cowdrey's father-in-law, brought the administrative flair of the boardroom to the committee room.

With the game's historical roots deep in its soil, the graceful serenity of Canterbury and a club well endowed with patrician support,

Kent was the ideal county for Cowdrey to captain. In the tradition of Lord Harris and Percy Chapman, he was an amateur to his finger-tips, travelling to matches in the stately splendour of his Jaguar, already kitted out in blazer and flannels, with his elderly secretary in attendance. Sometimes he would cut his arrival fine (it wasn't unknown for his vice-captain to toss in his lieu), not out of any casual breach of convention, but because of a prodigious workload at home, responding to a multitude of requests. These personal circumstances, however, could play havoc with team selection. John Dye, Kent's left-arm opening bowler during the 1960s, recalls the occasion at Canterbury when Cowdrey led his side on to the field, unaware that there were twelve of them. When this was pointed out to him he leant across to Alan Brown and said, 'Sorry, Brownie old boy. Would you carry the drinks out?'

With his extensive connections and his sense of duty, Cowdrey would spend nearly as much time conversing with committee men and other local dignitaries as with his players. In an age when formal meetings were seldom held, he cut a rather remote figure, especially given his dislike of hearty dressing-room banter or long sessions at the bar. He did, however, make it his business to organise golf days and social gatherings at his house to help foster team spirit. Youngsters were taken under his wing and they in particular were often the recipients of some act of Cowdrey generosity, be it a 21st birthday cake baked by Penny, or help with accommodation, or with winter employment. Derek Underwood remembers the evening in August 1964 when Cowdrey telephoned his parents to suggest their attendance at Canterbury the next day where Kent were playing the Australians. There, in full view of both crowd and players, Cowdrey presented Underwood with his county cap.

He would also act as chauffeur to those who lived within his vicin-ity, using these journeys to impart priceless gems of technical wisdom, particularly about facing quick bowling. Bob Woolmer, who often travelled with Cowdrey, recalls that his captain would become so engrossed in cricketing conversation that signalling was neglected as he overtook other cars on motorways. So riveting were these conversations that Woolmer – now a top coach himself – found a five-hour journey would pass in no time. The tuitions would continue in the dressing-room, when Cowdrey analysed individual dismissals, often posing questions for his batsmen to think about. Even more instructive was the opportunity to bat with him in the middle when, watching from close quarters, he would spot problems and ask how he could help to solve them. He made his protégés feel they could do it. Both Woolmer and Alan Knott found Cowdrey's advice invaluable in learning how to cope with Sobers at his most hostile. Woolmer recalls one such occasion against Nottinghamshire at Trent Bridge when he was all at sea against the swinging ball. Cowdrey came down the wicket and said, 'Let's have a bit of fun. We'll see if we can push Sobers back past mid-off, there's a single every time we can manage it.' He tried to follow the instructions and took two. Then Cowdrey would come down the wicket and say, 'Perhaps we can manage four off the next over,' a pattern of conversation repeated as the partnership became worth 141 in even time. It was not until driving back to the hotel, Woolmer later recalled, 'that I really appreciated what Cowdrey had been doing. He had been carefully teaching me how to play a very dangerous left-arm swing bowler merely by indulging in a game with me out in the middle.' On another occasion at Tunbridge Wells, Woolmer was struggling to lay a bat on Robin Hobbs's bowling when Cowdrey suggested that he hit the leg-spinner over extra-cover. Following the advice to the letter, Woolmer found that his troubles were behind him.

In the field there was the same benignity. Woolmer remembers that Cowdrey would nurse him into the attack and tell him where to bowl. Underwood also has reason to be grateful for Cowdrey's encouragement, particularly during his early days when he toiled for no reward. His captain's willingness to bring him back against the tail so that he could get a couple of cheap wickets did wonders for his morale. Always wanting the best for his charges, Cowdrey shared in their triumphs with a familiar refrain of 'Well played, old boy', or a congratulatory note afterwards, while those languishing in the doldrums invariably found him a sympathetic shoulder to cry on. 'You know just how fine the margin is,' Cowdrey once said. It was not in his nature to storm up and down a dressing-room berating his batsmen for getting out to bad shots. He knew all too well from his own experience the deflated feeling of returning to the pavilion after a soft dismissal. A diatribe from the captain in these circumstances achieved little. His tolerance was also evident when his own interests were affected. John Dye remembers being bowled out for 0 against Gloucestershire at Dover in 1965, leaving Cowdrey stranded on 99 but unperturbed at missing out on another landmark. One of the few occasions when Dye found his captain less than sympathetic was Kent's game against Yorkshire at Gravesend in 1963. They had kept going in a last-innings run chase right up to the fall of their ninth wicket. At which point, with 25 still needed, Cowdrey decided to put up the shutters and asked Dye to relay his instructions to Alan Brown, the not out batsman, as he went out to bat. Dye intended to tell Brown at the end of the over, but then became so preoccupied in conversation with Yorkshire's Don Wilson that he had still to carry out his instructions when play was ready to recommence. Oblivious to the change in plan, Brown continued to swing away merrily and was soon out stumped, leaving Dye to brave the frosty atmosphere in the dressing-room on his return.

With his easygoing tolerance, Cowdrey brought a lighter touch to a team still struggling to find its feet in the championship, chiefly because of their lack of a decent attack. Derek Ufton, Kent's wicket-keeper after Evans, recalls how Cowdrey was good at 'letting in the air', so that by 1962 Kent had become a delight to play for. They were also, according to John Murray and Colin Ingleby-Mackenzie, the most genial of opponents, who played the game in the right spirit, apart from their match against Middlesex at Tunbridge Wells in June 1963 when relations were slightly frayed. Contrary to norm, the Middlesex side had gone home for the weekend and were returning to Kent on the Monday morning when their convoy of cars became embroiled in heavy traffic in Tonbridge. So serious was the delay that by 11.30 a.m., the official starting time, only three players had shown up at the ground, including two who had already batted. As a result, the Middlesex innings, then standing at 120 for three in response to Kent's 150, was deemed forfeited by the umpires. Minutes later Middlesex stragglers arrived to witness the bizarre sight of their team taking the field with five Kent substitutes, one of whom caught Kent's opening batsman, Brian Luckhurst. The fiasco ruined the match, leaving Middlesex feeling aggrieved that Cowdrey had not displayed greater flexibility by agreeing to delay the start by half an hour, as the regulations apparently allowed. Cowdrey, for his part, felt affronted that Middlesex had failed to apologise for their tardiness.

If Cowdrey's gentle, reflective character made him a sympathetic captain, it did not necessarily make him an assertive one. It was perhaps with his own experiences in mind that he wrote in his book *Tackle Cricket* that 'the hardest job for the captain is to be able to make quick decisions and then have the courage of his convictions'. Godfrey Evans, who rated him highly as a leader, thought it extraordinary that Cowdrey would at times appear to undermine his own authority, a characteristic that periodically communicated itself to the team. Clearly the prospect of lording it over the established players was one which bothered him, especially with Arthur Fagg, the senior professional, who nursed a lingering resentment that Cowdrey had been chosen instead of him to go to Australia in 1954–55. In one of his early matches as captain, Cowdrey made a point of seeking his advice, only to be met with the caustic retort, 'You've been made the captain, so you can get on with it.' Gradually he found that through tactful gestures in the middle and by his own pedigree he could win over the professionals, but the hard choices associated with captaincy were invariably a weight on his shoulders. Discipline was one particular chore he hated, so that the task fell mainly on Ames, while selection was another onerous duty as it meant disappointing the unlucky ones. David Clark recalls how after team selection meetings, Cowdrey would turn to him and say, 'Will you tell him he's not playing?' which Clark refused to do, pointing out that it was not his responsibility. The dilemma was particularly acute at the beginning of a county match, when several players might be returning from Test match duty. With the decision rarely taken the night before, players often had to resort to the scorecard to find out whether they were playing. Peter Richardson recalls a game at Southampton when Cowdrey asked him to tell David Sayer that he was twelfth man, explaining that he himself had to go and see Desmond Eagar, the Hampshire secretary. With four quick bowlers of similar ability all fighting for two or three places, Cowdrey used to get round this dilemma by rotating them, a policy which kept them all refreshed but did not entirely alleviate dented pride. When Woolmer expressed his disappointment at being left out of the Kent side at Leicester early on in his career, Cowdrey told him that he felt let down by his response. 'Only eleven can play,' he said.

Cowdrey's lack of confidence could show itself in other ways. Mike Denness recalls how, as a youngster, his opinion would be sought by one of England's finest players, and opponents watching Kent in the field from the boundary habitually formed the impression that it was leadership by committee. Richardson has recollections of Kent's match against Hampshire at Southampton in June 1965. After Kent had bowled their opponents out for 113, Cowdrey was all set to enforce the follow-on, when Richardson was suddenly told to put his pads on. When he enquired about this change of heart, Cowdrey explained that he had consulted the team and the bowlers had informed him that they were tired. The decision, according to *Wisden*, probably cost Kent the match.

In the field Cowdrey gave much thought to how a particular batsman played, and was often astute at summing up his technical strengths and weaknesses. With these characteristics in mind, he would work out a field plan to suit all circumstances. John Murray remembers being driven up to Edgbaston by Cowdrey for his first Test in 1961, and how surprised he was to be asked what he thought about his captain's proposed field placings for the Australian batsmen. Brian Statham recalls that after the pre-Test dinner that evening Cowdrey approached both Trueman and himself with the same plan. Trueman took one look at it and dismissed it out of hand, with some typically choice language. Nothing more was heard of it. In general, Cowdrey would handle his bowlers with discretion, giving them every opportunity to ask for a change in the field; but those who became expensive would get short shrift. For all his romantic attachment to the leg-spinner, changes to the game in the 1960s meant that Cowdrey kept them on a tight rein. His ideal type of bowler was Underwood, who bowled for long periods giving little away. When convinced that the game was moving his way, he could, according to Underwood, be masterly in his tactics, particularly against a new batsman, with a combination of close in-fielders and others back on the ring to save one. On occasions such as his two tours of the West

Indies, he was adept at frustrating the opposition with his defensive field placings, but overall, as with most England captains of this vintage, he inclined too far in this direction. Jim Laker recalls MCC's first game against South Australia in 1958–59 when, with the home side in trouble, he noticed to his amazement that Tony Lock was bowling with a deep extra-cover, a square-point right out on the fence, and nobody close to the wicket. When Cowdrey ignored his advice to attack more, Laker had a word with Lock, who took it up with the captain. Eventually Cowdrey acted, and two men were caught close in before the end of the day.

His caution was evident in other areas, notably in his tendency to set stiff declarations and close up a game rather than take undue risks. Kent players in the 1960s recall some tedious games against Hampshire, such was Cowdrey's fear of Roy Marshall, Hampshire's dynamic Barbadian, after he and Ingleby-Mackenzie had made light work of a challenging Kent declaration at Southampton in 1958. In August 1960 Cowdrey became embroiled in an unfortunate spat with Bob Barber, after the Lancashire captain had taken exception to Kent's failure to chase his final-day target. He later apologised to Cowdrey for his harsh words. When quick runs were needed, Cowdrey tended to shrink from giving the lead, often dropping himself down the order. Mike Denness recalls sitting with Cowdrey and Alan Dixon during Kent's Gillette Cup semi-final against Sussex at Canterbury in 1967, when Ken Suttle, by then an occasional left-arm spinner, bowled a number of tidy overs. Suttle's spell so unnerved an already tense Cowdrey that he ordered Dixon, an honest lower-middle-order bats-man, to go and pad up with a view to promoting him above himself, so as to knock Suttle off his length. As it was, when the second wicket fell, it was Cowdrey who went in at his rightful position to play one of his greatest ever innings.

With Cowdrey an absent captain for so many matches because of Test calls, it was important that Kent had a sound deputy. Between 1961 and 1965 they had precisely that in Peter Richardson who, for all his outlandish humour, was a canny leader with attacking instincts. When he was in charge the cricket was rarely dull, and so infectious was his approach that many of the team preferred playing under him to Cowdrey. How evident this preference was to Cowdrey is a matter of conjecture, but a chance remark by one of his junior players, blown out of all proportion, undoubtedly rattled him. When Denness was guest of honour at a cricket dinner at Dartford in November 1962, he was asked why a talented team like Kent hadn't won a trophy for so long. He replied that to foster a healthy team spirit it was necessary to have the same captain there the whole time, unencumbered by Test calls. A journalist got wind of his comments and days later the *Daily Sketch* ran a story entitled 'Sack Cowdrey from Kent captaincy, says Mike Denness'. As Les Ames tried to repair the damage, a curt telegram arrived from the MCC management in Australia which read 'Cowdrey perturbed; explanation wanted.' John Murray recalls how, during MCC's match against South Australia, Cowdrey said to him, 'They're after me. We must succeed, because if we lose this game they'll be after me as captain.' When he returned from Australia a few months later, Denness, who had written to the MCC manager to explain himself, went to Cowdrey and suggested a talk, but he preferred to let the matter drop.

With the forthright Richardson himself willing on occasion to take his captain to task for what he considered to be tactical aberrations, their previous close relationship began to suffer. It was with some relief to Cowdrey when Richardson's waning enthusiasm for the game prompted him to seek premature retirement in 1965. He was succeeded by Dixon, and, in 1969 by Denness, by which time Kent were a much improved side. Had Cowdrey inherited a stronger legacy when he took over at Kent in 1957, he would probably have shown a more assured touch, as he was to do in later years. In retrospect, he acknowledged that he was not a natural leader, lacking the inspiration of his son, Christopher, the inner steel of May or the tactical flair of Illingworth. His strength, he felt, lay in his pastoral qualities, comparing his captaincy of Kent to a diocesan priest looking after his parish. The allegory was not an unreasonable one, and it is to Cowdrey's great credit that his long years of dedicated toil finally reaped a rich reward with a side that stood comparison with any in the county's history.

9

May's Apprentice

Ever since he became an England player Cowdrey had quite contentedly lived in the shadow of his great friend, May, with whom he was so often compared. Apart from being England's premier post-war batsman, May had won immediate acclaim for his leadership at both national and county level, and the gods continued to smile favourably upon him until the Australian debacle of 1958–59. Thereafter his luck changed, and with ill health ruling him out for the whole of 1960 it was time for his deputy to take command on a rather more permanent basis than hitherto. A quick look at the records and a reminder of Cowdrey's success against South Africa in 1960 suggests a smooth transition to the responsibilities of higher office, but sadly this was not quite the case. For in an unhappy summer, dogged by bad weather, slow scoring and controversy of all types, Cowdrey found himself exposed to some fairly scathing criticism, much of it patently overstated.

Part of his problem concerned his own form, which lacked consistency all summer. May did not yield one half-century, and two centuries against Hampshire and Sussex respectively in June were the exceptions rather than the rule. For the Tests he was once again pressed into opening, and on some indifferent pitches he found the formidable Neil Adcock to be his nemesis throughout. He started with three single-figure scores, and only twice during the series did he do himself justice. After two nail-biting encounters against South Africa in 1955 and 1956–57, a similarly even contest was expected this time. The prognosis soon proved to be wildly inaccurate. Unsettled by the vagaries of English conditions, the South Africans under Jackie McGlew rarely played to potential, their batting in particular proving no match for Trueman and Statham. At Edgbaston in the first Test they lost by 100 runs and at Lord's they fared no better. Geoff Griffin, their amiable quick bowler, made history not only by becoming the first man to achieve a hat-trick at Lord's in a Test, but more seriously by being no-balled for throwing, a felony which brought about his premature retirement from the game. Helped by 99 from M. J. K. Smith and 90 from Subba Row, England totalled 362 for eight, and with Statham's tail up South Africa's batting was obliterated in both innings.

They did no better at Trent Bridge, where England yet again won the toss and batted first. This time they were indebted to a masterly 67 from Cowdrey who, in the words of John Waite, the South African wicket-keeper, 'batted beautifully, his cover drives unfolding like tropical flowers of the scarcest delicacy'. England made 287 and promptly dismissed their opponents for 88. They were soon in the wars again following on, but with a plucky stand between McGlew and Sid O'Linn offered the semblance of a fightback before the former was run out in bizarre circumstances. The left-handed O'Linn played Alan Moss to extra cover and called his captain for a single. Moss dashed across the pitch to chase the ball and McGlew ran into him, stumbling in the process. By the time he had recovered, Statham had thrown the ball into the wicket with McGlew yards short. Unaware perhaps of what precisely had happened, Cowdrey and some of his team-mates close to the wicket promptly appealed and umpire Elliott duly raised his finger. Despite hearing mutterings from some of the England team about the manner of the dismissal, McGlew never hesitated when given out. As he made his way towards the pavilion, however, the Trent Bridge crowd let their feelings be known in a crescendo of booing. Cowdrey, who had by now been apprised of the situation by Moss, called for McGlew to return, which McGlew was reluctant to do. Eventually, at the third time of asking, he did pause while the England captain tried to persuade the umpire to change his ruling. This, according to Waite, was when Cowdrey understandably made a false step. He should have called to the umpire, 'I withdraw the appeal', since there is nothing in the laws of cricket which prevents a captain from with-

Above: 'Echoes of Dreamland'
– Cowdrey (middle row,
second from right) in his first
year at Tonbridge playing
against the Old Tonbridgians;
a match in which he scored
49. David Kemp (back row,
second from left), is his great
friend and was later
housemaster to all three of his
boys at Tonbridge.

Left: Captain of Oxford
University, 1954 – Despite
Cowdrey's outstanding
contribution to Oxford cricket
through his three years there,
it is a curious fact that the
university did not win one
first-class match.
(© POPPERFOTO)

Above: Ocean Bound – An apprehensive-looking Cowdrey on his first MCC tour, signing autographs aboard the SS *Orsova* at Tilbury before its departure to Australia in September 1954.
(© HULTON GETTY)

Left: In which we serve? – Cowdrey, in upbeat mood, as he arrives at RAF Cardington in May 1955 to begin his National Service. A month later he was discharged because of flat feet, a decision that gave rise to allegations of him dodging the column. Twenty years later he was still experiencing pain in his toes.
(© POPPERFOTO)

Above: The Queen and I –
Cowdrey being introduced to
the Queen by Peter May, his
England captain, at Lord's
during the second Test against
Australia, June 1956 – one of
his many encounters with
royalty over the years.
(© ALPHA/SPORT & GENERAL)

Right: Opening Salvoes –
Cowdrey and Peter
Richardson opening the
England innings against
Australia at Old Trafford, July
1956. Their stand of 174 gave
the team the best possible start
in a match made memorable
by Jim Laker's 19 wickets.
Opening was always
Cowdrey's least favoured
position, but it enabled him to
forge a firm friendship with
Richardson, which led to the
latter becoming Christopher's
godfather and a Kent player in
1960. Thereafter they went
their separate ways.
(© POPPERFOTO)

Left: One for the Album – Always the most sartorially elegant of cricketers, Cowdrey's photogenic features invariably made good journalist's copy. Here he poses for Trevor Bailey in Cape Town in October 1956 with fellow tourists Frank Tyson and Denis Compton.
(© HULTON GETTY)

Below left: The Recordbreakers – Cowdrey and Peter May leave the field at Edgbaston after their record 4th wicket partnership against the West Indies, June 1957. May was not only the greatest English post-war batsman, he was Cowdrey's closest friend; a friendship enhanced by their many hours at the crease together and their respective roles as captain and vice-captain of England between 1958 and 1961. Later, as chairman of the selectors, May was to appoint Cowdrey's son Christopher, and his godson, as captain of England.
(© HULTON GETTY)

Right: 'There is a Breathless Hush' – With England needing 6 runs to win with 2 balls left and one wicket remaining, Cowdrey, broken arm in plaster, gallantly returns to the wicket against West Indies at Lord's, June 1963. Fortunately, he was not on strike and the match was drawn.
(© ALPHA/SPORT & GENERAL)

Below: Cricket the Fickle Mistress – Cowdrey captaining England against the West Indies at Headingley, 1966, a match that they lost by an innings and led to his dismissal. One of the paradoxes of Cowdrey's career was that an essentially peace loving person and ardent devotee of the noble game had to grapple with so much controversy during his time as England captain; not, as he recalled in *MCC*, a gratifying or amusing experience.
(© ALPHA/SPORT & GENERAL)

Left: The Rivals – A mixture of dejection and bewilderment colours Cowdrey's reaction to losing the toss to Gary Sobers before the third Test at Bridgetown in March 1968. Opponents for the best part of twenty years and rival Test captains on eight occasions, their keenly contested duels were tempered by a high mutual regard for each other's ability.
(© ASSOCIATED PRESS)

Below: Casualty – Cowdrey leaving hospital in May 1969 after an operation on his broken Achilles tendon. His recovery was quicker than anticipated, but the injury all but finally quashed his hopes of leading an England team in Australia.
(© POPPERFOTO)

Above: High Noon at Canterbury – In common with many great players, Cowdrey was adept off his legs. Here he employs the leg glance to good effect against Worcestershire in the Gilette Cup at Canterbury, watched by his old friend Tom Graveney at mid-off and his legion of devoted supporters who revelled in his exquisite strokeplay. (© PATRICK EAGER)

Below: Master Class – Cricket to the Cowdreys is what the theatre is to the Redgraves and politics to the Kennedys. Here at his Surrey home in Limpsfield, Cowdrey gives Graham, aged five, an early tutorial in the art of batting watched by his wife Penny and his three other children. (© HULTON GETTY)

Above: 'If I was given a choice as to my last act on earth it would be to walk to the wicket at the lovely St Lawrence ground at Canterbury in the sunshine with the pavilion chattering and the small tents buzzing. I would then lead into a half-volley just outside the off stump praying the old timing still lived in the wrists to send it speeding down the slope for four. The cover-drive is the most beautiful stroke in batsmanship.' Colin Cowdrey in *MCC*. (© PATRICK EAGER)

Below: In his Pomp – Cowdrey playing John Snow with time to spare: Kent versus Sussex at Hove 1970. His 77 on a sporting wicket was crucial to Kent winning the match and the championship. (© ALLSPORT)

drawing an appeal. After some discussion with his fellow umpire, and to the acute embarrassment of Cowdrey, Elliot upheld the decision and waved McGlew from the field. In a statement after the day's play Cowdrey expressed deep sorrow for the incident and confirmed that the umpires, believing that Moss had not acted wilfully, had refused to change tack, a verdict which McGlew gracefully accepted. Although this explanation helped clear the air it did not prevent a fair amount of flak being hurled at the England captain for his part in the dismissal. The incident rather overshadowed England's eight-wicket victory and clinching of the rubber.

After the great gulf in standards so far, the South Africans pulled themselves off the floor for the final two Tests, although with a surfeit of interruptions the chances of a positive result were remote. At Old Trafford, England batted poorly and were made to sweat on the final afternoon before eventually wriggling to safety. In the dying stages of the match Cowdrey's token declaration drew barbs from a press thirsty for more dynamic cricket, but given the lack of options at his disposal, his resentment at this criticism was understandable.

South Africa continued to look the better side at The Oval. Cowdrey won the toss for the fifth time out of five, extending the sequence to ten consecutive Tests, a unique run, but with Adcock taking six for 65, England could only muster 155. The tourists, led by their vice-captain, Trevor Goddard, who made 99, in contrast indulged themselves, making 419.

Trailing by 264 runs, England had a mountain to climb on the fourth day. Before play began, the Australian cricket writer, R. S. Whitington encountered Cowdrey on the stairs of the Members' Pavilion and said, 'When are we going to see something of the real Cowdrey?' 'You want some of my 1938 form?' quipped Cowdrey. 'I'll do what I can.' As he walked to the middle with Geoff Pullar he calmly turned to his partner and said, 'I'm going to go out and play him [Adcock] as if the ball is not moving at all.' Adcock's first ball he duly stroked for four and, apart from one easy chance to slip off Pothecary when still in single figures, he did not look back. His 155 contained twenty-two boundaries which, according to John Waite, 'included some of the most handsome cover-drives, square-cuts and pulls that can have been played since cricket began . . . Long before Cowdrey had done, our fieldsmen must have resembled village green players.' With Pullar going on to score 175, England's opening stand realised 290, the highest then for the first wicket in any Test in England and the fourth highest opening partnership in the history of the game.

Their brilliance failed to inspire the rest of their colleagues, with the result that Cowdrey was forced to delay his declaration. Challenged to score 216 to win in four hours, South Africa were 97 for four before the rain returned to have the final word on a distinctly wretched summer.

With a rare winter off Cowdrey returned to work at the Chiesman's branch in Lewisham on a six-month apprenticeship on the shop floor. The highlight was a two-week trip to Ohio as guest of the National Cash Register Company to study out-of-town super-markets and their then revolutionary trend towards self-service, a visit which he found fascinating.

1961 was the year in which Cowdrey's enigmatic personality seemed to reveal all its facets, as a season which promised so much ground to a halt in misfortune and anticlimax. After several years of one-sided Test contests at home, the visit of Richie Benaud's Australians had the makings of an enthralling encounter, especially since England, with a revitalised team, were determined to revenge their humiliation 'down under' in 1958–59. They hoped to have May back in the saddle after his recovery from illness and meanwhile had appointed Dexter to captain MCC against the Australians at Lord's. Knee trouble forced Dexter to withdraw and at the eleventh hour Cowdrey was asked to deputise. His captaincy made little impression, except to irk some of the Australians with his defensive field placings, but his batting could not have been better. Having scored 104 and 67 in his previous match against Hampshire, Cowdrey walked to the wicket at 0 for one and found his timing immediately. His 115 in two and a half hours was pure pedigree. In the second innings he again excelled as he and M. J. K. Smith chased quick runs in search of an elusive victory.

Cowdrey's success merely whetted his appetite for the impending series, but with May expected to be fit after a minor ankle strain he had given little thought to the captaincy. It was thus with surprise bordering on astonishment when he was summoned to Gubby Allen's house on the Sunday before the first Test to be informed that his lease as England's captain had been extended because May had not recovered in time. Clearly unsettled by this turn of events, Cowdrey approached Edgbaston in a mist of confusion and appeared rather distracted throughout, not least in two undistinguished innings. After Australia gained a massive lead of 321 England were fortunate to secure a draw thanks to Dexter's 180 and bad weather.

Relieved to have escaped the tumbrils at Edgbaston, Cowdrey was in a much more positive frame of mind when he faced the tourists again days later at Canterbury. In this more relaxed setting, blessed by uninterrupted sunshine, he elevated the art of batting to its highest plateau with two unforgettable displays of brilliance as Kent came within a whisker of beating the Australians for the first time since 1899. After making 149 in Kent's first innings, he declared 92 behind and took up the challenge when they were left 291 to win in a shade over three hours. Coming in at 71 for three, Cowdrey immediately set about the task and reduced his opposite number, Neil Harvey, to despair as he constantly pierced the field with what *Wisden* called, 'an unending flow of beautifully timed strokes'. Ray Lindwall, in his book *The Challenging Tests* chronicling the 1961 tour, noted how Cowdrey, with a deceptive, casual laziness, butchered the Australian attack. Nobody could bowl to him. His century took only ninety-three minutes and although his 121 just failed to bring Kent victory, he could be consoled by his achievement in becoming the first player to score a century in both innings against the Australians in England.

As the Australians repaired from Canterbury to Lord's they had much to ponder besides Cowdrey's wonderful batting. Benaud, their captain, was unfit with a damaged shoulder tendon and handed over the captaincy to Harvey. Then, in the match against Kent, Davidson, their leading all-rounder, had damaged his back so seriously that he informed Benaud he was unfit to play. Benaud refused to contemplate this possibility and such was the loyalty he instilled in his players that Davidson, much to England's detriment, reported for duty at the appointed hour. Despite May's return to the team, Cowdrey was asked to continue as captain and, extending England's amazing sequence of winning the toss to twelve times, he batted first on a pitch of uneven bounce. Fortified by the help he received from the conditions, Davidson, summoning up the Gallipoli spirit, gave the performance of his life with five for 42 off 24.3 overs. He was well supported by an all-seam cast, of whom Graham McKenzie was making his Test debut. McKenzie's first wicket was the all-important one of Cowdrey, for 16, off a rearing delivery after the England captain had smote him for three fours earlier in the over. 206 all out, England struck back by taking the first four Australian wickets for 88, but a tenacious 130 from their young opener, Bill Lawry, and a stubborn half-century from Mackay steered their team into the lead. Mackay felt that Cowdrey had erred by allowing Statham to bowl to him without a slip, and 102 runs for the last two wickets was the result.

When England began their second innings 134 behind shortly before lunch on the third day, Cowdrey implored his batsmen to respond positively. The advice backfired as the upper order meekly surrendered to a series of rash shots. Cowdrey himself appeared a mere shadow of the cricketing giant on parade at Canterbury. He could have been out at least twice before hitting a half-volley tamely to cover when he was 7. Despite 66 from Barrington, England again barely passed 200 and Australia, needing 69 for victory, survived early alarms to win by five wickets.

In the aftermath of two disappointing performances the selectors now felt little compunction about restoring May to the captaincy, and it was with mixed feelings that Cowdrey returned to the ranks. The bitterness of the pill would have been eased by the fact that May was one of his closest friends, and they drove up to Leeds together discussing how England could improve on their limp showing so far. When they reached Headingley another substandard pitch, this time a grey, grassless one similar to the one in 1956, awaited them. Benaud, back for Australia, won the toss and chose to bat. His decision appeared well-founded at 187 for two before inspired bowling from Trueman blew away the rest of the batting like leaves in an autumn gale. 237 was all Australia could manage but, with the pitch already deteriorating, there was no gloating in the England camp. After the close of play Cowdrey, who had distinguished himself with two fine catches in the gully, popped into the Australian dressing-room and said, 'Well, boys, I'm off to Blackpool beach. I want some batting practice before I tackle this track.'

The next day he made his one telling contribution to the series with a masterly 93, ideally tailored to the vagaries of the wicket. Shunning front-foot drives unless the ball was of a full half-volley length, Cowdrey scored most of his runs with sweetly timed hits off the back foot and looked set for a century until caught down the leg-side by Grout as he attempted a hook off McKenzie. Australia, 62 behind on first innings, again collapsed in dramatic fashion to Trueman, losing their last eight wickets for 21 and leaving their hosts a mere 59 for victory. They lost by eight wickets.

With the series now tantalisingly placed at one game each, England, as in 1956, fancied their chances to come from behind and win, but before the Manchester Test had even begun their hopes had been dashed. On Saturday 15 July, Cowdrey fell ill when playing for Kent against Essex at Colchester and took advantage of a premature abandonment to retire to bed. There he stayed for five days, missing the Gentlemen versus Players fixture at Lord's, and he still felt far from perfect when driving down to Maidstone to play Essex on 22 July. One lap around the ground caused a new collapse and once again he became *hors de combat*. He immediately telephoned Gubby Allen to inform him of his condition as the team for Old Trafford was being selected the next day. On the assumption that he would have recovered by the following Thursday, Cowdrey was included in the team but the decision was made more in hope than on sound judgement. On the morning of the match Cowdrey was still running a temperature and although May kept pressing him to play, a chance encounter with a doctor sealed his fate. He took one feel of his pulse and told him that he could not play again for ten days. Pleurisy was the diagnosis. As a result of Cowdrey's withdrawal, Brian Close came into the team and was roundly condemned for his reckless batting on the final afternoon when England not only lost a pulsating match by 54 runs but any hope of recovering the Ashes.

Cowdrey's absence from the game provided no respite. His return in Canterbury Week, three weeks since his previous innings, proved sadly premature. He scored 156, it is true, against Hampshire and 57 in the next match against Gloucestershire, but the debilitating effects of his illness became increasingly more pronounced. By the time he arrived at The Oval for the final Test he was nursing a splitting headache. Reluctant to bother the selectors again with his various ailments, he made light of his fragile state. After a brief, tortured appearance at the crease on the first morning, when he failed to score, he felt progressively more wretched until by teatime he had returned again to his hotel with a temperature of 104. There he stayed until on the Monday, in a final gesture of defiance, he unselfishly volunteered once more for front-line service. Again, his efforts counted for nothing as he was the victim of a spiteful delivery from Mackay, signalling his final appearance on a cricket field that year.

For all the high hopes of springtime most of Cowdrey's flowers had failed to bloom. Not only had the Ashes remained with Australia, his batting had failed when it mattered, chiefly because he had developed stage fright. More important was the question of the captaincy. Believing himself to be a caretaker captain for May in 1960, on a match by match basis, and unaware at the time that his friend had little inclination to return, Cowdrey captained in his shadow without developing his own distinctive style. 'If I could now have that period of my life over again,' he wrote in *MCC*, 'I would have asserted myself without inhibition.' Similar feelings governed his approach the following year towards the Australians. 'Lord's 1961 was the Test in which I should have clinched the captaincy for years to come.' Instead, an undistinguished performance by both general and troops meant that the captaincy returned to May by default. The disappointment was such that Cowdrey could not even bear to discuss his demotion with his family. The pain in normal circumstances might have been temporary, because with the captaincy vacant for India and Pakistan that winter he would have been the obvious front-runner, but for family reasons he was unable to make the trip. His presence was needed at home.

10

The Last Boat to Australia

Having missed the long and tiring trek round the subcontinent, Cowdrey began 1962 with such aplomb that his first five matches for Kent brought him 542 runs and two centuries. Another one soon followed in the first Test against Pakistan at Edgbaston, when his 159 as an opener laid the foundations for a resounding victory. It was the beginning of a disappointingly one-sided series against unfancied opponents, and inappropriate preparation for the forthcoming tour to Australia.

Now that May had finally announced his intention to relinquish the English captaincy for good, the question of his successor loomed large in discussion for most of the summer. Ted Dexter's leadership in India and Pakistan had not won universal acclaim, and with the new chairman of selectors, Walter Robins, publicly demanding a more positive style of cricket any putative captain for Australia would need to make gestures in this direction. Having laid down his terms, Robins and his colleagues on the panel decided to use the Pakistan series as an opportunity to examine the main contenders. Dexter was invited to captain the first two Tests and Cowdrey the third. By common consent the former earned his stripes in the first Test but was less assured in the second. Cowdrey then took over at Headingley and put up a brilliant performance, in Dexter's own words, employing every trick to defeat the Pakistanis comfortably. It is probable that he would have continued in office for the fourth Test, especially since he had been appointed to lead the Gentlemen against the Players at Lord's in an unofficial tour trial with both Dexter and David Sheppard under his command – if kidney trouble had not forced his withdrawal. Dexter took over the captaincy but the spoilight was now fixed firmly on Sheppard, who by then was a cleric in the East End of London.

The fact that Sheppard should ever be in the running to be captain in Australia was little short of remarkable given his absence from the first-class game for two years and from Test cricket for five. What had prompted the spotlight to turn on him was a rogue article in the London *Evening News* by their maverick correspondent, E. M. Wellings, which happened to catch Robins's eye. The crux of Wellings's rationale was that it needed someone of Sheppard's calibre to restore the flair to English cricket, and given his own sentiments on this point, Robins's subsequent behaviour was entirely in keeping. He contacted Sheppard to see whether he might be available for Australia and was persuasive enough for Sheppard to consider the unthinkable. Within a few weeks he was making a comeback for Sussex against Oxford University in the Parks in the full glare of the nation's media, and crowning his return with a century. Thereafter run-scoring and fielding became more taxing and it needed Robins's support for Sheppard to continue with the experiment. Gradually the clouds began to lift, and with Cowdrey withdrawing from the captaincy of the Gentlemen the contest, according to the critics, became a straight fight between Dexter, his replacement, and Sheppard. On the first day of the match, Sheppard appeared to have cemented his claims with a skilfully made century and, encouraged by some mischief-making from Robins, the press almost to a man pronounced his impending coronation for Australia.

The next day the air around Lord's was thick with tension as onlookers waited for the white smoke to emerge from the Tavern chimney at close of play. Sheppard was relaxing in the bath in the dressing-room when a journalist dropped by to ask him about his reaction to Dexter's appointment. Apparently, Robins and his colleagues had been encouraged to have second thoughts about sending a part-time cricketer on such an important mission. Instead they had opted for Dexter, whose captaincy of Sussex at that time had been particularly inspiring, with Cowdrey as his deputy. Though Cowdrey's illness might have told against him, Woodcock thought he lacked the streak of ruthlessness required to tackle the Australians on their own broad plains.

Unfit for the fourth Test, Cowdrey returned at The Oval to inflict yet further punishment on the hapless Pakistanis with an imperious 182, his highest ever Test score, putting on 117 with Sheppard for the first wicket and 248 with Dexter for the second. On 32 at lunch, Cowdrey, observed Woodcock, went from 38 to 100 in fully fifty-five minutes 'with as majestic a succession of strokes as there has been all the year ... In full sail he was a magnificent sight'. England won again, this time by ten wickets, and Cowdrey returned to Kent to finish the season as he had begun it, with 465 runs in his final three matches including 148 against Gloucestershire and 155 against Middlesex. After a couple of lean years he had regained his appetite for plundering attacks and now eagerly awaited the opportunity for another crack at the Australians.

As a veteran of four major tours, Cowdrey had already established his own format for these lengthy expeditions away from home. Always a master of the formal occasion, Cowdrey could fly the flag as well as anyone and his legendary charm and good manners had won him a legion of admirers from Brisbane to Barbados. He could also be excellent company with his team-mates, entertaining them on board ship in such traditional rituals as the fancy dress ball, or mixing it with the best of them on the golf course, but long hours of soul-searching at the bar or informal nights on the town were not his style. This aloofness was partly his natural reticence and partly in accordance with the conventions of the time, which would have drawn somebody of Cowdrey's amateur status towards a different lifestyle, particularly in a country like Australia where private hospitality abounded. These distinctions were never better illustrated than in 1962–63 when the Duke of Norfolk as manager, Dexter as captain, Cowdrey as vice-captain and Sheppard as a former England captain, defying the official abolition of the amateur in November 1962, seemed to echo a Britain of a bygone era. Not only were they conspicuous by having their wives on tour or for the profusion of black tie dinners they attended, they also generated interest away from the cricket, be it the Duke's predilection for the racetrack, the captain's wife's talent for modelling or Sheppard's appearances in the pulpit.

A slight problem concerned the relationship between Dexter and Cowdrey which, for all their affinity off the field, remained a curiously one-sided affair. Dexter, with his striking presence, privileged background and natural air of command at the crease, looked every inch an England captain, but his aloof temperament and sudden flights of fancy made him difficult to work with. Tom Graveney recalls how Cowdrey would intermittently offer advice, which Dexter would greet with a bewildered cry of 'Oh, Colin' before wandering off.

Rebuffed by Dexter, Cowdrey found solace in Sheppard, a fellow member of the small selection committee, and like him an ardent devotee of Hutton in his scrupulous preparation for the game. Before the first Test, Hutton wrote to Cowdrey urging him to pick the people who really wanted to play. It took Sheppard and him some time to work out this inscrutable remark, since everyone, they assumed, wanted to play for England. 'However, the more we thought about it,' wrote Sheppard, 'the more sense it made. Making runs and taking wickets in Test matches can often be a very tough exercise.'

After flying to Aden to board the SS *Canberra*, the last time an MCC team travelled to Australia by boat, the tour started as usual in Perth, before moving on to Adelaide. For Cowdrey, earmarked to open, the early signs were anything but promising. After three matches and six innings his run tally was a paltry 67. What's more he suffered the indignity of three successive ducks, including a pair against the Combined XI in Perth, a match MCC lost by ten wickets. When he eventually scored a run in the second innings against South Australia in Adelaide he did a kind of war dance to celebrate.

Naturally concerned about this sequence of low scores, Cowdrey not only turned his back on opening thereafter (apart from in one innings in the final Test), but he practised with even greater intensity. Fred Titmus recalls Cowdrey summoning John Murray to bowl at him in the nets in Adelaide and suddenly announcing that he had rediscovered his timing. His labours paid off with 88 against an Australian XI when MCC, led by a rumbustious 102 from Dexter, raced to 633 for seven, the highest score on the Melbourne ground by an English touring team. 'Everyone made runs,' reported E. W. Swanton, 'and made them attractively, though of course the innings that mattered was Cowdrey's. By the time Dexter left, Cowdrey was playing well and in that vein he continually drew the short ball at the angles he wanted on the leg side and thrust the fuller pitched ones through the covers with that final persuasion of the wrists that those at home know so well.'

With a fifty against New South Wales to follow, Cowdrey approached the first Test in better heart, but his side's overall record of two losses, one victory and three draws did little to alter pre-tour thinking that Australia were clear favourites to win the rubber. Led by some superlative batting from Dexter, England overcame their traditional Brisbane hoodoo and emerged with a highly honourable draw. Had Cowdrey been in the mood they might conceivably have won, but he was out cheaply to long hops in both innings. According to Alan Ross, he 'gave the impression of being so absorbed in monk-like meditations of his own that when a really bad ball penetrated his consciousness he went haywire'.

Happily, in the return fixture against South Australia in temperatures of 105°, the red blood returned as he charmed the Adelaide crowd with a vintage display. Taking advantage of two missed chances at 43 and 91, his confidence increased throughout the day and by the final session he had the bowlers at his mercy. Some of his success should be attributed to Graveney, who persuaded him to keep going when he felt like throwing in the towel. Together, they put on 252 by the close, and when their partnership resumed in much cooler conditions on Christmas Eve the records continued to fall. Cowdrey took his score from 244 to 307 (four sixes and 29 fours), which was the highest ever score by a tourist in Australia, beating Frank Woolley's 305 against Tasmania in 1911–12. His stand of 344 with Graveney set a new fifth-wicket record for an English pair in Australia and was the second highest partnership ever by MCC there. 'His timing returned as if it had never been absent,' declared Ross, 'and he lofted four straight sixes with the diffidence of a man tilting a top hat.' Well before the end the opposition had lost interest but, tipped off by the morning papers of Woolley's record, Cowdrey was now in no mood to give his wicket away. When Dexter failed to declare at Cowdrey's 300, South Australia were distinctly unimpressed, even when Graveney explained the reason to Ian Chappell. The tourists in contrast were jubilant. Cowdrey had chosen his thirtieth birthday to break so many records and four parties were laid on in his honour that evening.

From Adelaide the caravan moved on to Melbourne for the traditional New Year's Test and the most exciting cricket of the series. Having dismissed Australia for 316, England were 19 for two when Cowdrey joined Dexter and together these two premier batsmen held a crowd of 61,000 at bay with a partnership of 175 in what Sheppard thought was the best batting of the tour. 94 not out overnight, Cowdrey reached his twelfth century in Tests before Graham McKenzie dismissed him for 113. With the tail falling quickly to Davidson, Endland's lead was only 15, but a lion-hearted effort from Trueman (five for 62), aided by two marvellous slip catches from Cowdrey to dismiss O'Neill and Benaud, gave England a fighting chance of victory. Needing 225 to win on the final day with nine wickets left, they started marginally as favourites before Sheppard, with 113, Dexter with 52 and Cowdrey with 58 not out turned victory into a formality.

One up in a series in which they previously had been written off, Dexter's men travelled to Sydney for the third Test in high spirits, but their reckoning was not long in coming. On a sluggish pitch, Cowdrey's attractive 85 stood out in England's 279 while Titmus's seven for 79 restricted Australia's lead on first innings to 40 runs. The match then turned on the third evening when total surrender to Davidson undid all the good work of Melbourne as Australia bounced back with an eight-wicket victory.

It was thirty years since the two teams had come to Adelaide all square and this beautiful ground was packed to the rafters in shimmering heat to see the Australians profit from some woeful English catching. Cowdrey, unusually for him, dropped two catches and Harvey, given four lives before he reached 30, needed no further invitation. He made 154 and Australia 393, enough to gain them a first innings lead of 62. With Benaud deciding to bat on till the final morning because he was a bowler short, all hopes of an English win disappeared. Indeed, with both openers out within minutes there was some anxiety in the camp before Barrington (132 not out), in partnership with Cowdrey and then with Graveney, avoided any further embarrassment.

And so with the Ashes at stake in the final Test for the first time in Australia since 1936–37 both teams returned to Sydney with everything to play for. Unfortunately, caution and the wretched state of the wicket combined to ensure that the match fell way short of expectation. The mood was set from the first day when England meandered to 195 for five. Cowdrey, opening instead of the injured Pullar, went early and only Dexter of the batsmen showed any real sense of urgency. With Australia's first innings lasting till lunch on the fourth day, the onus was now on the visitors to make up for lost time and set their opponents a target. Again they were overcome by caution and it was only on the final morning that Barrington (94) and Cowdrey (53) were able to raise their game, allowing Dexter to declare at lunchtime. Benaud, however, was unwilling to take up the gauntlet and the dying embers of the game were played out to catcalls from the Hill as spectators left the ground in droves. It was a desparately disappointing end to a series that had promised so much, proving once again that all the honeyed words about brighter cricket lacked conviction when put to the test.

Jaded and somewhat disillusioned, MCC travelled to New Zealand, but for Cowdrey this final leg of the tour enabled him for the first time in three visits to show the locals the full power of his weaponry. In the first Test at Auckland he made 86, and in the second at Wellington his late entry at no. 8 (he had a damaged thumb) proved all-important. Together with A. C. Smith, the wicket-keeper, he set a new record for the ninth wicket in Test cricket with an unbroken stand of 163. Cowdrey made 128 not out, Smith 69, and England again won by an innings. Another conclusive win in Christchurch, when Cowdrey made 43 and 35 not out, gave them a clean sweep, a small consolation after the disappointment of Australia.

Taking the tour overall, Cowdrey had let no one down with the bat and proved a perfect ambassador in performing the social chores which befell the vice-captain. Indeed Swanton wondered whether there had ever been a more popular player to visit Australia. About his leadership, however, the critics remained unconvinced. E. M.

Wellings found his captaincy in the less important games too frivolous for his taste. Alan Ross felt that as vice-captain his impact was limited to the point of invisibility, and although aloofness had not been a handicap to someone of Jardine's temperament, the feeling persisted that in strategic matters such as playing an extra seamer in Sydney in the third Test, the views of the officers were at variance with the rank and file. Similarly, despite a reluctance by Dexter to consult him, Cowdrey could not entirely be excused for the defensive mentality which blighted England's approach from Melbourne onwards. It is true that Australia were little better in this regard, but as the challengers for the Ashes it was up to England to make the running, particularly in the final Test. Their failure to do so not only disillusioned many supporters of the game, it did little to enhance Cowdrey's chances of becoming Dexter's automatic successor.

11

Cricketing Crusader

By playing as an amateur, Cowdrey's financial independence of Kent not only gave him greater influence at the club, particularly since his father-in-law was chairman, it enabled him to pursue his wider missionary role within the game. The trend was set during his first winter as Kent's captain, when he attended 164 functions, not just addressing cricketing aficionados, but also to learn about cricket in the county at the grass roots. Thereafter, he used what spare time he had to answer press enquiries, speak at dinners, open fetes, write letters, sign autographs, contribute forewords to books, write articles for *The Cricketer* and play in benefit matches. F. C. Bernardes, a close friend of Cowdrey's, recalls how between 1957 and 1967 he organised a Kent side to play a team of celebrities on the Bickley Park ground, including the only match involving a Prime Minister's XI (Harold Macmillan's) ever staged in this country, when 10,000 attended. He also gave voluntary support to the Guide Dogs for the Blind, became chairman of the Kent County Playing Fields Association in 1966, which consumed many hours of his time, and President of the Kent Association for the Blind in 1969, in succession to his father-in-law. Another important responsibility was his appointment to the board of Charlton Athletic in 1966 as a way of cementing links between the south-east London football club and Kent. As ever, he entered into his commitments wholeheartedly, once being the only member of the board to travel up to Hull for an away match, and is fondly remembered at the Valley by fellow director Tony Pocock.

For an essentially private individual who never sought the lime-light, Cowdrey was past master of the public occasion, with a distinctly regal touch. Jonathan Smith, the long-serving head of English at Tonbridge, admired the way he would glide effortlessly through a phalanx of strangers, shaking hands, exchanging pleas-antries and then moving on with perfect timing. With friend and stranger alike Cowdrey has always had that priceless gift of being able to make people feel better about themselves with a gentle smile, soothing aside or word of praise. Christopher Martin-Jenkins, the cricket correspondent of the *Telegraph*, recalls Cowdrey effusively complimenting him on his bowling while gently despatching him to all parts in the nets at Perth in 1974. Andrew Wingfield Digby, a useful lower-order batsman for Oxford University in the early 1970s, once batted with Cowdrey for the MCC against the University in the Parks. After Wingfield Digby had scored a four past cover point, Cowdrey sauntered down the wicket to put his hand on his shoulder and said, 'I haven't seen a cover drive like that since I played against Graeme Pollock.'

Robert Runcie, the former Archbishop of Canterbury, has reason to be grateful for the encouraging tone of Cowdrey's reaction to his speeches at cricketing dinners, making him feel that he had said something momentous. Others in a similar position concur, alluding to the invariable telephone call the morning after to extol their efforts in golfing parlance. 'Well done, old boy, you went round in 61 last night.'

Although his reluctance to decline an invitation placed undue constraints on his time, forcing him into a number of last minute cancellations, he charmed as many as he had to disappoint. Apart from his charm, Cowdrey's appeal stemmed from the trouble he took with his multifarious engagements. He has always been a felicitous speechmaker, combining a natural fluency with a keen antenna which captures the mood of the occasion. Humour of a P. G. Wodehouse type is a valuable tool in his armoury. Not only does he have a nice line in self-deprecation, he can embellish his rich fund of anecdotes with a gift for mimicry. A favourite target has been Alec Bedser in his cockney accent saying, 'Colin, a funny chap. All those strokes but goes in there and looks like a crab – doesn't deserve his talents.' The advent of J. R. Thomson into his life in 1974–75, what-ever the hazards to his safety, certainly gave him priceless new mate-rial for the after-dinner circuit thereafter.

Along with the style went substance. Almost everyone who knows him testifies to his kindness. Tony Greig recalls his first Sussex match against Kent at Hastings when Cowdrey befriended his parents, who were down from Scotland, and went out of his way to help them, arranging both their accommodation and transport. David Kemp, his contemporary at Tonbridge, was indebted to him for putting himself out to be an usher at his wedding, and Billy Slayter, a neighbour in Limpsfield, appreciated the trouble he took to talk cricket to his aged father and readily volunteer Test match tick-ets for his son, William, in Sydney in 1971. It was here, incidentally, that another of Cowdrey's typically thoughtful gestures backfired. The Yorkshire bowler Don Wilson recalls how Harold Larwood, the scourge of the Australians in the 1932–33 bodyline series, who had since emigrated to Sydney, was thrilled to be invited to the English dressing-room to join in the celebrations. All was going swimmingly until Sir Donald Bradman suddenly entered to offer his congratula-tions and saw Larwood reminiscing with some of the players. Without further ado he turned on his heel and left, refusing to drink with his old adversary in the same room.

It was not just close friends who benefited from Cowdrey's generosity. Michael Mitton, an Australian quick bowler with the Melbourne grade side, Northcote, came across Cowdrey in the nets at Canterbury when playing a few games for Kent second XI in 1963. Travelling to Lord's one day to watch MCC play West Indies, he was recognised by Cowdrey on his way to the ground and given a lift in his Jaguar. Once there, Cowdrey showed him round the Pavilion, turning a blind eye when Mitton breached protocol by photographing the exhibition in the Long Room, and entertained him for supper at his home that evening. The young were not neglected either. Charles de Lisle, a former columnist for the *Daily Telegraph*, happened to be scoring in an important match at Eton when Cowdrey was captaining Richie Benaud's XI against an Australian under-eighteen side. At its conclusion, de Lisle went into the dressing-room to give Cowdrey the scorebook and was given £5 for his labours.

Many were indebted to Cowdrey for his sensitivity. David Sheppard recalls his concern on the voyage out to Australia in 1962 when he was confined to his cabin with seasickness. He also came to his rescue at an important function on that tour. 'The Archbishop of Sydney, Hugh Gough,' he wrote, 'invited the team to dinner. Spouses were invited too. Mrs Gough had organised the evening meticulously so that we were all to move to a different table for each course. As mealtime arrived, she said, "No one is to sit next to anyone they know". My wife, Grace, was just emerging from agoraphobia and had found it pretty daunting to come to such a party at all. Colin was standing with her and said, "Let's not take any notice of that. Come and sit with me."'

Similar sentiments were expressed by David Larter, the Northamptonshire fast bowler. He has memories of Cowdrey walking him around the ground at Headingley during the New Zealand Test of 1965 to lend an ear to his frustration at his inability to become a regular in the England side. The following year he showed great sympathy when Ken Barrington had to withdraw from the Test side at Trent Bridge because of nervous tension. Another to whom he gave help was Basil D'Oliveira. Shortly after he had been omitted from the England party to South Africa in 1968, he was invited to stay at Cowdrey's home. Those who toured under his leadership would always receive a letter afterwards thanking them for their efforts. Those dropped from the Test side would normally be commiserated with by way of a personal note assuring them that their time would come again. Sadly, for some it did not.

On tour, Cowdrey was punctilious in discharging his duties as an ambassador for England and MCC. He was, according to Sheppard, perhaps more conscious than any cricketer of the value of fostering goodwill. In this rather soulless age of international jet travel and non-stop cricket, occasions such as cocktail parties, official dinners and up-country matches now tend to be regarded as superfluous. A generation ago, however, they were considered a valuable part of any itinerary, even by many of the players themselves. With his pukka background and celebrity status, Cowdrey was much in demand by the local bigwigs. He, in turn, enjoyed meeting prime ministers and governor generals, a number of whom, such as Sir

Robert Menzies, the cricket loving prime minister of Australia, became good friends. But he did not confine himself to dignitaries. Nobody was more conscientious in giving up time to visit schools and conduct coaching sessions for the pupils, and he was unfailingly courteous to local enthusiasts. Brian Booth, the former Australian captain, recalls how he and Cowdrey were waylaid by two young autograph hunters at the Sydney Cricket Ground as they were about to practise and Cowdrey saying, 'Excuse me, Mr Booth and I are just about to have a net. Could you come back later?'

His quintessential English gentility won him particular respect in Australia, where brash individualism goes hand in hand with social niceties. 'He needs no introduction,' gushed the *Melbourne Herald* in 1965. 'For the fourth time in twelve years, he has the middle-age set of women cricketing followers swooning. They gaze adoringly at the soft countenance and chubbiness of this grand player every time he goes out to bat. Really he could for all the world be walking out to have tea and scones with the local bishop.'

As captain he took endless trouble to involve the press with his team. It helped, of course, that a number of them, such as John Woodcock of *The Times*, E. W. Swanton and Michael Melford of the *Daily Telegraph*, were close friends who shared a similar background and outlook on the game. He was on amicable terms, too, with Ian Wooldridge and Alex Bannister of the *Daily Mail,* and able to discuss sensitive issues with them in the knowledge that they would not end up in print the next day. He also showed infinite patience to everyone, the best off-the-field captain Brian Johnston, the BBC cricket correspondent and another good friend, ever saw. An example of his benevolence came in Barbados in 1968 when Cowdrey and others were being entertained by Tom Crawford, the former Kent second XI captain. A chance remark by his host about the bowling skills of one of the waiters led to a spontaneous demonstration in the dining-room with bread rolls. The next day Cowdrey invited him down to the team nets, where he bowled flat out for ninety minutes and, much to his delight, rewarded him with his wicket.

Cowdrey's wholesome image was aided by the prominence given to his religious convictions. The significant part played by his former headmaster at Tonbridge, Lawrence Waddy, in igniting the spark, has already been referred to. Indeed, it was thanks to his influence that Cowdrey spent some time helping at the Stepney Boys' Club, the school mission in the East End of London, when still a schoolboy. At Oxford his spiritual awakening grew primarily because of his friendship with Cuthbert Bardsley, a football-loving Old Etonian oarsman, and Bishop of Croydon, who used to visit the university. By Cowdrey's last year, when he was still undecided over a career in the church or cricket, he asked Bardsley whether he would be justified in choosing the latter. Bardsley gave it some thought and then told him to play cricket because, through that medium, he would best be able to bring people together for the greater good. Years later, when, now Bishop of Coventry, Bardsley visited the English dressing-room at Edgbaston during Cowdrey's hundredth Test, he lightheartedly complimented himself on the shrewdness of that advice. For having gained a reputation as a Christian, Cowdrey repeatedly found himself invited to participate in spiritual gatherings, including a large Billy Graham rally in Melbourne. Sheppard recalls the 1962–63 tour to Australia, when he and Cowdrey were very close. 'We agreed that we make time to read the Bible together once each week. I was invited to preach on several occasions and Colin would come and read the lesson. Our friends, who teased us about these services, said that they had been made to think afresh about the value of church-going after the service in Melbourne cathedral. Brian Booth and Colin read the lessons and I preached. Three centuries were made in the Melbourne Test match – by the three of us.'

On occasion Cowdrey would preach, often using cricketing parables to illustrate his message, but applying these principles to his own life wasn't always easy. The controversy over apartheid was one such issue as the Church itself became divided. In 1968 Cowdrey sought spiritual guidance from Cuthbert Bardsley as to whether he should lead England in South Africa, in the light of the furore caused by D'Oliveira's omission from the team. He then released a statement explaining his reasons for going, only to be overtaken by events.

A more serious conundrum was the travails surrounding his marriage, which he had been wrestling with in private for many years and which ultimately resulted in divorce. The trauma not only brought him much unhappiness, it placed a great strain on his faith and led to him cutting back on his public preaching, feeling that the beam in his own eye would lay him open to charges of hypocrisy. It says much for his perseverance that he was able to come through his personal nightmare without any hint of public recrimination or bitterness.

12

Trials and Tribulations

In 1963, now turned thirty and just back from a third successful tour to Australia, Cowdrey was nearing the peak of his career. With May out of the reckoning for future Tests and Trueman and Statham on the downward slope, he, Dexter and Barrington now carried the hopes of English cricket on their shoulders. In the 1950s England had reigned supreme, but the advent of the 60s brought a shift in the balance of power within cricket as new forces wrestled with the established order. New Zealand and Pakistan apart, the number of painless triumphs was fast diminishing. England, beaten at home five years in six between 1961 and 1966, and successful only in seven out of thirty-four overseas matches during this period, lost their winning ways much to the disillusionment of their supporters.

With international cricket becoming a less forgiving environment, it is easy to see why to someone of Cowdrey's gentle character the return to the more tranquil ways of the county cricket circuit, with its (normally) appreciative crowds and decorous informalities, never lost its appeal. Every May, with its smell of freshly mown grass and the colour returning to the Weald, would find him with a spring in his step as he anticipated the fresh challenges ahead. Even a visit to the less salubrious grounds, such as the Bat and Ball ground at Gravesend, had its attractions because of its local character and the memories associated with it. It was here that Cowdrey had scored his first half-century for Kent, and now in May 1963, on a green wicket which completely flummoxed the rest of his team, he was to be the equal of Warwickshire's Tom Cartwright. Their duel fascinated the young Dennis Amiss, who even found Cartwright a handful to read from slip. 'Colin had no such problems,' he recalled. 'He kept going down the pitch to Tom saying "I can read your hand now Tom". No one else could lay a bat on him.' All out for 133 in their first innings, Kent looked to be heading for defeat before Cowdrey saved their blushes a second time with a superb century in eighty minutes, hitting twenty fours in his 107 not out. It proved an ideal warm-up for the impending clash with the West Indians.

Since their defeat at home by England in 1959-60 Caribbean cricket had undergone something of a renaissance under their first black captain, the charismatic Frank Worrell; and now, for his final campaign, he returned to his adopted country with a talented team under his aegis. Before the summer was out, such new names as Conrad Hunte, Basil Butcher, Charlie Griffith and Lance Gibbs had become engraved in cricketing folklore as West Indies, with a smile on their faces, took their revenge for 1957.

In the first Test at Old Trafford they never looked back after compiling an unassailable 501 for six. Wes Hall rocked the start of the England innings, accounting for Edrich, Barrington and Cowdrey in quick succession, the latter bowled round his legs, before Gibbs took over with eleven wickets in the match. With another failure in the second innings, the pressure on the Kent captain was considerable as he and his team-mates regrouped at Lord's for what turned out to be one of the game's truly great classics. Having dismissed West Indies for 301 in the first innings, England, led by an awesome 70 from Dexter, who smote Hall and Griffith to all parts of the ground, closed four runs behind. When they took the field again before lunch on Saturday morning it was Cowdrey rather than the injured Dexter who was in charge. The experience in front of the largest Lord's crowd for seven years set his stomach muscles churning but did nothing to affect his concentration as two neat slip catches soon came his way. Later on he picked up an even better one off Shackleton to send back Kanhai, his sixth catch of the game; but just as everything seemed to be running England's way, an inestimable 133 from Butcher restored the balance. 'As captain of the fielding side against him,' Cowdrey recalled, 'I found that every run seemed to cut through me.' His captaincy won staunch admiration from Dexter as England quickly cleaned up on Monday morning in front of another

112

capacity crowd, spiced with a vociferous West Indian contingent: 234 to win seemed well within their capabilities, before Hall and Griffith struck back. When Gibbs bowled Dexter for 2, England had subsided to 31 for three. If ever courage and skill was called for it was now, as Barrington and Cowdrey, desperately in need of a score after three successive failures, started on the long haul back. They withstood Hall at his fastest, thanks to what J. S. Barker in his book *Summer Spectacular* called incomparable technique allied to unflinching courage.

In increasing gloom Cowdrey had progressed to 19 when Hall switched to bowling from the Pavilion end – there was no sightscreen then. He let loose two very nasty short ones, then in the next over one kicked and turned into Cowdrey faster than even his reflexes could follow. As he thrust out his left forearm to protect his face, the ball struck him a sickening blow just above the wrist. Cowdrey staggered away from the stumps, head back, arms raised, and, gradually folding to his knees, lay prone. As the West Indian players gathered round, he eventually got to his feet before disconsolately making for the pavilion against a background of stunned silence interspersed with the odd sympathetic murmur.

Cowdrey's injury brought the best out of Barrington, who with splendid defiance swung Gibbs twice for six to reach 50 before bad light stopped play for the day at 116 for three. Rain delayed the start on the final day until 2.30 p.m. Then, against a sullen backdrop, England remained in contention for victory thanks to a heroic 70 from Close, who refused to be intimidated by the ceaseless bombardment from Hall and Griffith. Ignoring the bombardment of balls which cannonaded into his body and left his torso a mass of bruises, he took the game to the opposition, even to the extent of giving a perplexed Hall the charge. His bravery gave England the scent of victory. Despite his captain's strictures Cowdrey, with an hour to go, was changing back into his cricket gear with his left arm now encased in plaster, ready to rally to the cause even if this meant batting left-handed. While he practised improvisation in the dressing-room, England lost wickets at regular intervals as the game ebbed and flowed throughout those final pulsating minutes. Eventually, with two balls remaining and six needed for victory, their ninth wicket fell when Shackleton was run out by Worrell in a photo-finish at the bowler's end. With all results still possible, and with Cowdrey's intentions still unclear to the public, a mighty cheer now erupted as England's vice-captain made his way to the wicket twirling his bat in his right hand. Fortune decreed that it was his partner David Allen who was at the striker's end ready to face the final act of fury from Hall who, incredibly, had bowled unchanged since 2.30 p.m. With the tension mounting he was bombarded by frantic exhortations from his captain not to bowl a no ball. Heeding his instructions, Hall responded with two straight deliveries which Allen did well to keep out. The match was drawn, Lord's breathed again, and Cowdrey managed a wry smile at his premature curtain call for the year as, like some great actor, he temporarily vacated the stage for his aspiring understudies.

His injury had more lasting consequences than might have been imagined at the time. On the assumption that he would be fully recovered by December, Cowdrey had been invited in August to lead MCC in India that winter, since Dexter was unavailable. The optimism proved ill-founded. The arm took longer to heal than anticipated, and in October Cowdrey was forced to back out not only of the captaincy but of the tour altogether. M. J. K. Smith was appointed in his stead. The party left in late December and within weeks they were soon in the wars. Not only did Barrington break a finger, forcing him to return home, illness ravaged the camp in Bombay when up to half of them were laid low by stomach trouble. So dire was their plight that the team for the second Test picked itself, with bowlers playing as batsmen and the reserve wicket-keeper opening. This sorry state of affairs came up in a routine conversation on the telephone between Cowdrey and Billy Griffith, the MCC secretary, when the latter happened to mention a recent letter from the manager, David Clark, explaining their predicament. When they discovered that both the projected batting replacements were preoccupied in South Africa, Cowdrey on the spur of the moment volunteered his services. Within twenty-four hours he was on his way to India, to be confronted on his arrival with a lengthy casualty list. He had not touched a bat for seven months, and two long nets was the sum of his preparation before his immediate return to the front line.

On an easy-paced pitch in Calcutta he scored 107, and then went one better in New Dehli with 151. Even this fairy-tale comeback did not entirely meet with approval since his innings were in keeping with the sterile tenor of much of the series, which ended in stalemate. 'To resume playing in the heady atmosphere of international cricket,' wrote that harsh critic E. M. Wellings in *Wisden*, 'and then to score centuries in the next two Tests, represented a remarkable feat. But Cowdrey continues unaware of his vast potential and even after the first century had restored his touch, he stood suspiciously aloof in Dehli and left others to attempt the scoring rate his side needed.'

Amidst all his international commitments, the cause of Kent cricket remained very close to Cowdrey's heart. He had endured the lean years of the 1950s with fortitude, but with the emergence of promising new players such as Mike Denness, Brian Luckhurst and Derek Underwood the county's fortunes suddenly appeared much brighter. Indeed, Cowdrey felt able to inform the members at their annual general meeting after the 1963 season that they now had a team of good cricketers and that they actually stood a chance of winning something, provided that he could instil in them the necessary confidence. With these words at their back, Kent could not have begun 1964 on a more encouraging note, beating Yorkshire at Bradford in their opening match, their first win in that county since 1930. *Wisden* complimented Cowdrey on a delightful 85, and he remained in the spotlight during the next fortnight with 85 against Essex, 117 against Hampshire and 69 against Derbyshire as his team continued to make the early running. It was not entirely coincidental that they were unable to sustain their early momentum once England's claim on Cowdrey's services deprived them of his runs.

The visit of an Australian team to England invariably creates an additional allure to the cricket summer, and with Bobby Simpson's team dubbed the worst ever to visit these shores their hold of the Ashes seemed tenuous. In retrospect English optimism proved premature. In an unspectacular series the Australians, despite missing the talents of Harvey, Benaud and Davidson, lacked nothing in competitive edge and ran out deserving winners. Both the first two

115

Tests were badly affected by the weather and Cowdrey, with a top score of 33, had yet to make much of an impact when back trouble forced his withdrawal from the third Test at Headingley. With Ken Taylor of Yorkshire, his replacement, not quite looking the part, a rather prosaic England side were comfortably outplayed, losing by seven wickets.

A week after Headingley, Cowdrey was back in action for Kent as they rediscovered their winning ways, and although he did relatively little at first, the decision to omit him from the Old Trafford Test seems quite baffling. England's loss was Kent's gain as Cowdrey proceeded to enjoy one of his most fertile patches, making 83 and 109 against Lancashire at Gillingham before gracing Canterbury Week with 99 and 100 not out against Hampshire and 101 and 42 against Middlesex. His efforts were to some degree in vain, because although Kent pressed for victory in all three matches they had to settle for three draws, and lost their chance of finishing in the top three of the championship.

Recalled to the ranks for the final Test at The Oval, Cowdrey made only 20 as England, still one down after a dull draw at Old Trafford, were bowled out for 182. Another old stager back in favour was Trueman who, with the magical milestone of 300 Test wickets dangling enticingly in his sights, was beginning to show his years. On a fast improving pitch he couldn't find his rhythm as the Australians built up a useful lead and, after an innocuous stab at their middle order on the Saturday morning, he was unceremoniously banished to the outfield to curse his luck. As Ian Redpath and Tom Veivers consolidated in the overs up to lunch, Dexter began to get desperate and discussed the various options with Cowdrey, his vice-captain. When Trueman overheard the captain suggest that he might bring on Peter Parfitt, an occasional off-spinner, he snatched the ball out of Dexter's hand, saying 'I'm going to bowl'. His bravado amused Cowdrey, who tried his best not to laugh as he walked away leaving Dexter standing there a trifle shaken. Trueman's first over was good enough to guarantee him the last one before the interval. It was now that he dug deep into himself and found the inspiration to clean-bowl Redpath and have McKenzie caught by Cowdrey at slip the next ball, whereupon lunch was taken, leaving the large Oval crowd in animated suspension. During the interval Cowdrey recalls Trueman acting like a prowling lion, desperate to return to the killing fields as he paced up and down the dressing-room waiting for the minutes to tick by. Eventually, the clock moved round to 2.10, and with everyone back in their seats the players returned in a state of high tension to resume the uncompleted over. Neil Hawke, the new batsman, soon foiled any chance of a hat-trick, but Trueman, now that he had sighted his prey, was not to be denied. A few overs later Hawke edged one to Cowdrey and the whole of The Oval joined in jubilant celebrations as an exhausted Trueman slumped into Cowdrey's arms, the first man to take 300 Test wickets.

Trailing by 197 on first innings, England began sedately in their second. Geoff Boycott completed his maiden Test century and for the first time in the series Cowdrey played close to his best, with an unbeaten 93 during which he became the seventh man to complete 5,000 runs in Test cricket. 184 on with six wickets left when the last day began, England still had thoughts of victory, but rain prevented any further play; a fitting finale to another depressing summer. English cricket lacked panache, and it needed the artistry of Cowdrey's blade to set the grounds alight. Instead, he had missed one Test through injury, one through omission, and had 'failed' against the Australians at home for the second time running. The Australians' relief at what they had escaped was evident at Canterbury, where Cowdrey hit two sumptuous half-centuries in Kent's seven-wicket defeat. Although disappointed by their final championship position of seventh, Cowdrey could at least be reassured by the fact that his team had had their most successful season since 1947. It was another small ascent up the foothills, which in turn gave way to the higher peaks of the later years of the decade.

The news in midsummer that Dexter, with a general election pending, would be standing as a Conservative candidate in Cardiff South East against James Callaghan, a future Labour prime minister, once more created a vacancy for the England captaincy on their tour that winter. The fact that they were going to South Africa made it an attractive assignment, and Cowdrey might have fancied his chances. The dilemma with which he now wrestled was whether he should even consider going, given his commitments at home.

117

Penny Cowdrey was a devoted wife and mother of four (Christopher, Jeremy, Carol and Graham) who worked tirelessly on behalf of the family, particularly during the long periods when Colin was away on tour. Not only did she keep a large house and garden immaculately, she bore the brunt of the children's upbringing, coping with their education, their friends and multifarious sporting interests. In addition to bowling to the boys in the garden, she would ferry them to cricket matches and invariably support them in all kinds of sporting endeavours, both at Wellesley House prep school and at Tonbridge. She was also Colin's most ardent supporter, looking after him at home, graciously entertaining his many friends, and avidly following his career, either in the flesh or on the radio. Indeed, so intense was her adulation that it was not unknown for her to embarrass him with public utterances on his behalf.

With such a supportive wife to act as the perfect foil for the celebrated husband, the Cowdrey marriage, to the outside world, looked the ideal match. The reality was rather different, as Penny, for all her *élan* as a hostess, was essentially a loner, ill at ease with the celebrity lifestyle. She also found the challenge of raising a young family relatively single-handedly to be a taxing one; leaving Colin in a cleft stick as he tried to balance his commitments to his country and the needs of his wife. The strain of driving long distances from Test matches at weekends to be with her not only aroused the disapproval of the selectors, it also left him so exhausted that he was unable to devote the necessary energy to his leadership. His broken elbow in June 1963, painful though it was, at least gave him an unexpected opportunity to be at home with Penny, and it was in due consideration for her after Graham's birth in June 1964 that, for the second time in three years, he opted out of an overseas tour.

The decision was not lightly taken and, with Penny in surprisingly good fettle after Graham's birth, he began to have second thoughts. He sounded out Peter Richardson, and was told that he should go as he was the best player. Attracted by the advice, Cowdrey went along with it, informing the selectors of his change of heart days before the team was due to be chosen. The gesture made little difference since their priority at that stage was to find another opening batsman, and knowing his reluctance to fill this position, they opted instead for a promising young Cambridge graduate, Mike Brearley. The whole strange episode might have dwelt longer in the public consciousness had the repercussions been more severe. As it happened, MCC won in South Africa under Smith, with all the batsmen playing a leading part. For once Cowdrey wasn't missed.

13

The Elusive Urn

Unhappy with his mediocre Test record at home during the previous few years and sorry to have missed the trip to South Africa, Cowdrey had every reason to make 1965 a special year. As early as Kent's second match he gave notice of his hunger for runs with an undefeated 196 against Nottinghamshire, unselfishly declaring to keep his team on course for victory. With 34 and 49 against Oxford University, 64 and 57 against Leicestershire, 77 and 46 against New Zealand for MCC, and 145 against Worcestershire, the selectors would ignore him at their peril.

For the first time since the Triangular Tournament of 1912, two teams were scheduled to tour England in 1965, establishing a precedent which has remained periodically in vogue since. The first of the visitors, New Zealand under John Reid, were badly handicapped by unseasonal weather and this, coupled with the lack of pedigree in their team, led to spectators staying away in their thousands. In the first Test at Edgbaston, England established a daunting total around the dependable figure of Barrington, but his 137 in over seven hours carried caution to excess and he was dropped for his pains. Cowdrey's 85 in contrast was, according to *Wisden*, a charming display and a century seemed a near certainty until a ball from Collinge trickled on to his stumps via his body as he went to hook. One up at Edgbaston, England registered another easy win at Lord's thanks to Cowdrey's 119, even though he was suffering from back trouble, and again at Headingley where John Edrich scored 310 and Barrington 162.

Greater resistance came from the South Africans who, under Peter van der Merwe, boasted a formidable side based round the talents of Eddie Barlow, Colin Bland and the Pollock brothers. The first Test at Lord's ended with honours even, with England marginally ahead for most of the game but faltering in the final stages. Although he was top scorer in the second innings, Cowdrey's match return of 29 and 37 was a relatively modest one. He reserved his best for the next Test at Trent Bridge, a match made memorable by the accomplishments of the Pollock brothers. On the opening day it was the younger brother, Graeme, who stole the show with a vintage 125 in conditions tailor-made for seam bowling. Without him South Africa would have struggled to reach 150. As it was they made 269, and with brother Peter leading the way with five for 53 they soon had their hosts in trouble. It needed Cowdrey at his very best to keep his team on the straight and narrow. 'Hitting his seventeenth test century,' *Wisden* recorded, 'Cowdrey showed himself the true artist.' Finishing 29 behind, England, with a makeshift attack which included Boycott (26-10-60-0) did well to restrict the South Africans to 289. Wanting 319 to win, they again started catastrophically, and when Cowdrey was stumped for 20 at 41 for 5 their chances more or less disappeared. Despite a brave 86 from Parfitt and 44 not out from Parks, five more wickets for Peter Pollock meant the honours went to South Africa.

Undismayed by this reverse, Cowdrey returned to county cricket to continue to reap a harvest of runs. He scored 152 and 44 against Warwickshire at Edgbaston and 99 not out (termed masterly by *Wisden*) and 56 against Gloucestershire at Dover as Kent enjoyed a prosperous August. They won five of their nine matches and lost only once, a run which enabled them to continue their steady rise up the championship table to fifth.

For the final Test at The Oval, England recalled Statham for the first time since 1963 and gave a first cap to his Lancashire colleague, Ken Higgs. The hunch proved an inspiring one as they took nine wickets between them in South Africa's first innings of 208. England in reply made 202, with Cowdrey's pedestrian 58 in four hours top score. A century from Bland kept them toiling and ultimately they were left seven hours to make 399 for victory. To their credit, they responded with gusto and a spirited fourth wicket partnership of 135

121

between Barrington and Cowdrey gave cause for hope. At tea, with Cowdrey on 78, they needed 109 in 85 minutes, but rain soon prevented any further play, leaving South Africa winners of a rubber in England for the first time in thirty years.

Disappointed by this unwelcome interruption when possible glory beckoned, Cowdrey could rest content with his record for the summer. Not only had he scored 2,000 runs but he had topped the national averages with 63.42 (the only time he did so). In a year when only three players averaged over 50, and eight over 40, this was no mean achievement. The portents seemed encouraging for Australia as Cowdrey prepared for his fourth tour there. There were those canvassing his claims for the captaincy, but after his success in South Africa the previous winter, and his great rapport with the players, it would have been hard on M. J. K. Smith to cast him aside. Cowdrey had no qualms with this view, but as he assumed the vice-captaincy for the third time under yet another captain, his continued failure to secure English cricket's most coveted honour must have caused him more than passing regret.

Following the turgid conclusion to the previous Australian tour, and a depressing sequence of nine draws in ten matches on their two subsequent tours, MCC returned to Australia in 1965–66 with a determination to portray the game in a more favourable light. With this in mind, Billy Griffith, the MCC secretary appointed manager with overriding powers, together with Smith as captain, formed a harmonious partnership which brought credit to the team wherever they went. With no Trueman or Statham in the attack the bowling lacked penetration, but because Australia were suffering similar problems English hopes of regaining the Ashes urn were not entirely fanciful.

Six weeks later, after the initial round of state matches, on the eve of the first Test, the original prognosis still held good. Victoria had beaten them in a close game, it is true, but three wins and plenty of large scores had given England much to enthuse about. One obstacle to overcome, however, was the absence of Cowdrey from Brisbane, suffering from a viral infection just as he was beginning to move up a flight. With his replacement, Eric Russell, injuring a hand and being unable to bat, England were forced to follow on but with rain restricting play they had little trouble in holding out for a draw. Despite announcing his return with 63 not out against South Australia, Cowdrey still felt unhappy enough about his timing to request extra sessions in the nets with local grade bowlers on the eve of the Melbourne Test. His efforts were later to have their desired effect on the ground which so often was his talisman. Entering at 228 for three in reply to Australia's 358, he started full of confidence and was soon unleashing his full array of shots before an admiring crowd of 50,000. His classic 104 in little over three hours was the most fluent innings Bobby Simpson ever saw him play, while to E. W. Swanton it recalled his salad days. With Edrich also scoring a century and six other batsmen making over 40, England swept on to a mammoth 558, a lead of exactly 200. Had Jim Parks stumped Peter Burge when Australia were struggling to clear the deficit the home side might well have lost. As it was, centuries from Burge and Doug Walters saw them to safety.

In Sydney a few days later there was no such escape route. Bob Barber made a scintillating 185, England 488 and the Australians, without their captain, Simpson, who had chicken-pox, capitulated to Titmus and Allen on a turning wicket. They lost by an innings and 93 runs. Buoyed by this success, MCC headed for Tasmania where, in this relaxed setting, Cowdrey bounced back from a duck in Sydney with scores of 63, 108 and 70. Unfortunately these games, and a gentle workout against Northern New South Wales, were not ideal preparation for the crucial fourth Test in Adelaide where, under the revitalised Simpson, Australia stormed back with a vengeance. On the opening morning England were soon floundering at 33 for three, and it was left to their two senior batsmen, Barrington and Cowdrey, to pick up the pieces. They responded positively, and on a perfect pitch Cowdrey was in superlative form when there arose one of those misunderstandings which can help transform a game. Barrington pushed Keith Stackpole, the leg-spinner, straight to Neil Hawke at mid-on and Cowdrey, mistaking wicket-keeper Grout's call of 'Watch the one' for Barrington's 'Come on', charged down the wicket, only to be sent back and run out for 38. Barrington continued to battle it out for 60, but England's 241 was a paltry offering on such a bountiful surface. Lawry and Simpson showed up England's profligacy by putting on 244 for the first wicket, and when England began their second innings they had their backs to the wall. Once more they began disastrously and once again everything depended on Barrington and Cowdrey. They batted carefully on the fourth morning until Cowdrey, on 35, drove at a 'wrong 'un' from Stackpole and was unhappy to be given out caught at the wicket off an inside edge. With Smith and Parks following soon afterwards the game was all but up. Despite a fighting 102 from Barrington, England's hour in the sun had been all too brief.

With the series still hanging in the balance, all now hinged on the final Test in Melbourne. England again batted first and returned to their high-scoring ways, helped by another century from Barrington. At the close they stood on 312 for five, with Cowdrey undefeated on 43, but his innings was marred by a major umpiring row which left his opponents seething. On 15 he tried to sweep Veivers, the off-spinner, and Grout caught the ball down the leg side as it hurried through to his gloves. All the close fielders went up in unison and there were dismayed looks all round when umpire Rowan was unmoved by the appeal. The reason why some of the Australians did not let the matter drop was that this 'catch' was but the latest in a long line of contentious decisions involving Cowdrey in Australia. There were the two notorious occasions at Brisbane and Melbourne on the 1958–59 tour, two disputed dismissals at Adelaide in 1963 and 1966, and now the catch that never was in Melbourne. What riled Australians such as Simpson, O'Neill and Hawke was that Cowdrey's code of 'walking' operated very much on his own terms so that he, and not the umpire, seemed to be the arbiter on appeals for catches recalling the previous tour to Australia in 1962–3, when other Englishmen had allegedly failed to practice what they preached about walking. They much preferred the Australian practice whereby the umpire was the alpha and the omega of all decision-making, for in that way the scope for confusion and inconsistency was greatly reduced. These reservations about Cowdrey were not confined to Australia. They were shared by many within the game, with even Sobers, that most generous of opponents, writing in 1988 that, 'the former England captain, Colin Cowdrey, walked, but not always.'

124

That such a view became prevalent is surprising given Cowdrey's reputation for sportsmanship and the high esteem in which many former opponents continue to hold him. He, for his own part, would vigorously defend himself against such accusations, pointing out that he always walked unless there was an element of doubt, in which case he was entitled to wait for the umpire's decision. The fact that almost all the dismissals alluded to in Australia from 1958–66 fall into this category, gives some credence to Cowdrey's viewpoint. But, thereafter, the evidence is too elusive for the biographer to reach a definite conclusion.

Doubtless such moral considerations were far from Cowdrey's mind when England resumed their first innings in Melbourne. He and Parks took the game to the opposition and another century seemed a near certainty until a moment of indecision when he was on 79 brought about his downfall. Cowdrey later explained that as medium-pacer Walters let go of the ball he knew he could have hit it past cover's left hand, but then opted to glide it past third-man instead and ended up being caught at the wicket. He returned to the pavilion berating himself for havering over his shot deployment, little appreciating that such alternatives were not available to ordinary mortals.

With Parks making 89, England declared at 485 for nine, but this sterling effort was more than matched by Australia who, led by Bob Cowper's marathon 307, replied with 543 for eight. Once again, for all the talk about attacking cricket, inclement weather and limited bowling resources consigned the Test to oblivion, leaving England to rue their inept display at Adelaide. With a batting average of 53.40 from the Tests, his best ever against Australia, Cowdrey had certainly let nobody down but his opportunity to dominate was restricted by a mere five completed innings. The sense of anticlimax which clouded the end of the tour continued into the New Zealand leg where all three four-day Tests were drawn. Having celebrated his hundredth catch in Test cricket in the first Test in Christchurch – ironically more or less on the spot where Hammond, the only other man then to have reached this target, held his final Test catch – Cowdrey was in the runs in the next two but somehow, with the Ashes again eluding him, they seemed of little consequence. With England not due back in Australia for another five years, there was no guarantee that Cowdrey would be returning there as a player, let alone as a captain in pursuit of his ultimate dream.

14

Eclipse

1966 might well rank as Cowdrey's *annus horribilis*. A week after Bobby Moore had earned the gratitude of the nation by leading England to football World Cup triumph at Wembley, Cowdrey was unceremoniously axed as her cricket captain after being outplayed by the West Indians. It was not just the scale of the defeat that rankled. It was the unenterprising manner in which his side had succumbed, reflecting all too clearly the deficiencies then plaguing the English game. In truth, they had been mounting for a number of years and now, in another miserable summer, matters reached crisis point with the editor of *Wisden* remarking that the standing of English first-class cricket had never been so low, and the establishment of the Clark Committee to seek a way out of the malaise.

For the moment, such sombre thoughts were temporarily banished as large crowds flocked to the Duke of Norfolk's picturesque ground at Arundel one glorious Saturday in late April to welcome Gary Sobers's flamboyant West Indians. A dismal May did not dampen the hopes of an exciting, closely fought rubber, and when England gathered at Old Trafford they were confident enough to omit a batsman for an extra bowler. Sadly, their confidence proved to be illusory as the match followed a similar pattern to the one on the same ground three years earlier. Losing the toss on a wearing pitch, England laboured long and hard in the field as their opponents, with centuries from Hunte and Sobers, rattled up 484. They then cut a sorry sight as they were bowled out twice by Lance Gibbs to lose by an innings. Only Colin Milburn, with a robust 94 on his debut, and Cowdrey, with a skilful 69 during the dying stages of the game, offered any meaningful resistance as England slid to their first three-day defeat since 1938. The critics were not impressed and the selectors responded to the clamour for change by axing the unfortunate Smith as captain, not simply because of his double failure at Old Trafford but because of his run famine over the previous year. The decision to replace him with Cowdrey was broadly welcomed although, as the new captain himself recognised, the players' sympathy would linger on with Smith, who was never to captain England again.

Among the other changes for Lord's was the recall of the thirty-nine-year-old Graveney after a three-year exile, and it was his majestic 96 that placed England in pole position after they had dismissed West Indies for 269. The noose tightened even further on the visitors when, come Monday morning, they led by only nine, with five wickets down. Only Sobers, it appeared, stood between England and certain victory. Appreciating the immensity of the challenge in front of him, the West Indian captain quickly resolved to force Cowdrey on to the defensive by taking the attack to the bowlers. This he proceeded to do, and within a few overs Cowdrey obliged by spreading his fielders to distant parts. Although he justified his tactics by pointing to Sobers's dislike of defensive field placings since they helped to corral him, they certainly had little effect on his performance that day; Sobers, in retrospect, felt that Cowdrey should have gone for the kill. As it was he and his cousin, David Holford, not only escaped the noose, they increasingly turned their guns on the enemy as England's bowlers wilted in the fourth day's final session. By the close, Sobers was on 121, Holford on 71 and West Indies 202 to the good. The next morning they moved serenely on, with Holford making his debut Test hundred before Sobers declared, setting England 284 to win in four hours. For a time it looked as if his enterprise would pay off as Boycott, Barrington, Cowdrey (for the second time in the match) and Parks all went cheaply. It needed a swashbuckling, undefeated century from Milburn, well supported by the injured Graveney, to prevent further disaster and secure a drawn game.

This wonderful Test helped guarantee another healthy following when the two teams resumed hostilities at Trent Bridge. Losing the toss yet again, Cowdrey would have been more than happy to have seen off the West Indians for 235, but then, in a devastating retort, Sobers and Hall brushed aside the English upper order. At 6 p.m. on a dark, dank Nottingham evening, with the scoreboard showing 13 for three, the captain emerged unsmiling from the pavilion to join Graveney, and together they safely negotiated the final half-hour. They resumed with painstaking care the next morning but gradually raised the tempo, with both men reaching fifty before lunch. In an attempt to unsettle them, Sobers had constantly switched around his attack and himself bowled in all his different guises, but it made little difference as Cowdrey repeatedly late-cut him with precision. With Graveney going on to make 109, Cowdrey 96 and Basil D'Oliveira 76, England unexpectedly led by 90. They remained in control for the rest of Saturday, but thereafter West Indies reasserted themselves with a vengeance as they tore into some mediocre bowling. When Sobers declared at 482 for five, Cowdrey's men had been run ragged, and although Boycott and D'Oliveira resisted staunchly in the second innings, West Indies emerged worthy winners by 139 runs.

Two down with two to play, England recalled Titmus and Barber for Headingley, but Cowdrey's reluctance to use the latter won him few friends. When he was eventually given a bowl, the West Indian score was past 300, with Sobers doing more or less as he pleased. He eventually fell to Barber, but not before he had made 174, and Seymour Nurse 137. Up against a total of 500 for nine, England were soon in trouble against the fury of Hall and Griffith. Hall removed three key batsmen, whilst Griffith fell out with umpire Elliott after a vicious bouncer to Graveney delivered with a suspiciously bent arm. Despite a bravura 88 from D'Oliveira, England followed on 260 behind, and in their second innings folded feebly for 205. Shortly after 3 p.m. on the fourth day the match was over and the crowd swarmed across Headingley to acclaim the victorious West Indians. After taking his bow on the balcony, Sobers returned to the dressing-room for a celebratory party in which Cowdrey and a number of the England players joined in. The festivities, however, were soured by a few choice words from Griffith to Cowdrey, when the latter tendered his congratulations. It transpired that the West Indian was still upset that Cowdrey had done nothing when at the non-striker's end, to rebuke Graveney for supposedly encouraging the umpire to caution

Griffith for that much discussed bouncer. Taken aback by this unwarranted snub, the England captain then had to endure a raucous group of thirty youths chanting 'Cowdrey go home. We want Close' as he emerged from the pavilion, before discovering that the bonnet of his Jaguar had been damaged and his tyres let down. Not surprisingly, this tasteless episode greatly upset him. Yorkshire CCC deplored this wanton vandalism, and Stuart Chiesman said that if he had been there he would have tanned the youths responsible.

Leaving these outrages aside, the case for a major clear-out for the final Test, including a change of captain, was irrefutable. 'As for Cowdrey,' declared John Woodcock, 'he came back to lead England at a time when resources were lamentably weak and the opposition exceptionally strong, though the country's resentment runs high after England's showing at Headingley and by his handling of his limited attack both there and at Lord's, Cowdrey invites criticism.' His replacement by Brian Close was not surprising but no less painful a blow for all that. Cowdrey was at a dinner at The Oval when news of his ousting was relayed to him. He rang Penny to tell her and she later informed a reporter that their son, Christopher, asked, 'What has Daddy done wrong?' 'How can you tell a boy of eight?' she wondered. 'He is so disappointed.'

This was not the only blow to befall Cowdrey. His batting had been disappointing for much of the summer, and after scores of 17 and 12 at Headingley the selectors decided to dispense with his services altogether. 'It is unbelievable that a player of such brilliant natural ability as Cowdrey can also be left out of an England side as a specialist batsman', lamented Ian Wooldridge of the *Daily Mail*, but such was the mood for change (there were originally six new faces for The Oval Test) that few people were prepared to go to the barricades for him.

As ever, Cowdrey took his punishment stoically, returning to play his best cricket of the summer as Kent beat Lancashire and Hampshire. After that week, he recalled in *MCC*, 'I was determined to win my place back in the England team as a player and hoped that the captaincy would never again be an issue. I enjoyed cricket too much, and I did not enjoy the infighting which the press liked to highlight.' With these comments in mind it was ironic that Kent's last fixture of the year happened to be at Harrogate against Yorkshire, who were on the cusp of the championship. The clash of captains past and present was, of course, too good an opportunity for the press to miss. After a spirited fourth innings' chase, Kent lost a thrilling match by 25 runs, giving Yorkshire the title, and Cowdrey boosted his following in the broad acres with a gracious speech complimenting his victorious counterpart. For the moment Close was the saviour of English cricket and likely to remain in place as the country sought refuge in his robust style of leadership.

15

The Turn of the Tide

With no winter tour to recover from, and unlikely to be returning to Test duty in the near future, Cowdrey could really make Kent his priority when the players reconvened in April 1967. The three previous years had seen them continue their slow but steady rise up the championship, finishing seventh in 1964, fifth in 1965 and fourth in 1966, as the years of careful husbandry began to bear results. Not only had Mike Denness and Brian Luckhurst developed into one of the most successful opening partnerships on the circuit, Kent had in Alan Knott, their wicket-keeper, and Derek Underwood, their left-arm spinner, the two most promising youngsters in the country. Now, as the new season beckoned, they were to be further strengthened by the recruitment of John Shepherd, an all-rounder from Barbados, who had attracted Cowdrey's attention on a short tour there in 1965. He, along with Asif Iqbal, who arrived in 1968, and to a lesser extent Bernard Julien in 1971, were all to become splendid servants of Kent cricket, fully justifying the great faith Cowdrey and Ames placed in them. But this was all in the future.

May revealed little – the weather was terrible – apart from a sweeping innings victory over Somerset at Gravesend built round a painstaking 150 from Cowdrey, his first championship century for two years. By June the sun was shining and so were Kent's prospects. Having lost to Leicestershire at the beginning of the month they gained the better of a draw against Middlesex, with Cowdrey's 97 causing *Wisden* to wax lyrical. Days later his undefeated 55 at Blackheath ensured that Middlesex did not escape a second time, and after two overwhelming victories in Tunbridge Wells week confidence was sent rocketing throughout the county. Cowdrey continued to lead from the front, with an admirable unbeaten 80 against Northamptonshire when the next top score was 18, before further success against Surrey at The Oval and Lancashire at Folkestone in early July placed them firmly top of the table.

There was encouraging progress, too, in the Gillette Cup, the one-day, 60-over competition which since its inception in 1963 had failed to bring Kent any joy. A powerful 66 from Cowdrey, earning him the man-of-the-match award, saw off Essex in the second round, and a deadly seven for 15 from Alan Dixon accounted for Surrey in the third. On 19 July the sun beat down on Canterbury as 17,000 spectators packed the St Lawrence ground to watch Kent play their old rivals, Sussex, in the semi-final. The situation was ideal for Cowdrey when he entered at 138 for two, and he responded to the manner born with a regal 78 in eighteen overs, earning him another man-of-the-match award and his county a trip to Lord's. Such was the effortless quality of Cowdrey's strokeplay that the large number of fielders protecting the boundary, like troops guarding a disputed frontier, were helpless to stop the ball from crashing into the boards. The cricket writers to a man applauded, and many advocated his return to the Test team. Another choice offering against Sussex, 118 in a championship match, gave added substance to their claims; and when England performed indifferently against Pakistan in the first Test, the selectors decided on a cull. Six changes were made for Trent Bridge, although Cowdrey's pleasure at his recall (as opener) was tempered by a reluctance to tear himself away from Kent's championship campaign when they were neck and neck with Yorkshire in the final straight. On the journey up to Nottingham he found himself constantly stopping at telephone boxes to find out how Kent were faring in his absence, and during the next week his thoughts never veered far from Canterbury.

As for the Test itself, a sodden pitch made batting a laborious business and Cowdrey's contribution to England's ten-wicket win was a sedate 14 and 2 not out. His absence from Kent had coincided with their vital clash with Yorkshire, which was settled very much in the latter's favour. In retrospect, it was a body blow. Although Kent won their last three home matches, their away form was not good enough to topple Yorkshire from their perch. Their triumph, however, did not come without a cost following a major rumpus at Edgbaston which left Close's credibility in tatters.

Since crowning his return from the wilderness with laurels at The Oval against West Indies, Close had consolidated his hold on the English captaincy with a three-nil whitewash over India and the victory over Pakistan at Trent Bridge. On top of this he was on course to lead Yorkshire to a second consecutive championship, but his tough, uncompromising style was sometimes overplayed, as was evident from the delaying tactics used at Edgbaston to deny Warwickshire a well-merited victory. The fact that Yorkshire could only manage twenty-four overs in 100 minutes and two in the last eleven – and that Close refused to apologise – left him vulnerable to the whims of a disciplinary hearing of the Counties' Executive Committee at Lord's. On 23 August, the eve of the final Test against Pakistan, after having heard from Close, they unanimously concurred that Yorkshire's tactics had constituted unfair play and that Close, as the instigator of these tactics, should be severely censured. The verdict left Close flabbergasted but, immediately bolstered by the support of Doug Insole, the chairman of the selectors, and by his team when he arrived at The Oval, he turned his attention to immediate matters. What he could not have bargained for was the speculative nature of the press comment the next morning as they mulled over the verdict and its implications for the English captaincy. An editorial in *The Times* was more reasonable than most. 'To condemn the offence is right,' it declared, 'but it is no less important to show a sense of proportion towards the offender. Close has erred, but this one episode should not be enough to deprive him of the England captaincy.' Unfortunately for Close, the full MCC committee, meeting on that same day, saw things differently and vetoed his appointment – the likely choice of all four selectors – for the forthcoming West Indies tour, thinking it inappropriate to send such a controversial leader to a politically sensitive part of the world.

The public debate continued. Meanwhile, Boycott withdrew from the Test because of sickness and, with Close electing to go in first with Cowdrey after Pakistan had been dismissed for 216, the scene was a photographer's dream as England's leading titans ventured out together. Neither survived for long, with Cowdrey's 16 in ninety minutes drawing censure from John Woodcock for his reluctance to hit the ball.

Ever since the controversy over Close broke and the press began hounding Cowdrey as to whether he was available to captain in the West Indies, he had sought to keep the lowest of profiles while the political machinations continued behind closed doors. Rebuffed by their superiors over Close, the selectors informally sounded out M. J. K. Smith, but he had just announced his retirement so with little joy either on this score they began to retrace their steps. As Cowdrey was leaving the dressing-room at lunchtime on the Saturday of the Test match, he was accosted by Insole who, as he recalled in *MCC*, informed him starkly, 'The selection committee will select the captain for West Indies on Monday morning. I want to know that you are definitely available for West Indies and that if the disciplinary committee at Lord's takes action against Close . . . in spite of a very embarrassing set of circumstances you would be a candidate to be considered for the captaincy. . . . I shall take it that you will say Yes unless I hear by the start of play on Monday morning.'

Shaken by the way that the Sunday newspapers reduced the captaincy issue to a personal showdown between Close and himself, Cowdrey consulted Les Ames, the tour manager, as to whether he should declare himself unavailable for the tour. Ames, one of his supporters in committee, firmly counselled against such action, arguing that withdrawal would be in nobody's interest. Thus when the question was put to him on the Monday evening after England's resounding victory in the Test, Cowdrey accepted without demur. The next day, as the press tracked Close's every movement, he joined the selectors at Billy Griffith's home to pick the team for West Indies. Given the rushed nature of his appointment, he went in unprepared but, buttressed by the professionalism of the other selectors, he found this meeting an oasis of peace before the storm broke next day when the team was announced. 'The hot throne of England's cricket captain has never been so scalding as it awaits Colin Cowdrey to ascend it for the fourth time in his career,' wrote one correspondent.

His discomfiture had been increasd by an unfortunate admission from Insole – sympathetic to Close's plight – that Cowdrey had not been the selectors' first choice as captain. This prompted Cowdrey to remark that he felt like coming third in the school egg-and-spoon race but had won the prize because the first two had been disqualified. While substantial sections of the northern and tabloid press, led by Michael Parkinson, railed against Cowdrey, claiming that he was the nominee of the public school élite which ran the game, more measured support came from John Woodcock in *The Times*. 'Cowdrey must feel to some extent that he gets the job by default. Nevertheless he possesses many of the qualities it requires. Where I think Cowdrey lets himself down is in his reluctance to go after his prey. What this side needs from him is assertiveness whether with the bat or in the field.'

With the furore over the captaincy, it was a relief for Cowdrey to return to the unfinished business of the season: Kent's appearance in the Gillette Cup final against Somerset at Lord's. The first Saturday in September dawned bright and fair and a colourful crowd paraded their respective loyalties with stylish good humour. Kent, with the more glamorous team, were certainly favourites and, led by half-centuries from their opening pair of Denness and Luckhurst, played accordingly in the early stages. After lunch, however, the pendulum swung sharply when 138 for one became 193 all out as Cowdrey and the rest of the middle order missed out. Somerset in turn began confidently, but gradually the Kent attack turned the screw, causing wickets to fall at regular intervals. When they eventually folded for 161 and Cowdrey gratefully received the Gillette Cup from the MCC President, Sir Alec Douglas-Home, the county was able to celebrate its first trophy since 1913. It was an auspicious end to another unpredictable season. Little was Cowdrey to know that in the months to come his star was to burn ever brighter in the firmament.

16

A Wolf in Sheep's Clothing

Third in the queue or not, Cowdrey soon revelled in having the captaincy restored to him, assuming, probably correctly, that provided he acquitted himself well in West Indies it was now his for some time. During the four months before departure he planned to the last detail, even summoning the players for a two-day squad session at Crystal Palace in late November, which was then something of a novelty. Here Cowdrey spoke with a real sense of purpose about the future. Not only did he want to develop a strategy to win in the Caribbean, he also wanted to forge the nucleus of a team which would achieve success for England over a longer period, culminating in the tour to Australia in 1970-71. After some gentle net practice, the two-day get-together ended with a dinner at the Little Carlton Club, hosted by Edward Heath, the leader of the Opposition, who like Sir Alec Douglas-Home, his predecessor, was a good friend of Cowdrey's. Conceived as a pre-tour tonic, Cowdrey's initiative appeared to have done the trick. 'Even before we got into the aeroplane,' said Graveney, 'the attitude of the MCC party was better than I experienced before.' They travelled very much as underdogs after their hiding in 1966 but, apart from a lack of depth in the spin attack and a dearth of agile outfielders, there were no obvious weaknesses.

In the era before American culture began to impinge upon West Indian traditional loyalties, MCC tours generated enormous interest throughout the Caribbean, and wherever the team went large crowds accompanied them. One early highlight was a crowded New Year's Eve party in Bridgetown, where Colin Milburn stole the show with his rendition of 'The Green Green Grass of Home'. With his gargantuan size, warm-hearted personality and buccaneering batting, Milburn soon became a particular local favourite, eclipsing even the resident calypso king when he appeared on stage in Trinidad during carnival season. He was to experience a lean time on tour with the bat, but his capacity for enjoyment (sometimes to excess) added a nice Cavalier touch in a team of Roundheads bound up with their own performances. At first the camaraderie of Crystal Palace seemed threatened, but as the series proceeded, the team came together under Cowdrey's benevolent leadership. Tolerance had always been one of his hallmarks and now he used it in abundance. Boycott (on Close's advice) was told to bat how he wanted, irrespective of any general instructions, and was excused some of his more annoying traits. Pat Pocock, the Surrey off-spinner, was given permission in Barbados to stay with his wife at a friend's house provided he was back by breakfast, and the waspish asides of one or two malcontents, unhappy about their lot on the tour, were tactfully ignored. A blind eye was also turned to some embarrassing umpiring decisions, and when discipline was required there was Ames, as manager, to administer it. He and Cowdrey formed an excellent partnership, and with Graveney and Barrington, the senior professionals, providing extensive support Cowdrey's position as captain was immeasurably strengthened.

Cowdrey's men started shakily in Barbados with a near-embarrassment against the local Colts and an indifferent performance against the President's XI, despite centuries from Boycott and the captain himself. This mediocrity only hardened Cowdrey's determination to stress the work ethic. Net practice was ordered for the scheduled rest days, including Sundays; fast bowlers indulged with new balls were requested to go flat out; and fielding practice was sharpened. The results of this additional sweat were not immediately obvious in the drawn game against Trinidad, so that on the eve of the first Test in Port-of-Spain, West Indies remained firm favourites to win. An indication of England's caution was the omission of the mercurial Milburn for the more circumspect Edrich as opener, and the selection of the experienced Parks as wicket-keeper in preference to the youthful Knott, on the grounds that his batting was the stronger suit.

When Cowdrey won the toss and chose to bat first, the large crowd sat back in gleeful anticipation of the expected grilling of the English batsmen by the West Indies bowlers. It never happened. For the past year there had been ominous signs that Hall and Griffith were no longer the force of old, and now, on a docile pitch, these premonitions were amply confirmed. Boycott and Edrich saw off the new ball before Cowdrey and Barrington took over, so that by the close on the first day England were 244 for two, a massive boost to their confidence. Cowdrey was out first thing the following morning for 72, but a painstaking 143 from Barrington and an exquisite 118 from Graveney helped England on their way to 568. West Indies, for their part, seemed well placed at 240 for three, but subtle bowling changes and careless batting saw them fold for 363, enabling Cowdrey to enforce the follow-on. Again, they seemed in little danger on the last afternoon until a seismic collapse before tea, with six wickets falling for 16 runs, made England confident of victory. Had fortune not smiled so favourably on Hall, they surely would have won. As it was, the big no. 10 rode his luck and managed to stay with Sobers throughout the final session to deprive the visitors of first blood.

Disappointed by their near miss, the team moved on to Jamaica where Cowdrey continued his voyage of plenty with a century against the island XI. More important to him, however, was the return to prominence of John Snow, who hitherto had been handicapped with a virus. Indeed, so lethargic had he looked during the opening game of the tour that Graveney recalls a despondent Cowdrey turning to him and saying, 'I think he's going to be a waste of time.' Omitted from the team for the first Test, Snow now had his chance to stake his claim and he did so in convincing fashion. His inclusion in the second Test was critical to England's chances, particularly as the wicket, damaged by a recent storm, looked a lottery from the outset. On winning the toss again, Cowdrey said, 'We'll bat, whatever that means', and after losing Boycott relatively early, he again steadied the ship with 69 as he and Edrich took charge in a partnership of 129. The next day Cowdrey, despite nursing a heavy cold, went on to make 101 and put on 99 with Barrington to help England to a respectable 376. With the wicket now revealing deep cracks and the ball skidding through, the West Indians had no answer to Snow, whose seven for 49 included the prize wicket of Sobers, first ball, the second consecutive time Snow had achieved this feat in a Test. All out for 143, they were once again at Cowdrey's mercy. He made them follow-on and confined his troops to barracks over the weekend to keep them fresh for what he hoped would be the *coup de grâce*. Resuming at 73 for no wicket, Sobers's men lost wickets at regular intervals and looked all but doomed when, once again, a Test match in the Caribbean became subject to unruly passions.

For all the tranquil allure of those parts, with its sparkling blue water and sunkissed beaches, three of the four Test venues were situated in industrial centres associated with grinding poverty and crime. Kingston, Jamaica, was probably the most notorious, and in this tightly compact ground emotions would often run high, particularly when the home team played below potential. At 204 for four, Basil Butcher glanced a ball from D'Oliveira down the leg side and was athletically caught by Parks behind the stumps. Once informed that the ball had carried to the wicket-keeper, Butcher walked, but his hesitation proved fatal, sending all the wrong signals to a combustible crowd at the mercy of an extremist fringe.

As Butcher left for the pavilion, howls of protest erupted from the cheaper seating before a hail of bottles rained down. The arrival of baton-swinging policemen to restore order served only to antagonise them further. Seeing no sign of the storm abating, Cowdrey, joined later by Sobers, walked over to the boundary to appeal for calm but found an inferno of anger as protests turned to insults, such as 'How much did you pay dat Chinkee, Cowdrey?' in reference to Douglas Sang Hue, the Chinese umpire who had given Butcher out. In *Cricket Over Forty* Graveney too recalls walking over to assure the crowd that Butcher was out. 'Yeah, we know he was out,' one of them replied, 'but if it had been Cowdrey or May in England [remembering Edgbaston 1957] he would not have been given out.'

With the protestors immune to reason, it was now time for the riot police, armed with plastic shields and tear gas, to restore order. Safety decreed that Cowdrey, however reluctantly, led his team from the field to the sanctuary of the pavilion, but any hope of a quick resumption was frustrated by the incompetence of the authorities. By failing to take into account the prevailing wind, they fired their tear gas towards the troubled area only to see the fumes being blown back across the field into the pavilion and the stands on the other side of the ground. Spectators gasped for breath as they rushed for the inadequate exits, and the players, tears running down their cheeks, were forced to seek relief with wet towels in the dressing-room.

When the gas had cleared, Cowdrey, along with Ames and Arthur Gilligan, the visiting MCC President, met the Jamaican officials to discuss the options. In their distraught state their hosts, apprehensive about the continued volatility of the crowd, pleaded for as speedy a resumption as possible and Cowdrey, moved by their distress, agreed to their request. His gesture found little accord with his team, especially Graveney, who thought the decision madness. By the time they trooped back on to a still simmering arena, seventy-five minutes later, accompanied by a few boos from a sullen residue, the momentun had been lost. Fully alive to the tension, Cowdrey had instructed his players to appeal only when absolutely certain and, unsettled by this surreal atmosphere, the bowlers and fielders seemed distracted. No further wickets fell that evening and the next day, in conditions alien to batting, Sobers scored an astonishing hundred, which put the game out of England's reach. Then, true to character, he declared, took the new ball himself, and sent back Boycott and Cowdrey for ducks. When bad light stopped play forty minutes early, they were teetering at 19 for four and Sobers, much to Cowdrey's dismay, claimed the extra seventy-five minutes the following day for the time lost in the riot. Subjected to the pitch at its most venomous, and with the locals baying for blood, it was an enormous relief for England to crawl to safety at 68 for eight.

From Jamaica, via Antigua, to Barbados and trouble of a different type. A day out at the exclusive Sandy Lane beach ended in tragedy, when the propellor of a speedboat, driven by Cowdrey's wife Penny, got caught up with Titmus's foot, depriving him of four toes while he, Cowdrey and Hobbs frolicked around in the water. By his own admission in *MCC*, Cowdrey was consumed by panic as he went in search of help. Two local beach-hands pointed them in the direction of the neighbouring Speightstown hospital, but the gravity of an accident involving both his wife and his vice-captain left him incon-solable. Titmus recalls trying to comfort him in the car taking him to the hospital, assuring him it was nobody's fault, but it was still a distraught England captain who was comforted by Hobbs as Titmus was wheeled into the operating theatre. Fortunately there was an eminent surgeon on hand to take control. Two hours later he was able to telephone Cowdrey to inform him that not only had the oper-ation been successful, but Titmus's absence from the game would only be temporary.

With Titmus out for the tour, Graveney took over as vice-captain and Tony Lock was summoned from Australia, where he had been captaining Western Australia in the Sheffield Shield. The third Test, on a lifeless wicket in Bridgetown, ended in stalemate despite another brave effort from Snow which briefly gave England hopes of victory. Disappointed with their performance so far, West Indies now took the momentous decision to drop Hall and pack their side with spinners for the fourth Test in Port-of-Spain. Losing the toss on a perfect pitch, a grinning Cowdrey pretended to thump his opposite number as Sobers predictably elected to bat. They ran up 526 for seven, with centuries from Kanhai and Nurse, before getting a taste of their own medicine as Boycott, Cowdrey and Barrington led the fightback. By close of play on the third day Cowdrey had scored 61, and he continued to dominate the next day as he reached his sixth century against West Indies. 'If ever there was such a thing as an impenetrable technique,' commented John Woodcock, 'this seemed to be it.' When a dangerous spell by Willie Rodriguez, the Trinidadian leg-spinner, caused jitters in the middle order as they failed to read his googly, Alan Knott, in his first match of the series, helped his captain through the crisis. They had added 113 when Cowdrey, on 148, was bewildered to be given out, caught at the wicket off Butcher's rarely employed leg-spin.

The fact that Butcher fiddled out the English tail in no time to finish with five for 34 seemed of little consequence, as only a day of the match remained. On the final morning, in sweltering heat, both sides seemed simply to be going through the motions as a jaded England slowed down the over rate to eleven an hour and West Indies ambled to 86 in two and a half hours. 'The whole atmosphere as we returned to the field after lunch was one of sleepy indifference,' recalled Cowdrey, before a sudden burst of activity on the balcony alerted him to the remarkable events in store. Frustrated by England's time-wasting and confident that his spinners, particularly Rodriguez, could pose them problems, Sobers suddenly declared, leaving England to score 215 to win in 165 minutes, at 78 runs an hour. Since they had never come close to this scoring rate in the series, Sobers reasoned that England would not be tempted, but on a still unblemished pitch, with a quick outfield and an attack deprived of the injured Griffith, their one fast bowler, the opportunity was there for such an experienced batting line-up.

They started solidly, and when Edrich was out for 29, Cowdrey, unhappy with the delaration, settled in quickly enough without suggesting a man intent on a mission. Several threatening overs from Rodriguez before tea gave him further food for thought, and left him in a cautious mood at the interval as a debate raged in the dressing-room about their tactics. It needed some forthright comments from the senior professionals, notably Barrington and Graveney, to convince Cowdrey that victory was within their grasp and they should seize the hour. Geoff Boycott recalls that as he went to put his pads on, Cowdrey came out and told him to play his normal game and he would see if he could push it along. Helped on their way by a plethora of full tosses and long hops from the spinners at the beginning of the final session, Cowdrey quickly took command. For the next hour Sobers found it difficult to set a field to him as the England captain now led the victory charge with a series of sweetly timed strokes which enchanted all but the most partisan of spectators. When he was eventually caught by Sobers off Gibbs for 71, 38 runs were still needed, but helped by the exceedingly generous over rate and an innings of impeccable precision from Boycott, England completed their triumph on the stroke of time, leaving Sobers to rue his folly. As first Trinidad, then the rest of the Caribbean, clamoured for his head, the victors repaired to the Pelican Inn in Port-of-Spain for a night of celebration, with Cowdrey the toast of his team. He had, as John Woodcock observed, outmanoeuvred his opposite number and batted when it mattered in his finest style.

In the fifth Test in Georgetown, played over six days because the series was still undecided, Sobers won the toss yet again and condemned England to more hard toil in the field. He and Kanhai shared a rare lengthy partnership of 250 *en route* to the West Indies total of 414. Boycott (116) and Cowdrey (59) were again the main-stays of the English batting, but with the middle order contributing little the runes looked unfavourable. It needed an unlikely saviour in Lock with an aggressive 89, his top score for England, to help keep them in the game. When West Indies went in again on the fifth morning their lead was a mere 43. Their second innings was built round a sublime 95 not out from Sobers, who, following his 152 and three wickets in the match so far, was doing his best to atone for Trinidad.

England began the final day needing 330 to win or, more realisti-cally, to bat out six hours for a draw. The first hour produced little excitement, but the introduction of Gibbs to the attack caused mayhem as within a few overs England slumped to 41 for five. As a procession of batsmen came and went, Cowdrey stood there impas-sively at one end. Then Knott arrived in support, and together they survived to lunch. During the afternoon a battle of wills was played out as the Kent pair withstood everything the West Indian spinners threw at them, if necessary by Cowdrey's frequent use of the pads. Such tactics won him few friends amongst the Guyanese crowd, and when he paused for their barracking to subside he was told by the umpires to get on with the game.

Soon afterwards a tense crowd were again in on the act, when Knott turned Gibbs to Sobers at leg-slip, who swooped it up on the half volley and threw it up a mile high. Their delirium immediately turned to anger when Sobers, once the ball had alighted, proceeded to throw it along the ground indicating to the umpire that the bats-man was not out. Grateful for such small mercies, Cowdrey strolled up to Sobers a few minutes later and commended him for his sports-manship. 'Ah man, I did not catch it,' he replied. 'If I do not catch the ball, no fun in that. That's not cricket!'

With Cowdrey and Knott still together at tea it appeared that England might have weathered the storm, but twenty minutes after-wards Cowdrey padded up once too often to Gibbs and, much to his consternation, was given out lbw for 82. He left the field to boos, uncertain whether all his efforts had come to nought. Ten minutes still remained when Glamorgan's Jeff Jones, one of nature's no. 11's, made his way to the middle to join Knott as Cowdrey and others huddled in the dressing-room unable to watch. In scenes of unbearable tension Jones somehow negotiated Gibbs's final over to save the game, ensuring that England were victorious in the Caribbean for a second consecutive series.

Disillusioned by England's escape, many of the locals were in an unforgiving mood as they hung around the pavilion to vent their spleen on the English players. Lock was hit by a stone and a police escort was needed to shepherd Cowdrey and Ames back to the hotel, where the celebrations began in earnest. 'Men of Kent and Kentish Men have done great things for England but have they had a day of such triumph as this?' asked E. W. Swanton as Cowdrey's men returned home to a hero's welcome. He had achieved what few thought possible, and had done it by leading from the front. 'Cowdrey took a tremendous weight on his shoulders on that trip', recalled Tom Graveney, 'more than I've seen an England captain accept before. He skippered the side brilliantly, batted magnificently, sprinted through the social chores and did everything right.' Similar sentiments were expressed by Ian Wooldridge, who, looking back on a series in which personal relationships were often frayed, saw Cowdrey in a rather new light. Having had severe doubts about his appointment in the first place, he went on to call his leadership ruthlessly brilliant. 'England have set the pace throughout the tour only because Cowdrey, at 35, has become more professional than any of the professionals beneath him. He is the classic exception to the rule, the smooth man who has deliberately acquired rough edges. In the process, he has undoubtedly alienated a few cronies who believed the sun shone out of his Oxford cap, while he continued to lose with good grace. I can only hope that to compensate he has made a million new admirers in the back-to-back streets of Bermondsey, Huddersfield and Sunderland.'

A final postscript on Cowdrey's leadership came from J. S. Barker in his book *In the Main*. 'Cowdrey's personal triumph lay in the manner in which he moulded his ragged party into a team in which he became the leader as of right rather than by appointment, and in

145

which he became the key figure in the English array. When Sobers said after the fifth Test that Cowdrey won the series for England, it was no end of tour gallantry: it was the simple truth.'

17

The D'Oliveira Affair

Rarely can Cowdrey's position have been stronger or his confidence greater than at the beginning of the 1968 season. Not only had he triumphed against the odds in West Indies, he had rarely ever so excelled either in his batting or in his captaincy. Soon to be confirmed as captain against Australia for the whole summer, he now entertained great hopes of regaining the Ashes, as well as winning the championship for Kent. With a shade more luck, he could have achieved both. Instead, as August gave way to September, he once again had to settle for silver rather than gold, as well as seeing his dreams of leading MCC in South Africa disintegrate amid a welter of controversy.

After the sunlit splendour of the Caribbean it must have been somewhat disconcerting to return to the frustrations of another damp English spring. Nevertheless, in between the showers Kent began where they had left off the previous year in a championship now open to overseas players without residential qualification, and boosted by the introduction of bonus points to promote more attacking cricket. By the end of May they remained unbeaten in the first-class game and Cowdrey had recorded consecutive centuries against Somerset at Gravesend and Essex at Romford, the perfect overture for that summer's five-act opera.

With the Australians handicapped as much as anyone by the weather, and fielding a young untried side in English conditions, few pundits gave Bill Lawry's men much chance for the first Test at Old Trafford. In the event, they confounded the sceptics by winning easily, thanks to a supine English performance marred by undue defensiveness. The trouble began at the outset when Cowdrey, desperate to strengthen the batting after Barrington's late withdrawal through injury, omitted Brown, Underwood and Cartwright – three front-line bowlers – from the original fourteen. With Lawry, Doug Walters and Paul Sheahan all topping 80, Australia took control from the first day and on an uncertain pitch, eased themselves into a near unassailable position. All England could do, with some insipid batting, was to avoid the follow-on, and when challenged to score 413 for victory they never threatened, especially once Boycott and Cowdrey had gone early. Despite D'Oliveira's 87, they lost by 159 runs and all the previous reservations about Cowdrey's diffident captaincy were once again revived.

He and his fellow selectors resolved to approach the Lord's Test – the two hundredth between the two teams – in more positive vein, making five changes and fielding a more balanced attack. After a rain-interrupted opening day, a wonderfully aggressive 83 from Milburn helped make up for lost time before Cowdrey, with a patchy 45, and Barrington proceeded at a more leisurely pace. With most of Saturday also lost to the weather, England declared at their weekend score of 351 for seven. Then, exploiting the heavy overcast conditions, they decimated the Australian batting with an adroit display of controlled swing bowling and flawless close catching. Cowdrey held a beauty at slip during the opening overs to send back Redpath, and when he swooped later on to dismiss Gleeson and Hawke to finish off the innings, he not only had the pleasure of seeing Australia scuttled for 78, he had also broken Hammond's Test record of 110 catches.

Determined to press home the advantage, Cowdrey asked the Australians to follow on, but further progress that day was impeded by several interruptions for bad weather. More rain the next morning kept the players cooped up till 3.15 p.m., and hard though England hunted their prey thereafter they were unable to complete the kill in the limited time available.

Fortified by their showing at Lord's, England kept up the pressure at Edgbaston. The match was particularly special for Cowdrey, as it marked his hundredth Test – the first player ever to reach this milestone. 'The strain of Test cricket in these days of mass publicity and exaggerated criticism is great,' mused John Woodcock on the eve of the match, 'especially for the captains and the kings. It is one of Cowdrey's worthiest achievements that he has stuck it for so long.' Rain washed out the first day, but English spirits were sent soaring on the second when Cowdrey celebrated his day of days in style. Undeterred by the emotion of the occasion, which saw him cheered all the way to the wicket by 18,000 people and the Australian team, he immediately took control as he unleashed a series of vintage strokes which left the fielders floundering. His cover driving in particular was a joy to watch. A damaged hamstring, which required Boycott of all people to run for him once he was past 50, only briefly interrupted the flow, so that by stumps England had made 258 for three, with Cowdrey on 95.

The next morning, clearly handicapped by his hamstring which had seized up overnight, Cowdrey struggled to recapture his earlier fluency. It took him another half-hour to get the five singles needed to complete his century. He was out soon afterwards, but a commanding 96 from Graveney helped take England to 409. Australia replied with 222, and were once again involved in a rearguard action when rain again came to their rescue.

Cowdrey's hamstring injury kept him incapacitated for over a month and prevented him from playing in the fourth Test at Headingley, when Lawry, his opposite number, was also indisposed. In a dour, colourless encounter characteristic of Ashes cricket throughout the 1960s, England, under Graveney, found a challenging fourth innings target beyond them, and had to settle for a draw, ensuring that Australia kept the Ashes.

Deprived of cricket's most sought-after prize, Cowdrey at least was able to mark his return to first-class cricket with a well-crafted century against Surrey at The Oval, as Kent again chased Yorkshire for the championship. The next week he was back at Surrey's headquarters for the final Test, determined to salvage something from the rubber. By retaining Dexter after his surprising return to Test cricket at Headingley, as well as recalling both Milburn and D'Oliveira, England fielded their most enterprising team of the summer. They had first use of an easy-paced pitch and amassed a formidable 494, built round marathon efforts from Edrich (164) and D'Oliveira (158). Their opponents began confidently, and at 136 for one on the third afternoon the match seemed destined for a draw, but Cowdrey's men kept pressing and gradually they gained the upper hand. When Australia, set 352 to win, were 86 for five at lunch on the final day, the match looked as good as over, but then a violent thunderstorm deluged the ground, leaving it under water within half an hour.

As the Australians celebrated in their dressing-room, thinking that the elements had once again come to their rescue, and most of his own team began to pack their bags, Cowdrey, once the storm had relented, headed for the middle to survey the desolate scene. Although the water was an inch deep in places, Cowdrey, knowing The Oval to be an extremely quick-drying ground, was confident that with a concerted effort they would be playing again by five o'clock. At his instigation, an appeal was made for volunteers to help the ground staff clear the surface water with buckets and brooms, and when hundreds responded he loitered in the middle to encourage them. Thanks to their efforts and the return of the sun, play duly recommenced at 4.45 p.m. Cowdrey went straight on to the offensive by posting men round the bat, but the sodden wicket appeared so lifeless that neither Illingworth nor Underwood troubled the Australian batsmen. With time running out, Cowdrey threw D'Oliveira the ball with a gambler's last throw of the dice. His hunch did the trick. In his third over, D'Oliveira found a way through Barry Jarman's defence, causing a major breach in the floodgates. Cowdrey immediately recalled Underwood at the Pavilion end and now, aided by a drying pitch, he scythed through the Australian tail. Precisely six minutes remained when John Inverarity, the only batsman to take root, was lbw for 56, giving England victory and some belated compensation from a series which, after Old Trafford, had seen them play much the better cricket. For Cowdrey, too, it was an exceedingly satisfying moment as he savoured the thrill of defeating Australia on home soil for only the second time since 1956, not least because his captaincy, as *Wisden* remarked, had been magisterial throughout. There was, however, no time for celebration as he was due at Lord's by 8.00 p.m. to help pick the team to tour South Africa that winter.

These meetings have often given rise to considerable controversy when the views of the selectors have failed to find favour with the press or the public. This one, after the events at The Oval, was charged with political dynamite as much of it was bound to centre around the candidacy of D'Oliveira, the highly popular Cape Coloured all-rounder. D'Oliveira had first come to England through the good offices of John Arlott, the eminent writer and broadcaster, and, after some spectacular performances for Worcestershire, he was included in the England squad for the first Test against West Indies in 1966. Still a relative stranger, Cowdrey arrived at net practice on the eve of the Test and had to introduce himself. 'I saw you play in a Test match once in South Africa in 1956,' D'Oliveira said, 'I never thought I would one day play with you. Times have changed.' In the event he was made twelfth man, but he made his début at Lord's when Cowdrey was in charge. He felt moved enough by the occasion to present D'Oliveira with a special memento from the Lord's shop. Thereafter they became firm friends, with Cowdrey warming to D'Oliveira's old-fashioned courtesy, not least in the field where he was a pleasure to captain.

Once selected for England, D'Oliveira showed that he had what it took to succeed at the highest level, and in a summer when little went right for England his flamboyant strokeplay won him many a new admirer. His stock remained high throughout 1967, but thereafter his England career entered a more chequered phase with a disappointing tour to West Indies in 1967–68. He retained his place for the first Test against Australia on the basis of his bowling, but it was his 87 not out during the closing stages of the match which provided England with one of their few redeeming features. Having escaped the scaffold prior to Old Trafford, it seemed rather ironic that after his heroics there the axe should now fall on him. With England one down in the series, and the need for greater penetration in the attack, D'Oliveira was tossed aside for Barry Knight in the Lord's Test, though he was no doubt comforted by his captain's assurance that 'before the season is out, you'll be back'. By August, these words had begun to sound increasingly hollow as D'Oliveira lost all form with the bat. Only a sudden haul of wickets for Worcestershire kept his name in vague contention for the final Test and the tour to South Africa. The fact that he had not earned a recall when the team for The Oval was announced on 20 August came as little surprise, but here

151

the story of D'Oliveira's topsy-turvy summer took another unexpected turn. In the week before the selectorial meeting for The Oval, Cowdrey had played there for Kent against Surrey and had noticed that the pitch had favoured the medium-pacers more than the quick men. Consequently, he struck a deal with his fellow selectors that should the pitch continue to favour the medium-pacers he would be within his rights to call up another seamer with Cartwright being the first choice, Knight second and D'Oliveira third.

By the Tuesday before the Test, Cowdrey's plans were in disarray when it was reported to him that both Cartwright and Knight were unfit, and so he now called the Worcestershire ground and asked for D'Oliveira to report to The Oval the following day as a stand-by for the Test team. It so happened that while Cowdrey had been trying to contact him, D'Oliveira had been in London discussing with his agent, Reg Hayter, a handsome coaching offer in South Africa that winter. That evening he had returned to Worcester for the forthcoming match against Yorkshire, only to learn of his summons to The Oval through a chance encounter with Fred Trueman. The next day, during the pre-match practice, England's opener, Roger Prideaux, dropped out of the team with a viral infection, and after seeking reassurance from Graveney, his Worcestershire captain, Cowdrey persuaded the selectors to opt for D'Oliveira. He more than justified his selection over the next two days by scoring 158 in his most peerless style.

Now, with the selection to South Africa immediately pending, the focus was inevitably back on him. The following evening, when everyone else had left the dressing-room, Cowdrey asked D'Oliveira to stay and talk to him about the kind of pressures which might crop up if he accompanied the team to South Africa, which for sentimental reasons was his burning ambition. The fact that D'Oliveira had given some thought to the potential pitfalls of being a Cape Coloured 'Englishman' in the land of his birth, where apartheid was still very much entrenched, and how best he might avoid them, clearly impressed Cowdrey. Just before they parted, D'Oliveira remembered him saying, 'I want you in South Africa. If anyone at the tour selection meeting asks me if I'm prepared to accept responsibility for anything which might happen on tour should you be selected, I'm prepared to do so.' Similar sentiments were expressed three days later to Jack Bailey, the assistant secretary of MCC, as he recalled in his book *Cricket Conflicts*. 'After the match Colin Cowdrey was kind enough to offer me a lift to Lord's where he would be attending the meeting of the selectors that evening. I climbed into MCC 307, the captain's Jaguar, and virtually his first words in reply to my congratulatory offering were "Thanks. It's good to have beaten the Aussies. It looks as though we shall have problems with South Africa though, they can't leave Basil out of the team. Not now." '

Six hours later they had done precisely that, sparking off one of the biggest controversies in the history of the game. Inevitably, much of the furore centred around the suspicion that D'Oliveira's omission owed more to political factors than sporting ones, as Lord's went out of its way to appease the racist government in South Africa in order to safeguard the tour. Certainly, the political storm clouds had been gathering in the months preceding this meeting once it had become clear that D'Oliveira was likely to be in MCC's party. In January 1968, the MCC's letter to the South African Cricket Association, asking for an assurance that no restrictive pre-conditions would be imposed on their selection, had met with no immediate answer. Then in March, on a visit to South Africa, Lord Cobham, a former president of MCC, had been told by the prime minister, Dr Vorster, that D'Oliveira's presence on the tour would not be acceptable. Cobham passed this information on to the MCC hierarchy, but they chose to sit tight on it for fear of prejudicing the minds of the selectors when they came to make their decision. What political advice they had received had come from the former Conservative prime minister and president of MCC, Sir Alec Douglas-Home, who had visited South Africa in February 1968. When he met Cowdrey at Old Trafford in June, he urged him to choose the strongest team available, with or without D'Oliveira, and then await political developments there rather than force the issue beforehand. Despite all the conspiracy theories to the contrary, there seems little evidence to suggest that the authorities deviated from this path. For if they had been truly intent on excluding D'Oliveira from the tour at all costs, why would Cowdrey have gone to such lengths to bring him back into contention at The Oval? If he had seemed unfortunate to be dropped after Old Trafford, he

153

was lucky to earn his recall. The fact that he had seized his opportunity superbly undoubtedly enhanced his chances for South Africa and, with his captain's apparent support, it is understandable that D'Oliveira felt so confident about his place on the tour.

Given the impression Cowdrey had left with D'Oliveira, and his comment to Jack Bailey before the selectors' meeting, it might seem something of a mystery why hours later he had a change of heart, and why he later felt compelled to write: 'D'Oliveira himself, I feel sure, believed he had done enough to justify his selection for the tour. On purely cricketing terms, I was not so sure.' In *MCC*, Cowdrey went on to advance a theory that, in a recent conversation with Bill Lawry, who had toured there the year before, he had discovered that because South African wickets were increasingly grassed the need for a top-class seamer such as Cartwright was paramount. But even if we allow for this, and for the fact that at least one selector, as quoted in E. W. Swanton's *Sort of a Cricket Person*, was hostile to D'Oliveira going, despite his century at The Oval, on the grounds that he had failed in the West Indies, it is difficult to believe that Essex's Keith Fletcher, with one unsuccessful Test during the summer had advanced a better case for the final middle-order batting slot. One has only to glance at their respective Test records in Pakistan in 1968–69, and Australia and New Zealand 1970–71, when D'Oliveira averaged 40.25 and 40.87 to Fletcher's 39.25 and 21.

It was now in all probability that other cricketing reasons helped tip the balance, as some of Cowdrey's fellow selectors, the majority of whom he greatly looked up to, weighed in with arguments he could not or would not refute. Ray Illingworth, in his autobiography *Yorkshire and Back*, recalls that when he was helping to pick the side for Australia two years later, he came up against a residue of anti-D'Oliveira feeling stemming from the 1967–68 West Indian tour. Christopher Sandford, in his biography of Tom Graveney, records that D'Oliveira and Milburn, another surprise rejection for South Africa, had to be gently upbraided by Les Ames, the manager on that tour, for their hectic social life. 'D'Oliveira,' wrote the same author in the November 1991 issue of the *Cricketer*, 'an essentially uncomplicated, open character, found it hard to refuse the near continuous hospitality to visiting cricketers.' Now, with the same captain and manager in harness for South Africa, the authorities felt that on such a politically sensitive tour they could not afford to take a risk with D'Oliveira, in a country where the opportunities for sampling the good life were many. The most they were prepared to do was privately to list him as one of their replacements, and they decided to take a risk with Cartwright, despite his unsuccessful tour to South Africa in 1964–65 and his known susceptibility to injury.

After the selectorial meeting had ended in the early hours of the morning, and the full MCC committee had approved the team, that afternoon they released it to the media and waited for the impending storm. Its ferocity was even greater than they had feared, as the more reasoned objections of many of the cricket correspondents gave way to a campaign of vitriol by politicians, churchmen and some MCC members, much of it directed against Cowdrey himself. Attempts by Insole and his colleagues to explain away D'Oliveira's omission on purely cricketing grounds were brushed aside in this febrile atmosphere. Pressure on the England captain to withdraw from leading the tour prompted a statement from Cowdrey, following consultations with Cuthbert Bardsley, that he had accepted the captaincy only after being assured that the team would be chosen on cricketing ability alone.

Until now, ironically, the only real body of support for MCC's position came, embarrassingly, from the National Party in South Africa. Even their enthusiasm proved ephemeral when on 16 September, in another extraordinary twist to the saga, Cartwright was forced to pull out of the tour because of a recurrence of back problems, and D'Oliveira stepped in as his replacement. The decision now to include him primarily as a bowler would have contained more credibility had the selectors not originally pinpointed his lack of penetration on overseas wickets as the fundamental reason for his original exclusion. To many, this *volte face* reeked of political opportunism, not least to South Africa's hardliners opposed to D'Oliveira's presence in their country. It so happened that prime minister Vorster was due to give a speech in Bloemfontein the following evening, and here, in the heart of Afrikanerdom, he denounced MCC for caving in to political pressure and made clear his opposition to a team 'being thrust upon us'.

Devastated by this development, Cowdrey now volunteered to go to South Africa in person and plead his case before the government, but in truth before such closed minds there was no case to put. A few weeks later MCC, bowing to the inevitable, cancelled the tour, and South Africa began its descent into the sporting wilderness from which it took over two decades to re-emerge.

18

The Unkindest Cut of All

After political shenanigans had put paid to MCC's visit to South Africa, alternative venues for the winter were quickly sought and within a month an itinerary had been drafted to another of the world's great trouble spots. Given the extreme turbulence then gripping Pakistan, and the dangers which faced the players, it is difficult to disagree with E. M. Wellings's assertion in the 1970 *Wisden* that 'the tour should have been called off even before it got there'. As it was, the determination of those on the bridge to surge on through the tempestuous waves brought murmurings of dissent from an increasingly mutinous crew.

News of the turmoil in Pakistan reached MCC as they warmed up in Ceylon, where the hospitality and facilities were first-rate. Essentially, the discredited authoritarian regime of Ayub Khan was the focus of mass riots and strikes which were reducing large parts of Pakistan to paralysis, and towards the end of the MCC's stay in Ceylon the East Pakistan section of their schedule was cancelled. The day after the team landed in Karachi, on 2 February, Ames and Cowdrey were locked in consultations with the Deputy High Commissioner and the Pakistan cricket authorities. A persuasive case could now have been made for the abandonment of the tour. Instead, the second Test was restored to Dacca and the first three fixtures were rescheduled away from the main trouble areas. John Snow recalls that for the first of these games, at Bahawalpur, the team was forced to rise at 5.30 a.m. and take a special chartered plane for a two-hour journey to the ground. They were behind schedule when they arrived and the match began late, because Cowdrey told the local officials that no England side started a game of cricket without first having a cup of tea. Two or three times the umpire looked into their dressing-room asking when the game would start, but the captain insisted on tea first. He got his way.

The games in Bahawalpur and Lyallpur were dull affairs, barely worth the discomfort and inconvenience caused to the team. After the match in Lyallpur was abandoned prematurely, the team returned to Lahore for three days' practice before the first Test, although demonstrations near their hotel kept them marooned at their headquarters for most of that time. When eventually they could get down to the nets, a further headache for the captain appeared in the form of Snow, who declined Cowdrey's request to bowl off his long run, believing that in the hot sun it would achieve little. That evening at the bar, dark hints were dropped by his team-mates that his obstreperous attitude had incurred displeasure on high. Next morning, Snow recalls, Cowdrey went up to him, placed his hand on his shoulder, and without a word of explanation told him he had failed to make the final eleven.

The Lahore Test took place against a background of constant inter-ruptions, some of which were violent, as a noisy crowd clashed constantly with policemen and army guards patrolling with rifles at the ready. Unperturbed by the commotion around him, Cowdrey scored a century which *Wisden* rightly called magnificent. When he resumed with Fletcher after tea, they were jostled by dozens of spec-tators, and Fletcher was almost dragged to the ground. Later, Cowdrey's departure after scoring his twenty-second Test century, which placed him on level terms with Hammond, was the signal for renewed uproar, with quarrelsome groups of students throwing chairs at each other. He waved to D'Oliveira, the incoming batsman, to follow him off but Aftab Gul, one of the student leaders conve-niently playing for Pakistan, begged him to stay. Although England experienced some uneasy moments in their second innings, at the close it was Pakistan who had more reason to be grateful for a draw.

The relief of leaving Lahore for Dacca soon gave way to anger, since Dacca, contrary to the British High Commissioner's reassur-ances, remained a city in the grip of mob rule. When Ames found out that the match was to be marshalled by student leaders, even his considerable resolution was taxed to the hilt. For the first and only time he rang Lord's to seek advice. They left it to him to act as he saw fit, and Ames decided to brazen it out, a decision which was by no means universally popular. But despite the unnerving atmosphere in this concrete stadium and the scores of pickpockets milling around the English dressing-room, one of whom divested Cowdrey of his loose change, the match passed off reasonably peacefully. So relieved was Cowdrey that during the game he showed by several gestures his appreciation of the student leaders. Any fears that England might fall foul of a crumbling pitch were stilled by an undefeated century from D'Oliveira, and they finished the stronger of the two teams.

The one consoling feature of the stay in Dacca had been the arrival of Milburn from Australia as a stand-by for Cowdrey, given that there were some doubts about his fitness. The whole team turned up at the airport to greet him, and immediately his ebullient humour shone out like a light in the darkness as fears over their safety became ever more paramount. Their reservations in no way lessened when they returned to trouble-torn Karachi for the third and final Test. Conditions there had deteriorated, and with Cowdrey appearing increasingly distracted, the team looked to Graveney, the vice-captain, as their spokesman. Sympathetic to their concerns, he fell out with his captain and manager after a meeting with the Pakistani board on the eve of the Test to discuss their security, in which Cowdrey had stressed the need for normal relations.

The truth was that local conditions were making a mockery of Cowdrey's deeply cherished beliefs about the game and its capacity for the greater good. Brilliant centuries by Milburn and Graveney on the first two days of the Test were constantly interrupted by unruly pitch invasions. Then, when England awoke on the third day to the news that a leading anti-government leader had starved himself to death, their fate had effectively been sealed. Shortly after play began, six hundred politically motivated students stormed the arena and engaged in such wanton destruction that there could now be no question in anybody's mind of the tour continuing. By late that evening the team were gratefully airborne following in the wake of their captain who had flown home the previous evening because of the death of his father-in-law.

159

For such a peace-loving man the traumas of the two previous months, on top of the South African fiasco, must have taken their toll. Faced with the problem of keeping his cool when everyone about him was losing theirs, Cowdrey was ultimately a victim of forces beyond his control. Michael Melford, covering the tour for the *Daily Telegraph*, reckoned that Pakistan in 1969 was no place to be going for a cricket tour, but once there the manager and captain were right to soldier on, given that the hostility in the country at the time was not directed at them (not a majority view, it is fair to say). The fact that when the cancellation came it was made at the behest of the Pakistani board and not MCC, meant that the latter could at least leave with a clear conscience. This view in fact corresponded more to that of the manager than to that of the captain, who for some time had wrestled with the conflict of public duty on the one hand and personal preference on the other. E. M. Wellings, in *Wisden*, wrote that Cowdrey found the making of decisions more and more difficult in the bewildering circumstances, and Keith Fletcher, one of the youngest members of the party, felt that Cowdrey's leadership during the troubles had not been strong enough. To the majority it now appeared that most of the credit his leadership had banked the previous winter had, once again, been frittered away – though in circumstances which would have tried the patience of a saint.

For all the frustrations of the winter, the portents continued to look favourable as Cowdrey contemplated the year ahead. Apart from his championship aspirations for Kent, the slightly less demanding challenge from West Indies – then in a rebuilding stage – and New Zealand that summer, followed by a winter at home, would be a welcome interlude before South Africa (still scheduled to tour in England) and Australia in 1970.

With two wins and a draw from their first three championship games in 1969 and three wins out of three from the new John Player League 40-over competition, Kent were the early pace-setters during the opening weeks. On 25 May, the day Cowdrey had been appointed captain of England for the summer, Kent entertained Glamorgan in a televised Sunday match at Maidstone. On a damp wicket they struggled to get the ball away until Cowdrey arrived.

Immediately he found his best form and had reached 39 in ten overs before tragedy struck. Having negotiated a lifting ball from Malcolm Nash, the Glamorgan seamer, which placed undue pressure on his heel, he set off for a sharp single, slipped on the wet surface and then heard a loud crack, audible around the ground, which signified a snapped Achilles tendon in his left leg. In great pain, Cowdrey lay outstretched on the pitch and had to be carried off by the Kent masseur and Alan Brown, the twelfth man. In the dressing-room cold compresses were applied to the ankle, and after a medical examination he was admitted to St Nicholas's Hospital, Plumstead, for an operation the next day. Amidst a flurry of get well messages, he cheerfully left hospital in plaster three days later and returned home to recuperate with bicycle rides in the Kent countryside.

In the immediate aftermath there was some speculation whether Cowdrey, at 37, had the appetite to come back from such a crippling injury, but the sceptics did not know their man. On 18 August he had his first gentle work-out against the English Women's XI at Sissinghurst. Four weeks later a crowd of over 3,000 turned up at Dover to welcome him back to first-class cricket for Kent's final fixture against Essex. He made only 2, but in a season where high hopes had turned to disappointment because of a number of serious injuries to leading players, the mere relief of seeing their captain restored to fitness was enough for most supporters.

After winning a Pro-Am golf tournament at Turnberry that autumn, playing off a handicap of five, with his friend Brian Huggett, Cowdrey's rehabilitation continued during the winter when he accompanied an International Cavaliers XI to Jamaica and captained a team of young English hopefuls, under the aegis of the Duke of Norfolk's XI, to the rest of the Caribbean. With the scenery on the smaller islands stunning and the hospitality accorded them sumptuous, the month-long trip left a legacy of happy memories. What's more, with three half-centuries in three first-class matches Cowdrey not only topped the averages, he lay to rest any doubts about his fitness and seemed ready to resume his position at the helm of English cricket after his enforced absence. The fates, however, were to decree otherwise.

19

A Canterbury Tale

Had the events of the summer of 1970 been left to a scriptwriter it would be hard to conjure up a more intriguing or compelling tale than the one which actually occurred. Not for the first time in Cowdrey's career, he had to endure the hard, lonely slog of the foothills before finally scaling the high peaks.

The year was always going to be special for Kent because they were celebrating their centenary and, given their recent renaissance, it was not entirely fanciful to hope that they might celebrate in the appropriate way. Such optimism as there was faded fast in May and June as the team bumped along the lower reaches of the table, managing only one championship win in their first nine matches. Their batting in particular lacked conviction, none more so than that of the captain himself, with only 152 runs in his first thirteen innings, the nadir of which was a pair against Northamptonshire at Dover. Since he was mired in such a trough, the selectors, with Cowdrey's consent, decided to leave him out of the England XI to play the Rest of the World, the all-star team cobbled together at the last minute to replace the cancelled South African tour, and to continue with Illingworth as captain. While Illingworth was emerging from the heavy defeat in the first match at Lord's with great credit, top scoring in both innings with 63 and 94, Cowdrey at last turned the corner with two centuries in Tunbridge Wells week. His recall for the second match against the Rest of the World was now assured, and his 64 in the second innings at Trent Bridge, helping England to an eight-wicket victory, moved E. W. Swanton to comment that 'he batted admirably in his quieter vein, still palpably the best equipped of contemporary English batsmen'.

He could not find anything to inspire Kent against Sussex in the third round of the Gillette Cup two days later. An abject collapse caused them to lose a match they should have won, much to the dismay of their supporters. With the county making no headway in the championship – they were actually in bottom place – something dramatic was called for. Cowdrey convened a team meeting at Maidstone and Ames gave the players a withering broadside. The meeting was then opened to the floor, and at its conclusion there was unanimous agreement that as part of their quest to be more enter-prising Kent would make the attainment of championship bonus points a greater priority than hitherto.

With the air now clear, Kent approached Maidstone Week with a renewed sense of purpose, determined to put words into practice. Denness, Cowdrey and Asif all batted adventurously in the draw against Derbyshire before Denness captained an under-strength team to an audacious win against Hampshire. They then travelled to Sheffield and drew against Yorkshire, while Cowdrey wrestled with one of the great dilemmas of his life at Edgbaston, venue for the third match against the Rest of the World side. Fate had determined that the appointment of the captain for Australia would be made on the penultimate day of the match, adding to the drama of the announce-ment, especially since the two leading contenders had so little in common. Given the unfortunate circumstances of his accident the previous year when he was very much the man in charge, justice as well as romance seemed to point to Cowdrey. He was after all the Grand Old Man of English cricket, the survivor of four previous Australian tours, three of them as vice-captain, as well as being victor in the Caribbean. Illingworth, however, with his tactical shrewdness and his unflinching approach, had done everything asked of him since becoming captain, with convincing wins against West Indies and New Zealand the previous year. In addition, his batting in particular had been a revelation since assuming the captaincy, as demonstrated during that summer when he averaged over 50 against the world's best. Taking all these things into consideration, the four selectors and David Clark, the tour manager, faced a hard choice. Ultimately, they plumped for Illingworth (with only Clark voting for Cowdrey) on the grounds that his assertive nature made him a more effective leader. Yet again Cowdrey had to be content with the consolation prize of the vice-captaincy.

Once the deliberations were over both men were to hear the verdict separately after long spells at the crease in England's second innings. 'I realised the news would be painful to Cowdrey,' recalled Alec Bedser, the chairman of the selectors, 'so I arranged to see him in the Secretary's office. . . . As I feared, Cowdrey was very disappointed and asked for time to consider his position as the vice-captain elect. Naturally his wish was granted.' In retrospect, Bedser conceded that they were wrong to accede to his request for, as Richie Benaud commented in the *News of the World*, 'Anyone who had to think more than one second about it should forget it.' Clark recalls that the next day Cowdrey rang him at home and asked whether he should accept the vice-captaincy. Clark said he would love to have him on the tour but warned him of the problems ahead, given his fractious relationship with Illingworth. Only he could decide whether he should tour in these circumstances. As Cowdrey continued to agonise, the selectors encouraged Illingworth to write him a letter acknowledging past differences but urging a fresh start in the interest of English cricket. This somewhat prickly olive branch drew no obvious response, because Cowdrey was still procrastinating when he met Bedser for over two hours at Harrogate a week later. Aware, however, that rejection might be interpreted as sour grapes, and keen to assist his friend as manager, he finally fell in with the selectors' wishes. 'The circumstances of those successive subordinations have been different each time,' declared Ted Dexter in the *Sunday Mirror*, 'and one by one have been stoically endured. But the cumulative damage to his spirit can only be guessed at.'

Drained by all the hullabaloo surrounding the captaincy, Cowdrey drew comfort from the harmonious atmosphere in the Kent dressing-room when he returned to lead them against Sussex. On a typically lively Hove wicket, Luckhurst (80) and Cowdrey (77) needed to be at their very best on the first morning to keep out Snow and his colleagues. Thereafter the conditions eased and Kent's 308 for seven was the basis of their ten-wicket victory. Two draws in Canterbury Week rather hampered their progress, but creditable wins over Somerset at Weston-super-Mare, and Gloucestershire at Cheltenham when chasing 340 on a turning wicket, made them dark horses for the championship, especially as they were now picking up plenty of bonus points. After a draw against Northamptonshire, the match against Surrey at Blackheath assumed a critical significance. Making up lost time for bad weather, Kent, taking a lead from their captain, played wonderfully attacking cricket. Not only did he bat with *élan* in both innings, Cowdrey judged his declaration and bowling changes to perfection. Encouraged to keep going for the target of 263 in three and a half hours, Surrey remained in the chase throughout until with 12 needed off eight balls Pocock, the no. 11, was brilliantly caught by Asif on the long-off boundary.

From Blackheath to Folkestone and two more memorable matches for the Kent faithful who flocked to this historic ground, now sadly no longer a championship venue. In the first match against Nottinghamshire they had to contend with Sobers at his most domineering as his team rattled up 376 for four. When Kent slumped to 27 for five in reply, they looked doomed, but they were saved by a pugnacious 156 not out from Luckhurst, who found willing allies in Alan Ealham and John Shepherd. When challenged by Sobers on the final day to score 282 for victory in three hours, it could have been Port-of-Spain in 1968 all over again, for Kent needed no second invitation. Denness and Luckhurst gave them a wonderful start, and a late flurry from Knott guided them home with eight balls to spare.

With two matches to go, Kent were twelve points behind Glamorgan, the reigning champions, with a game in hand, and six points ahead of Lancashire. Another twenty-pointer was needed against Leicestershire, captained ironically by Illingworth. Having dismissed them cheaply on the opening day, Kent then batted with such panache that they collected eight batting bonus points in their eighty-five overs, with 21 runs coming off the last. While Kent romped to an innings victory, Glamorgan could only draw against Lancashire, so that Cowdrey's men travelled to The Oval on 9 September for their final match against Surrey as clear favourites, intent on making history. A tidy bowling performance, restricting Surrey to 151 for nine, and a Cowdrey century (one of his best) gained them the necessary points. Then as the match meandered to a draw on the final afternoon, Kent supporters could sit blissful in the knowledge that after the long years of darkness the dawn had well and truly broken. The champagne certainly tasted sweet as Cowdrey and his team toasted their triumph in the dressing-room along with Ted Heath, the newly elected prime minister, whose support for Kent cricket stretched back many years. A few weeks later he organised a celebratory dinner at Downing Street, where Cowdrey presented him with the ball his team had been playing with on the day of his election victory.

With Kent also second in the John Player League, 1970 proved to be their *annus mirabilis*. That Cowdrey was able to put his earlier disappointments behind him and play such a leading part in securing their first championship pennant for fifty-seven years was a considerable triumph of character. It goes without saying that he owed much to Ames, his manager, Denness, his vice-captain, and indeed the talented team at his disposal. Equally, it is fair to point out that during that purple passage from the beginning of the Maidstone Festival up to The Oval, when the county were unbeaten in thirteen matches, the doubts which so often seemed to assail Cowdrey's captaincy were notably absent.

20

A House Divided

It was with mixed feelings that Cowdrey set off to Australia for the fifth time and his fourth as vice-captain, serving four different masters. Good friends of the first three, his relationship with each of them had varied on the field, but nothing surpassed the tensions which existed between him and Illingworth, only some of which could be attributed to their different backgrounds. Whereas Cowdrey had always been part of the magic circle which controlled English cricket, Illingworth was an outsider, unafraid to speak his mind. Given his unglamorous Yorkshire roots, it would be easy to depict him as a man who railed against privilege, but for all his undoubted reservations in this field he had held May in enormously high regard and was on friendly terms with Dexter. With Cowdrey, however, things were different. Not only did Illingworth rate his captaincy poorly, feeling that he lacked the courage of his convictions, he had also fallen out with him personally in Australia in 1962–63, a tour which saw Illingworth forfeit part of his good conduct bonus of £150. A couple of incidents had drawn his fire; the most notable being when Cowdrey turned up late at the end of an exhausting practice session and ordered Illingworth to bowl at him, a demand he firmly rebuffed. A rarity, it must be said, given Cowdrey's predilection for practice over the years. From Cowdrey's perspective, he greatly admired Illingworth, both as a cricketer and as a captain, and tried to maintain a civil relationship with him. But in contrast to his friendship with other Yorkshiremen, there was something about Illingworth's aggressive philosophy which niggled him. Given this frosty relationship, it is easy to see why both men and the manager had misgivings about the vice-captaincy. Any hope that Cowdrey's eventual acceptance would herald the beginning of a more constructive partnership proved shortlived, for it soon became clear that his disappointment at losing the captaincy ran too deep. There were those in the party who sympathised with his position, and according to Don Wilson, the Yorkshire slow bowler, a deep schism developed right from the outset and widened as the tour progressed. He recalled the Christmas celebrations in the West Point Riviera Hotel in Hobart when John Hampshire and he organised a team cabaret, but there was still a residual element of separatism within the party, with the Kent–Surrey axis not wishing to become fully embroiled in the season's geniality. Wilson's views on internal dissension were fully supported by Keith Fletcher, who increasingly realised that Cowdrey and Illingworth would never settle their differences during the tour. 'They were total opposites and now there was the added needle between them of the captaincy issue. Their antipathy created two camps, a most unhealthy situation for any touring team.'

Personal differences aside, there was also considerable disagreement within the team hierarchy about the precise nature and priorities of a modern tour, best illustrated at Melbourne over the New Year. Faced with a massive financial loss from the abandonment of their most lucrative Test because of diabolical weather, the Australian Cricket Board of Control went out of their way to restructure the tour to accommodate an extra Test. Their wishes were met sympathetically by Clark, Cowdrey and MCC officials, who, in the interests of Anglo-Australian relations, went along with their request. This benevolence, however, found little favour with Illingworth and the majority of the players. Apart from objecting to an arrangement which gave them no additional revenue, unlike their opponents, they disliked the idea of having to play four Tests in six weeks since such a schedule would place undue strain on a touring party. A team meeting was called in the captain's room, boycotted by Cowdrey and two others, where the mood became distinctly militant. It needed a number of phone calls to Lord's and significant financial concessions before the majority were pacified.

The tour continued on a jarring note, with England's over-zealous approach on the field causing further headaches for the management. At Adelaide, Boycott fiercely remonstrated with the umpire after having been given run out, and at Sydney, in the final Test, Illingworth led his team from the field after the uproar caused by Snow injuring Terry Jenner, an Australian tail-ender, with a bouncer. For old-style diplomats such as Clark and Cowdrey (now a bystander), who clung to traditional images of MCC touring sides as ambassadors for the game, these unseemly spats were deeply embarrassing, an unwelcome reflection of a new, meaner era. They tried to apply the healing touch but, as with earlier incidents, there was no meeting of minds and the recriminations continued for some time after the tour had become history.

Clark recalls how Cowdrey would always help out at a social function if Illingworth decided not to attend and, according to R. S. Whitington, he was the only member of the party who cared what impression they created off the field. Whitington remembers staying at the English team's hotel in Brisbane and barely laying eyes on anyone except Cowdrey, who ate in the dining-room every night and crossed from his table to talk to old friends. 'Cowdrey did all he could to compensate for his comrades' shyness or for whatever it was that caused them to stay in their bedroom hideaways. Despite his poor form, despite those dropped chances in Melbourne, Cowdrey was regularly on view and I'll not forget the smile he gave when entering the Brisbane Park Royal Motor Inn dining-room alone with a lovely young brunette, seated her at a table and crossed to my table and said, "It's only Tom Graveney's daughter, you know. Can't think where the beggar's got to." '

Out of sympathy with the captain and out of step with the ethos of the game, Cowdrey saw his unhappiness seep into his cricket so that the whole trip soon became his *via dolorosa*. Beginning with 14 and 3 against South Australia, he followed with 0 and 101 against Victoria, but his century was so laborious that even the normally restrained *Wisden* felt moved to criticise it for being tediously slow and marked by wasteful running. With two more failures against New South Wales, he began the Test series totally out of sorts. His 28 – which at least enabled him briefly to become the leading run-scorer in Test cricket – was the lowest score among the first seven batsmen in England's 464. He looked little better in the second Test in Perth, where he scored 40 and 1 in yet another inconclusive draw. A fluent 66 against the Combined XI in Tasmania did just enough to salvage his place for the abandoned Test in Melbourne, but the writing was on the wall. A tortured 37 against the gentle bowling of the New South Wales Country XI finally convinced his fellow selectors that he should make way for a younger player in Sydney. England won handsomely, but when Fletcher, Cowdrey's replacement, damaged his wrist in the next game, Illingworth resisted the calls for a tour replacement, a generous gesture since it enabled Cowdrey to reclaim his place for Melbourne.

Alas, his reprieve brought Cowdrey no joy. The malaise which had affected his batting now spread to his fielding: in Australia's first innings he dropped four slip catches, including chances given by Ian Chappell when he was on 0 and 14. They proved to be expensive misses. When a pitch invasion celebrating Chappell's hundred got out of control and someone made off with Cowdrey's hat, his whole world seemed to be caving in about him. His batting did nothing to compensate. 'He seemed to all of us,' recalled Doug Walters, 'to be not a little bit past it with regard to his footwork and co-ordination, but he looked as though he thought that himself. He appeared a very worried man every time he came out to bat and I do not think he believed in himself enough, nor did he seem to believe that he was going to make runs against us.' With another dropped catch in Australia's second innings Cowdrey's misery was complete, and not surprisingly he was omitted from the final two Tests, prompting Clive Taylor of the *Sun* to write that 'The Test match career of Colin Cowdrey is over'.

Fresh from their Ashes triumph in Sydney, Illingworth's men made for New Zealand and here at last Cowdrey's luck began to change. Restored to favour for the second Test in Auckland in place of Fletcher, Cowdrey delighted his many followers there by making 54 in what *Wisden* termed 'a grand display'. His services were called upon again in the second innings when defeat stared England in the face. Despite nursing a cold and a leg injury he put on 76 with Knott for the fifth wicket to help his side to safety and gain them a one nil win in the short series.

With something at last to cheer him, Cowdrey returned home determined to put his Australian nightmare behind him. He was back among friends at Kent and from the outset both captain and county struck oil. A commanding 83 in an innings win against Yorkshire at Bradford was followed by 132 and 77 not out against Leicestershire at Dartford, 82 and 11 against Surrey at Canterbury, 40 against Surrey at The Oval and 51 against Worcestershire. His reward for this rich crop of runs was his inclusion in the first Test against Pakistan at Edgbaston. His 16 and 34 in a tepid England performance was not enough for the selectors to keep faith with him, and he returned to Kent to mastermind the defence of their title, but after they had beaten Middlesex at the end of June he was suddenly struck down with pneumonia. The attack was serious enough for him to be rushed to hospital, and he was not to play again that season. This was a major disappointment since Cowdrey had announced the previous September that this would be his last season in charge. Now, through no fault of his own, his tenure was ending with a damp squib, especially since Kent's championship aspirations fell away during August. Nevertheless, with a strong, well-integrated squad of international players, a solid infrastructure and a loyal membership, he could rest content that he was bequeathing a handsome legacy to his successor, Mike Denness.

21

One Hundred Hundreds

Fully restored to fitness by April 1972, Cowdrey, who was honoured in the New Year's Honours List with a CBE, returned to Kent to begin the final phase of his playing career. Now in his fortieth year and no longer captain, he could take nothing for granted, for in a side crammed full of batting there was little room for sentiment. A further imponderable concerned his suitability for the rigours of the limited overs game, at which Kent, with their plethora of talented all-rounders, excelled. Denness decided that Cowdrey's main value would lie in the three-day game, although an early season century against Middlesex, the first ever in the newly inaugurated Benson and Hedges 55-overs competition, showed that there was no substitute for class, whatever the form of cricket.

Cowdrey had now settled back into his favourite no. 4 position. His early outings in the championship contained little that was memorable, but a brilliant 91 against Nottinghamshire at Trent Bridge in mid-June gave notice of better things to come: 59 not out on a rain-affected wicket against Sussex at Hastings, 107 against Northamptonshire at Dover, and 51 against Middlesex. During Canterbury Week the sun shone, and large crowds were quick to show their appreciation when the Kent president, Oliver Grace, presented Cowdrey with a clock and a cheque to mark his fifteen years as captain. In the first match against Glamorgan, he put on 141 for the fourth wicket with Denness in the first innings, which turned things Kent's way. Another victory in their second match against Sussex saw them leap up the championship table, and although Warwickshire were too far out in front, Kent's achievement in winning five of their last six games ensured that they finished second for the third time in six years. With 57 not out against Warwickshire, 101 not out against Somerset and 43 against Yorkshire, Cowdrey finished strongly and could be well pleased with an average of 43.43.

He missed out in Kent's John Player League triumph, but was included in their Gillette Cup team, since the 60-overs game gave more scope to batsmen such as Cowdrey who liked to build an innings. In the semi-final, Kent were pitted against their old rivals Lancashire, who had beaten them in a memorable final at Lord's the year before. Rain at Old Trafford had delayed the start until after lunch, whereupon the home team scored 224 for six. The Kent innings started in murky light shortly after 5.30 p.m., and they were in some trouble when Cowdrey joined Denness at 34 for two. Three times the umpires gave them the option of coming off for bad light, and three times they refused, pointing to the 20,000 spectators in the ground. George Pope, one of the umpires, later said that in a long career he could not recall a comparable action to that of Denness and Cowdrey. Whether their selfless act altered the result of the game is impossible to say. Having put on 76 for the third wicket, Cowdrey was lbw to Peter Lee, Lancashire's medium-pacer, in the final over of the day, leaving the middle order an even chance of victory the next morning. In the tightest of finishes they ultimately failed by seven runs, but they had left behind a residue of goodwill. Lancashire went on to overwhelm Warwickshire in the final.

With ninety-eight centuries now to his credit Cowdrey had one final landmark to aim for as he began his twenty-fourth season. He just missed out on his ninety-ninth century in Kent's match against the New Zealanders in early May. With competition for batting places as stiff as ever, and Cowdrey short of big scores in the championship, he twice suffered the indignity of being dropped. Restored to the side against Hampshire at Tunbridge Wells, he found himself batting in the unusual position of no. 7 but, undeterred by what many, including himself, deemed to be a slight, he responded with two undefeated innings of 23 and 58. He continued his fightback at Bristol with a masterly 73 not out, guaranteeing his participation in the game at Maidstone. There, on the lovely Mote Park ground, he made 123 against Somerset, figuring in a stand of 241 with Denness, and then, in the next against Surrey, he finally reached his goal. It was just before lunch on Thursday 5 July that Cowdrey came to the wicket with Kent, in reply to Surrey's 367 for six, in some bother at 124 for five. He continued where he left off against Somerset, scoring at nearly a run a minute. Once he got past 50, the historical significance of his innings became evident, but with Asif an inspired partner throughout Cowdrey headed for the home straight at a full gallop rather than at a leisurely trot. It was only during the nineties that he had his anxious moments and Asif, seeing him gripped with tension, went down the wicket to relax him. On 99 he told him, 'Just keep your eye on the ball and push it anywhere and I'll run.' Moments later he placed Robin Jackman wide of cover and, seeing Asif half-way down the wicket, charged off for the other end. It was indeed his hundredth run and, immediately, Denness declared. A fraction misty-eyed but smiling broadly, Cowdrey left the field to a delirious reception, with his team-mates forming a guard of honour at the pavilion steps. Later the revelry continued, and the next morning all the members of the press corps who witnessed his achievement were presented with a bottle of wine. One of them, John Mason of the *Daily Telegraph*, wrote that 'Cowdrey's innings in no way was a poor imitation of the batsman of summers ago. This was brisk, hugely entertaining, and of considerable importance to Kent.' Later, during Canterbury Week, he was photographed with Kent's two other great players who had performed this feat, Frank Woolley and Les Ames.

If Maidstone was undoubtedly the highlight of his year, his form in no way deserted him thereafter. A regular from now on at no. 5, he remained a model of consistency and finished the year with an average of just under 50. Two weeks after his hundredth hundred, Cowdrey was back in the spotlight when by sheer weight of runs, he forced his way into the Kent side for the Benson and Hedges final against Worcestershire, despite having not featured in any of the earlier rounds. On a sun-filled day at Lord's he was given a rousing reception by the crowd as he appeared for the closing stages of their innings. Eight overs and 29 runs later, he returned to the pavilion after a partnership of 53 with Knott, which was just what the doctor ordered. Despite a noble effort from D'Oliveira, Kent were always in control and Cowdrey looked on with pride as his successor as captain collected another trophy to add to their rapidly growing collection.

Cowdrey also played some part in the John Player League – Kent retained the title with ease – and during that summer the feeling persisted that age did not weary him nor the years condemn. He might well have added a couple of inches to his waistline, and building an innings was now a more leisurely business than of old, but overall he remained in remarkably good shape, well able to take the strains of an English summer programme. As a batsman, the profusion of vintage cover-drives had given way to neat deflections off his legs, while more discretion was now employed in despatching the short ball, but otherwise the old familiar traits were still evident in the traditional three-day game. (The 40-overs game did call for some improvisation which he never fully came to terms with.)

As a slip fielder he remained among the best, with two diving efforts against Yorkshire in Canterbury Week as good as any taken over the years. When one-day skirmishes decreed a sudden evacuation from familiar terrain behind the wicket, he would take up residence at mid-wicket or square-leg, where he was safe if unspectacular. Occasionally a full-length dive or an accurate shy at the wicket, accompanied by a vigorous surge of the arms and a heartfelt appeal, would bring the crowd to life as he indulged in a rare display of theatrics.

No longer burdened with the daily cares of captaincy, Cowdrey had even more opportunity to share his undiminished enthusiasm with all and sundry. There were the hours before a day's play when a privileged posse of young boys would take it in turn to bowl to him in the outfield. There were the endless number of friends and acquaintances to catch up with, and the infinite mementoes to sign. These were heady years for Kent cricket, when nearly every game seemed to be a sell-out, and Cowdrey's prestige as the revered elder statesman had never been greater. In a team where each and every member had his own loyal following, nothing could surpass the special reception accorded him when coming out to bat, or the collective groan if he made an early exit.

After the triumphs of 1973, Kent had their hands on the silverware again in 1974, although they had to wait until the final days of the season. It was a year when injury disrupted their progress, beginning with a nasty joust at Basingstoke where, on an ill-tempered surface, Cowdrey fell foul of Hampshire's West Indian quick bowler Andy Roberts. Attempting to hook him, he was late with the shot and took a nasty thud on the chin for his pains. The concerned looks on the Hampshire faces as they gathered round the stricken figure told their own story, but Cowdrey was battle-hardened and soon he was walking off unaided. He was incapacitated for several weeks, but marked his return with an accomplished century against Cambridge University and retained the no. 3 position for the rest of the year by virtue of five first-class centuries. He also hit another in the second round of the Gillette Cup against Durham, when he and Luckhurst set a new second-wicket record of 204. *Wisden* accorded it high praise and it earned him his fifth man-of-the-match award. He failed to score in the third round and was bowled for 8 in the semi-final against Somerset by a strapping young all-rounder called Ian Botham. When Kent's depth in batting saw them through to the final, their opponents again were Lancashire. Heavy rain prevented any play on the Saturday, and after a rough and ready dogfight on the Monday, it was Kent who this time narrowly emerged victorious. With Lord's half-empty and shrouded in stygian gloom, the occasion lacked the atmosphere of previous finals, but a win was still an appropriate way for Kent to finish the season. Now that autumn was upon them Cowdrey swapped his bat for his pen to work on a coaching manual, while four of his team-mates prepared to defend the Ashes in Australia. They departed with confidence, unaware of the rude awakening that was soon to come their way.

22

The Final Trumpet

On the evening of Wednesday 4 December 1974, Cowdrey was at home in Limpsfield watching the television highlights of the final day of the first Test at Brisbane. It made grim viewing as Denness's team received their come-uppance from a revitalised Australian team under Ian Chappell, with the new pace duo of Dennis Lillee and Jeff Thomson being their chief tormentors. Lillee, of course, was of known pedigree but Thomson, the long-haired surfie from Sydney, whom Cowdrey had never heard of, was the new sensation as he pulverised England in the second innings with six for 46. With his powerful whip action and his ability to generate steep bounce from some underprepared wickets, he was a constant danger as he persistently probed the limits of the Englishmen's technique. When he had Amiss caught in the gully in the second innings with a snorting lifter, the Australian commentator was moved to speculate as to where were all those classic players like May and Cowdrey.

Unknown to Cowdrey as he witnessed the carnage on television, events on the other side of the world were unfolding in such a way that they were to lead to one of the most dramatic comebacks in the history of Test cricket. It so happened that Cowdrey's form had been good enough in 1974 to justify consideration for the original tour party and he admitted to a sneaking disappointment when his name was passed over. Now, six weeks into the tour, not only had England been comprehensively beaten in the first Test, but two of their leading batsmen, Amiss and Edrich, had suffered injuries thought serious enough to rule them out of contention for the next Test. In these circumstances a replacement was thought advisable. Unwilling to throw a newcomer to the lions, on the grounds that the experience might ruin him, the unanimous choice of the tour committee was Cowdrey, such was his continued dexterity against really good quick bowling. The next morning Denness phoned him at home and asked him to help out. 'I'd love to,' was the reply.

Two days later he was on the plane to Perth and – after a twenty-four hour delay in Bombay because of engine trouble – the whole of Australia seemed to be waiting at the airport to welcome back a familiar figure for the sixth time, equalling the record of Johnny Briggs, the Lancashire slow bowler, who toured between 1884 and 1898. But for all the nostalgia of Cowdrey's comeback, the decision to recall him seemed both illogical and retrograde in a country where the accent had always been on youth. The Australian press talked of Santa Claus and Dad's Army, and Thomson spoke of Cowdrey 'copping it as fast as anyone', inducing a humorous reaction from England's veteran performer. 'Why should I worry?' he confided. 'After all, I faced Gregory and MacDonald.' Once Cowdrey had caught up with some much needed sleep, his main problem was to get fit and acclimatise as quickly as possible since the news from the sick bay was not encouraging. For the next three days he subjected himself to rigorous net practice with Graham McKenzie and Tony Lock, now resident in Perth, in between fielding countless telephone calls from his army of well-wishers. By Thursday, on the eve of the Test, it became clear that Cowdrey would play, batting at no. 6, but having won the toss, Denness asked him to take the no. 3 position. It was in one sense a dream come true, but it also contained its night-mare element, since the challenge facing him was a daunting one. Not only was a forty-one-year-old (almost forty-two) being plucked straight out of an English winter into a Test match, he was being asked to perform on the quickest wicket in the world against one of the most fearsome bowling combinations of all time. It was the near-est Greg Chappell had ever come to feeling sorry for an Englishman. Max Walker, the Australian quick bowler, seeing Cowdrey arrive at the ground by taxi in a businessman's pinstripe suit and with pale complexion, immediately thought to himself, 'Lillee and Thomson will kill him stone dead.' When Cowdrey opened his cricket case in the dressing-room, Tony Greig remembers a mountain of foam rubber springing from the interior. 'This was his protection and he had obviously been well briefed. He padded almost every part of his body but nobody laughed. We had seen enough to convince us he was right.'

At first, England's openers, David Lloyd and Brian Luckhurst, made sound progress as they saw off the new ball. Then, just as they were beginning to relax a little, Luckhurst was out, caught off Walker, and a crowd of 16,000 stood to a man to greet Cowdrey as he strode out, bat aloft, to acknowledge the cheers in his 110th Test, twenty years almost to the day since he had made his Test début. He was perilously close to being lbw first ball and was badly beaten in the same over. Fortunately, the gods were with him, and Australians forgot their partisanship as he opened his account with a sweetly timed pull off Walker, who, fine bowler that he was, posed less of a threat into the breeze than the rampaging Lillee. To help his partner play himself in, Lloyd opted to take on Lillee, an act of selflessness which earned him Cowdrey's perpetual gratitude. Eventually, he too faced the music from both Lillee and Thomson, and after repeatedly taking evasive action he came down the wicket and said to Lloyd, 'This is rather fun, old chap, isn't it?' Still there at the mid-afternoon drinks interval, Cowdrey watched from the non-striker's end as Thomson bowled the last ball of his over, at which point the players moved towards the drinks trolley. Finding himself walking towards him, Cowdrey took the opportunity of stretching out his hand and introducing himself, 'How do you do, I'm Colin Cowdrey', he said. 'G'day, I'm Jeff Thomson,' came the gruff reply. It was, as Cowdrey later recalled, a Livingstone and Stanley greeting. Shortly on resumption, Lloyd was out for 49, another victim of the slick Australian close catching, a vital part of their success that summer. He was replaced by the ebullient Greig, fresh from an audacious century at Brisbane and ever ready for a challenge. Greig recalls how in his own inimitable way he took the game to the opposition by slicing the ball over the slips and picking up several boundaries. At the end of the over he walked down the wicket to explain his tactics. 'Interesting,' Cowdrey mumbled with a smile.

After 125 minutes and 22 runs, Cowdrey's gritty effort ended when he shuffled across his wicket and was bowled by Thomson around his legs. His dismissal triggered a familiar English collapse, as 119 for two became 132 for six and 208 all out, a hopelessly inadequate total in relation to Australia's reply of 481. When England went in a second time, they had an awkward three hours to survive in front of 24,000 people scenting blood, and without the services of Luckhurst, who had damaged his hand in the first innings. With few rushing forward to volunteer, it was the reassuring figure of Cowdrey who appeared with Lloyd to murmurs of approval from the members. His courage was rewarded when he was missed in the slips during Thomson's first over. Thereafter, he warmed to his task, and with his basic technique of playing back and across in line serving him well, he was altogether more fluent than in the first innings. A younger generation who had been brought up on the deeds of his youth now had the chance to see something of the Cowdrey of old as he drove and glanced with finesse. His efforts did not impress everyone, however. As the shadows began to lengthen, Cowdrey later recalled, a little old suntanned Australian sitting in front of the scoreboard amidst a pile of beer cans started to heckle him and a piercing cry of 'Cowboy' kept bellowing across the ground. At the end of one over, Cowdrey walked a few yards in the man's direction and took off his cap to acknowledge him. This gesture brought a huge cheer from the crowd, but the Australian had the final laugh by shouting, 'Cowboy, I used to come here and watch your father and he wasn't very good either.'

After two hours, with Lloyd on 19, Cowdrey on 40 and England 59 for no wicket, it looked as if they might get through to stumps without loss, but then a nasty lifter from Thomson dealt Lloyd a vicious blow in the groin, sending him into paroxysms of agony. Cowdrey later reckoned that he had never seen anyone so badly injured, and for the first time ever in his memory an ambulance was summoned onto the field to remove the stricken player. Next, it was Cowdrey's turn to endure the treatment when another Thomson thunderbolt cannonaded into his elbow, causing further delay while he tended to his wound. No sooner had he recovered than he too was back in the pavilion, lbw to Thomson as he once again shuffled across his stumps to play to leg. The next day, despite a noble effort from Titmus, who played in a manner similar to Cowdrey, it was all

England could do to make Australia bat again. Shell-shocked and subdued, they lost by nine wickets.

Having survived this baptism of fire, Cowdrey was happy to move on to Adelaide where, in more tranquil surroundings, he used the game against South Australia to good effect. 'It was,' wrote Christopher Martin-Jenkins, 'the artist using his softest colours, hitting only four boundaries in his 78 runs, but caressing the ball through gaps on either side of the wicket with poised control.' Most spectators were happy enough simply to see him perform, but one barracker, obsessed with his age, yelled out to Barnes, the opening bowler, 'Play a tune on his false teeth, Barnsey.' His jibe was not quite as cruel as the one which Knott heard in Perth. 'Hey, Thommo, I've searched everywhere for a vet, but can't find one. You put the old boy to sleep.'

After their welcome break in Adelaide, England headed for Melbourne, knowing that something out of the ordinary was needed to reverse their ailing fortunes. Amiss and Edrich were once again fit, and it was the latter who battled it out with Cowdrey in England's first innings after early losses. This demonstration of motionless defence won plaudits from their team-mates. 'It gave us confidence,' Amiss recalled, 'to see how fast bowling could be played. Cowdrey would drop his wrists to anything short of a length and take his bat down and across his body away from the ball. That casual sway of the head, while the rest of us were all arms, legs and undignified scuttling, was a wonderful technical effort.' The trouble was that there was very little to drive, and Bob Willis recalls being very sorry for Cowdrey. He could survive with his wonderful technique but couldn't score runs. In just under four hours he made 35, before once again falling lbw to Thomson. In the second innings, he edged a lifter from Lillee and was acrobatically caught by Greg Chappell at second slip, much to the indignity of Ian Chappell at first slip, who accused his brother of poaching. With Amiss scoring 90, and Greig 60, England in a slow-scoring match at last competed on even terms. Set 246 to win, Australia's fortunes fluctuated wildly as they scored runs and lost wickets in equal measure. Denness recalls that with the game entering its vital phase he delayed taking the new ball, only to see Rod Marsh mete out heavy punishment to Bob Willis when he did. In the midst of this onslaught, Cowdrey came up to him and said, 'You've got to think about this when you talk to the press', a prospect Denness quickly dismissed from his mind. With Underwood returning to call a halt to the victory charge, Australia lost their nerve and finished on 238 for eight.

Sadly, Melbourne proved the lull in the storm for England, as Australia re-established their superiority at Sydney. The tourists went into the match without Denness, their captain, who decided to omit himself because of barren form, but the decision made little difference as their failings against really top-class bowling were once again painfully exposed. Their nadir came on the second afternoon when they began their reply to Australia's 405. Australian crowds are more partisan than most, and now in the brash 1970s, under a radical Labour government out of sympathy with the relics of British imperialism (a year later, the Queen's representative in Australia, the Governor General, caused a constitutional crisis by dismissing Gough Whitlam, the prime minister), the traditional baiting of the mother country reached new and feverish heights. There had been trouble at Sydney on the previous tour under Illingworth, and now in January 1975 a large holiday crowd out in force on the Hill were again in gladiatorial mood as they urged on their hero with a sustained cry of 'LI-LL-EE, LI-LL-EE'. Amiss, unsettled by the commotion, soon departed and into this seething cauldron stepped Cowdrey, already convinced that Lillee and Thomson were the fastest combination he had ever faced. He played skilfully for well over an hour but once again met his match in Thomson. With successive balls he hit Cowdrey high on the body, and as he went back to defend himself against another lifter the ball lobbed off his bat to Rick McCosker at short-leg. 'One could almost see Cowdrey shrugging as he walked out,' reported Christopher Martin-Jenkins, 'defeated and wondering to himself what means of survival were possible against this man.'

Despite spirited resistance from Knott (82) and Edrich (50), who was captaining in place of Denness, England closed on 295, 110 behind Australia, who quickly extended their lead to over 400. Forced to bat for seven hours to save the match, England started confidently with Amiss and Lloyd but, as often was the case in this series, it took only a minor gust of wind to blow the English galleon off course. With the score on 67, an impetuous shot off Thomson cost Lloyd his wicket. The next ball struck Cowdrey on the shoulder, raising in his mind once again the old demons. For half an hour he defended stoutly, but with only a single to his name he was caught at first slip off Walker. 68 without loss had become 74 for three and, bravely though the lower order fought, they could not prevent the Ashes from changing hands.

At Adelaide, with Denness now restored to the captaincy, it was a similar story as England once again bit the dust. For the third match running Cowdrey mixed stoical defence with a few strokes in the first innings and a single figure score in the second, the victim of superb close catching. With the umpires adopting a lenient attitude to the short ball throughout, it was not only the constant pounding from the quick men which disconcerted Cowdrey. It was also the absence of decorum on the field of play, as bad language and provocative comments became increasingly commonplace. Ian Redpath recalls how after one ill-tempered altercation between an Englishman and an Australian, Cowdrey sidled up to him and, in a tone of voice that seemed to indicate something between sadness and indignation, said, 'It's just not cricket.'

Even allowing for these unpleasantries and the one-sided nature of the series, Cowdrey found this tour much more congenial than his previous one, when he had cut an isolated, brooding figure. Now as the elder statesman, returning by popular demand to the fray, he felt himself wanted once again and in a country which had always worshipped the underdog his sheer cussedness under fire raised his stock even higher. Tony Greig remembers accompanying him to several private functions and being spellbound by the scintillating discussions which raged over battles past.

As on the ill-fated 1950–51 tour under Freddie Brown, England at last found some consolation from the final Test in Melbourne. On a sweating pitch Australia batted first and were dismissed for 152. With Lloyd unfit, Cowdrey once again found himself pressed into opening, and saw out the closing overs with some skill after Lillee had dismissed Amiss for his third successive duck. The next morning he hoped, in what was to be his final Test, to go out on a high but, alas, it was not to be. Another steepling delivery from Walker brushed his gloves on the way through to the wicket-keeper, Marsh. Cowdrey made only 7, but with Thomson not playing and Lillee soon indisposed, the English batsmen at last had their revenge. Led by centuries from Denness and Fletcher, they totalled 529 and dismissed Australia for 373, to win by an innings and four runs. As England at last had something to cheer about at the end of a traumatic series, Cowdrey, wearing a large straw hat, could be found in the outfield consorting with a group of Australian spectators who had constructed a large banner which read 'MCG thanks Colin for six tours'.

If this was truly the end of the road after 114 Tests, it seemed highly appropriate that Cowdrey should make his exit on the ground that twenty years earlier had seen him rise to glory with the first and greatest of his twenty-two Test match centuries. Although his final average was a disappointing 18, his willingness to shoulder the full fury of Lillee and Thomson at his advanced age was tantamount to a mention in dispatches for extreme gallantry under fire.

With the Australians due back in England that summer after the inaugural World Cup, Cowdrey had visions of extending his Indian summer, but whatever hopes he might have cherished were soon to be dashed. Despite his substantial following in the county he could expect no preferential treatment from Denness and Les Ames when it came to picking the best Kent XI from an almost embarrassing array of riches. Come the end of May, and with Cowdrey no longer an automatic choice for the three-day game, let alone the one-day, he must have felt that his days were numbered. Knowing of the pressures to give the youngsters their fill, and unhappy about his spasmodic appearances, he decided with Denness's approval to forestall any embarrassment by announcing in early June that this would be his last season. On hearing the news, Tony Greig paid him the compliment of inviting him to Sussex on a three-year contract to act as a mentor for the younger players. Cowdrey was sorely tempted by the offer, but decided to remain with Kent in the hope that on occasions such as Test calls on other players they would still find room in the cast for an old stager.

Left: Recognition – Cowdrey with his wife Penny and sons Christopher and Jeremy after receiving the CBE from the Queen at Buckingham Palace in February 1972, the prelude to a Knighthood in 1991 and a Peerage in 1997, making him the most decorated cricketer of all time. Only the Lord Warden of the Cinque Ports still eludes him. (© HULTON GETTY)

Below: 'Be Ye Men of Valour' – On the eve of his 42nd birthday and after an absence of over three years from Test cricket. Cowdrey was delighted to answer an SOS from the struggling MCC team in Australia, December 1974. Within days he was facing one of the most hostile bowling combinations that he'd ever come up against on the quickest wicket in the world. Here he unavailingly attempts to hook Jeff Thomson, Australia's new bowling sensation. (© PATRICK EAGER)

Above: Nemesis, Cowdrey Bowled Around His Legs – Cowdrey Bowled by Thomson for 22 in Perth. The long-haired surfie from Sydney was to claim his wicket five times in four Tests. (© PATRICK EAGER)

Above right: Continuing on the Comeback Trail – Cowdrey emerging from the pavilion at Perth with David Lloyd to open England's second innings in place of the injured Luckhurst. His 41 in the most testing circumstances won him acclaim from both friend and foe alike. (© PATRICK EAGER)

Right: Breaking out of Mallett's Stranglehold – Cowdrey cover-drives the Australian off-spinner, Ashley Mallett. (© PATRICK EAGER)

Above: Cricketing Aristocrats – Cowdrey with Sir Donald Bradman at Adelaide. Ever since watching the ship carrying Bradman's 1938 side to England glide by, at the age of five, Cowdrey has never lost his sense of awe for cricket's greatest ever maestro. A regular visitor to his home in Adelaide and keen competitors on the golf course, Cowdrey was forcibly struck by Sir Donald's quest for perfection in all matters great and small.
(© PATRICK EAGER)

Left: A Man For All Seasons – Ever since his first tour there in 1954–5 Cowdrey had enchanted Australians with the artistry of his strokeplay. Six tours and 20 years later the old class was still apparent.
(© PATRICK EAGER)

Above: 'This Blessed Plot' – Cowdrey with Lavinia Duchess of Norfolk (his future mother-in-law) and the West Indian tourists at Arundel 1976. The death of the Duchess's husband the previous year had raised doubts about the future viability of the family ground at Arundel, one of the most beautiful in England, but thanks to the work of Cowdrey and others the game thrives there as never before. (© PATRICK EAGER)

Above: Mid-wicket Conference – Cowdrey locked in earnest conversation with match referee, Sunil Gavaskar, the former Indian opening batsman, Kingston, Jamaica, 1992. One of Cowdrey's achievements as Chairman of ICC was to introduce match referees to oversee the conduct of the players and reverse the decline in standards in the game. (© ALLSPORT)

Below: The Sport of Kings – Cowdrey playing Real Tennis with Prince Edward. Both he and the Prince were excellent presidents of the Lord's Taverners during the mid-90s. (PATRICK SHERVINGTON)

Above: 'Charity Never Endeth' – Cowdrey (front row, fifth from the right) and his second wife, Lady Anne Herries (on his right) presiding over the Lord's Taverners Umpire's dinner at the London Hilton. Among the luminaries, most of them ex-presidents, on view are Prince Edward (middle row, seventh from the left) is next to his fiancée, Sophie Rhys-Jones and Patrick Shervington, the dynamic Director of the Taverners, is in the back row, second from the left.

Below: Political Interference with a Difference – Cowdrey with the Prime Minister, John Major, promoting their School Sports initiative at Millwall Football Club in 1996. During his time as President of the ICC, Cowdrey found Major's support invaluable, while Major for his part greatly appreciated Cowdrey's notes of encouragement during the darker days of his government. (© ALPHA)

Having made his fateful decison, Cowdrey yearned for a glorious finale at Canterbury, and in the final week of June his wish was fulfilled. The opponents, appropriately enough, were the Australians, who, true to character, were hardly in festival mode. Having held the upper hand throughout, Ian Chappell declared early on the last day, setting Kent 354 to win. Two early wickets did little to alter the belief that the match would not last its course, and so confident was he about the outcome that Chappell ordered the team's coach driver to the ground before tea so that they could be at Southampton, their next destination, by dinner. Little did he reckon with Cowdrey, who had rarely missed out in this fixture over the years. He began in confident enough manner, and soon Chappell, according to Alan Turner, the Australian opener, was telling Lillee to give Cowdrey several bouncers on the assumption that if he went the rest would follow. Lillee did as instructed, but instead of causing him trouble the balls were promptly despatched in front of square, recalling his pomp of yesteryear. He reached his century in under three hours, and with Woolmer supporting him at the other end with 71 not out, he continued to run the Australians ragged. Shortly before 6 p.m. on a beautiful sunlit evening, the sparse crowd at the St Lawrence ground rose to acclaim a memorable victory, Kent's first over the Australians since 1899, while Cowdrey's opponents vied with each other to compliment him on his masterpiece. 'As he came running in after what must have been one of the most satisfying innings of his life,' wrote Alan Gibson, 'he looked less like the familiar archdeaconal personage than a skipping lamb finding enough spring.'

Not even a pair for MCC against the Australians at Lord's the following week could dim Cowdrey's enthusiasm as he embarked on a long farewell around the cricket grounds of England, committed to the game as much as when he had started twenty-five years earlier. It helped that Kent was once again in the hunt for the championship. I well recall a friend of my parents, John Scotland, staying with us for Canterbury Week and visiting Cowdrey, whom he knew through the Anglo-Australian Society, during Kent's match against Hampshire. Their meeting took place on the players' balcony as Kent chased vital batting bonus points, and Cowdrey's sense of animated glee when another one unexpectedly came their way left Scotland dumb-founded.

After his great epic against the Australians, and 52 and 119 not out against Gloucestershire at Cheltenham, the runs rather dried up, but an elegiac 45 against Somerset at Folkestone in late August gave a vivid reminder of what his many supporters would be missing. The end came on Saturday 14 September when Kent, now out of the championship race, played Surrey at The Oval. As he made his way to the middle, Cowdrey, batting at no. 7, received a standing ovation from the rather thin gathering and was given one off the mark by Intikhab. Forty minutes later, the pavilion was on their feet again as he returned, c. Skinner b. Smith 20. The match ended in a quiet draw and Cowdrey, after twenty-six years on active service, was left to experience withdrawal symptoms as he contemplated the reality of a life away from the front line.

23

A View from the Boundary

Even after the abolition of amateur status in 1962, Cowdrey continued to derive no money from his Test match and county appearances, although he was generously remunerated from his writing, endorsements and occasional commercials. The handsome bequest Penny received from her father on his death in 1969, and the selling of Cowdrey's shares in the Chiesman firm in October 1970, helped the family's financial position, but with an expensive home to maintain and four children to educate, there was little room for complacency. Once his playing days were nearing their end, Cowdrey had to think of alternative employment. Through the good offices of Lord Cornwallis, a former Kent captain, he managed in 1974 to get a part-time promotional job with Whitbread Fremlin, a highly regarded firm of brewers who were extremely supportive of cricket in the county. This entailed him spending many an evening in their pubs answering questions about the game, having first conducted a tutorial with youngsters. It was work of a most fulfilling kind with which he was very much at home. Most Easters he used to give a batting demonstration to the MCC Young Professionals at the Indoor School at Lord's. Chris Stone, one of the coaches, admired the quality of his instruction and his uncanny ability to cover-drive good length balls, only later discovering that he had moved the stumps forward.

In addition to this work, Cowdrey took up a position with Barclays Bank International Division in the City, who had cultivated strong links with sport and the Commonwealth and whose chairman, Anthony Tuke, was an old friend. In his capacity as a PR executive, Cowdrey travelled extensively to the Test-match playing countries, speaking at functions and presenting prizes, a role tailor-made for his talents. It was while visiting South Africa on business in the late 1980s that David Moore, a close friend of a senior Barclays man in Johannesburg, came across him on the golf course.

> By the time we got to the nineteenth we were all on very friendly terms and after a couple of beers I felt bold enough to ask him if he would consider doing me a very big personal favour. My 91-year-old father, I explained, was living by himself in London and had only two interests in life – cricket and television. If Cowdrey were to ring him and say he had seen me, it would, I felt, be a wonderful moment in his rapidly ending life. Cowdrey asked for his phone number and I'm ashamed to admit that as I gave it to him I felt that was the last that would ever be heard of it. After all, he had known me for all of one afternoon.
>
> I was wrong. A few weeks later my brother wrote from England. 'Dad had a phone call the other evening. The voice said it was Colin Cowdrey. Dad decided it was a hoax, but then he mentioned your name and Johannesburg. Since then we can't get him to talk about anything else.'
>
> He died six months later.

Later Cowdrey became an advisory director of Barclays in Kent, and although he retired in February 1988 he continues to act as a consultant.

Once Cowdrey had finally retired from first-class cricket (although he did play one match for Kent in 1976, scoring 25 and 15 against Surrey), he could return to his autobiography, aptly named *MCC*, which he had been working on for a number of years. To help him write it he had hired the services of Ian Wooldridge of the *Daily Mail*. Wooldridge, who was surprised to be asked, adopted a relaxed approach, gently leading Cowdrey through his life and omitting anything he did not want to touch on. He found him charming and helpful but their partnership somewhat foundered on Cowdrey's desire to send off certain chapters to eminent names such as Sir Len Hutton and Sir Donald Bradman to seek their approval. The most embarrassing moment came when an agitated Cowdrey and Wooldridge went to the Foreign Office to seek Sir Alec Douglas-Home's approval of the chapter on the D'Oliveira affair. Surprised by their version of events, Sir Alec, much to Wooldridge's dismay, insisted on excising certain points, and Wooldridge now gave way to Tony Lewis, who finished the project. Between them they managed to produce a generous and eloquent commentary on Cowdrey's life and times, and the book became a best-seller on its release in 1976. 'It is a highly readable book,' declared Clive Taylor, adding perceptively, 'yet its silences are as interesting as anything.'

With the first-class game behind him, Cowdrey now turned to other forms of cricket to satisfy his continued desire to play. There was *The Cricketer* Cup, the prestigious knock-out competition featuring former pupils of thirty-two of the leading independent schools. Four years earlier he had followed in the footsteps of Peter May and Ted Dexter who had previously represented the Charterhouse Friars, and Radley Rangers respectively by turning out for the Old Tonbridgians. Once again he found the burden of expectation considerable. Bob White, a canny slow left-armer for the Berwick Club, recalls bowling to Cowdrey for the St Edward's Martyrs. Cowdrey had batted conventionally throughout the innings until he suddenly played a series of lap shots to leg, each one going for a boundary. He then apologised for the shots. 'I am sorry about the pantomime but I have to get a move on,' he explained. His 66 helped see off the Martyrs in the second round and an elegant 49 in the final at Burton Court, Chelsea, set up a comfortable victory against the Old Malvernians. Now in 1976 he teamed up with his son Christopher in the semi-final to see off the Eton Ramblers, father scoring 112 and son taking three for 27. Then in an overwhelmingly one-sided final against the Old Blundellians, Cowdrey scored 74 as the Tonbridgians strolled to victory, earning them a visit to the French vineyards, courtesy of the sponsors Moët and Chandon. Thereafter most of the cricket he played was in benefit and youth games, causes to which he had always given unstintingly of his time. He was, according to Christopher Martin-Jenkins, the ideal captain at Arundel when in charge of the Duke of Norfolk's XI, because of his efforts to ensure that everyone was properly involved. After his heart by-pass operation in 1987, Cowdrey might well have hung up his boots but, undeterred, he was back in action the following year, aged 55, playing for Old Kent against Kent at Tunbridge Wells, and he continued to cheerfully turn out for the Old England XI for several more years. He also appeared in 1988 for the Governor of the Bank of England's XI against the Archbishop of Canterbury's XI at Canterbury in aid of the Church Urban Fund. Robert Runcie, then archbishop and like Cowdrey a Brasenose man, recalls bowling two wides to him in front of the television cameras, a *faux pas* which finally persuaded him to retire from the game. He did, however, thanks to Cowdrey, become a Lord's Taverner and never ceased to delight him by telling the story about one of his predecessors as archbishop, Michael Ramsay, a rather donnish figure with little knowledge of cricket who once visibly stirred a congregation in Barbados by announcing his intention to preach on the 3 W's. There was an audible groan, however, when instead of elaborating on the local heroes, Weekes, Worrell and Walcott, he pronounced on Worship, Witness and Work.

Few causes have been closer to Cowdrey's heart than the future of Arundel, the beautiful cricket ground owned by his old friend the Duke of Norfolk, adjoining his castle in Sussex. When he invited the Australians there in 1956 the Duke inaugurated a tradition which became part of every major cricketing itinerary as players and spectators revelled in the quintessential English setting. As a regular participant on these occasions, Cowdrey was quick to the fore when the Duke died in 1975, leaving an heir with little interest in cricket. In conjunction with Ronnie Aird and Billy Griffith, former secretaries of MCC, and Eddy Harrison, secretary of the Sussex Marlets, who played their matches there, he encouraged Lavinia, the former Duke's widow, to set up the Friends of Arundel Castle Cricket Club. He launched the appeal to ensure the survival of cricket at the ground and became vice-chairman of the new set-up. This worked in the short term, but he soon realised that more needed to be done as not enough players were on hand to benefit. Consequently, with Sir Roger Gibbs and John Knight, he formed the Arundel Castle Cricket Foundation in 1986 to enhance the cricketing education of young people through coaching and playing at Arundel and elsewhere.

The means to realising this was the building of a stylish Indoor School behind the pavilion, financed largely by Sir Paul Getty and opened by the Prince of Wales in 1990. Since then some 100,000 boys (and girls), including groups from the Prince's Trust and the London Boys' Club, have taken advantage of the excellent facilities, or have been coached in the school by the excellent Director of Cricket, John Barclay, the former Sussex captain, and his small staff. Although Cowdrey now plays only a supporting role at Arundel, he can rest content that with the sixty matches staged there in 1998 and the Foundation's missionary work amongst the younger generation, the memory of the sixteenth Duke has been properly honoured.

Like Arundel, Tonbridge became another leading priority for Cowdrey. Given his close links with the school over the years, it came as no surprise that in 1980 he should join the Court of the Skinners Company, the school's trustees and governing body. Having risen through the hierarchy, learning the work of the livery company, he became Master in 1985–86, dazzling his Tonbridge audience on Speech Day with a spellbinding speech. His year as Master was immensely time-consuming but richly rewarding and enjoyable. Since then he has remained on the Court, was chairman of the last school appeal, and uses his many contacts to make things happen. David Kemp recalls how Cowdrey organised the Director of Grounds at Tonbridge to spend a day with the head groundsman at Lord's during a test match there to discuss problems and exchange ideas. When the school wanted advice on creating a new rugby ground he was quick to arrange a visit from the head groundsman for the Rugby Football Union at Twickenham. So deep has been his affection for the school that it seemed entirely appropriate that when elevated to the peerage in 1997 he should take as his title, Lord Cowdrey of Tonbridge.

In addition to becoming President of the Oxford University cricket club in 1976 for a three-year tenure, and beginning his twenty-three years' service on the board of *The Cricketer* magazine, Cowdrey was elected on to the Kent committee. With two more one-day trophies won that year, giving Denness a total of six in his five years as captain, it should have been a time of celebration but sadly, this was not the case. Not only did senior members of the committee feel that

Denness had been too remote a captain, it was also thought that he had been unduly insensitive in the way he had treated Cowdrey (not a charge that Cowdrey, an admirer of Denness, himself would lay). Despite the majority of players wanting Denness to stay, their views were overruled by the committee who dispensed with his services as captain at the end of that year. Denness never played for Kent again, becoming the first of a number of stalwarts reluctantly to transfer their allegiances to another county in acrimonious circumstances.

His successor, Asif Iqbal, did well to lead Kent to a share of the championship with Middlesex in his first year before he, along with Knott, Underwood and Woolmer, became embroiled in the Australian media magnate Kerry Packer's World Series Cricket which split the cricketing world. As an unabashed traditionalist, Cowdrey was horrified at this alternative vision with its crude commercialism and raucous aggression. To him there could be no compromise with Packer, and when the question of Asif's leadership was mooted he found it difficult to continue his support. For an instant the committee toyed with the possibility of coaxing Cowdrey out of retirement to lead the side but, realising that such a move would impede the development of their younger players, they chose Alan Ealham instead.

Although he stayed on the Kent committee until 1991 and played an important part in securing the services of his friend Jim Woodhouse as chairman of the Cricket Committee in 1987, his influence was otherwise largely compromised by the presence of his sons Christopher and then Graham in the team. This is one of the main reasons why he has never been President of the club. He does, however, keep closely in touch with its affairs (he is always turning on Ceefax to see how Kent are faring) and now that Graham has forsaken cricket for a career in the City, that anomaly may yet be corrected.

Cowdrey's committee work at Kent was the prelude to an administrative role at national level. With his abiding interest in the game, and a record second to none, it was only a matter of time before he was co-opted on to the MCC committee, on which he had first served when captain of Kent in the late 1960s. He kept a relatively low profile at first until the vexed question of South Africa returned with a vengeance in 1983 to haunt the hierarchy at Lord's. Back in 1971 Cowdrey had gained official blessing to take a multiracial tour to South Africa, which included Basil D'Oliveira. When he visited the Republic to drum up support, he faced a wall of resistance from the non-white South African Cricket Board under Hassan Howa, the rival to the all white South African Cricket Association, who saw the tour as a cosmetic exercise which would do little to eradicate the blight of apartheid. Cowdrey's plans fell away, leaving him to contemplate the future with foreboding as the argument that there could be no normal sport in an abnormal society increasingly found favour.

A decade later the game in South Africa, thanks to the work of its enlightened Cricketing Association, had become more racially integrated but because this was still the exception rather than the rule South African players and officials remained helpless pawns in the larger political battle between the supporters and the opponents of apartheid. Their plight was well documented in Britain and continued to draw sympathy from businessmen, sportsmen and Conservative MPs who saw the virtues as well as the vices of South Africa and felt that sportsmen should be free to go there regardless of what politicians decreed. One such organisation which persistently championed their cause was Freedom of Sport, boasting five MCC members on its executive of six. A group of them, led by the idiosyncratic right-wing MP for Luton, John Carlisle, and supported by such cricket luminaries as Bill Edrich and Denis Compton, managed with the help of fifty MCC members' signatures to call a special general meeting to discuss the issue.

On the evening of 13 July 1983, a thousand MCC members crowded into Westminster Hall to listen to Carlisle – deploring political interference in sport – propose that MCC should implement the selection of a touring party to South Africa in 1983–84. He was opposed on behalf of the committee by Hubert Doggart and Cowdrey who both, according to Matthew Engel in *Wisden*, disguised some sharp debating points beneath their gentle demeanour. They acknowledged hypocrisy and double standards among South Africa's opponents, but argued that a tour would breach the 1977 Gleneagles Agreement, which imposed a sporting

193

boycott on South Africa by Commonwealth countries, and would endanger MCC's position within the game.

'If members think that by voting for it, they're taking cricket out of politics that is a pipe dream,' declared Cowdrey. He and Doggart had put their case persuasively enough to win the vote in the hall 534 to 439 and the postal vote by 6,604 to 4,344. The fact, though, that 40 per cent of the membership had defied their committee was indicative of the strong emotions which the topic continued to arouse. It was the prelude to a more turbulent relationship with the same membership four years later, when the accent should have been overwhelmingly on celebration.

Sir Pelham Warner had called MCC a private club with a public function, for besides being the oracle of English cricket for the best part of two hundred years it tended to the game worldwide with benign authority. But by the 1960s dark clouds had begun to appear. With crowds fast dwindling, and its finances in a parlous state, the temptation for sporting bodies to accept government funds became overwhelming. A cost, though, would have to be paid in the form of diminished status, since a private club with an unelected president receiving public money from the government – particularly a Labour one – would be considered an unacceptable anomaly. Thus MCC in 1968 voluntarily signed away much of its authority to the newly formed Test and County Cricket Board, who in future would control the first-class game, within the ambit of the Cricket Council, the official new governing body of English cricket.

On the surface the new arrangements seemed to have bred a good working relationship but behind the scenes there lay much friction as the TCCB resented the undue influence MCC still exerted through its secretariat who did the bulk of their work. Prior to Billy Griffith's retirement – he having been secretary of the MCC, TCCB, the International Cricket Council and the Cricket Council – it became clear that the multiplicity of titles in the hands of one person was no longer acceptable to those in the TCCB who yearned for greater autonomy. Thus when Griffith retired in 1974 his responsibilities were split between Jack Bailey, one of the assistant secretaries since 1967, who became Secretary of MCC and ICC, and Donald Carr, his colleague, who became Secretary of the TCCB and Cricket Council after seven years' work for these bodies. With the split in the roles of the secretariat for the first time the discord between MCC and TCCB now became more clearly defined as the balance of power increasingly shifted towards the latter by dint of its hold on the game's purse strings. At the heart of this secret war stood the imposing figure of Jack Bailey.

A former quick bowler for Oxford University, whom he captained, and Essex, Bailey proved to be an enlightened administrator who successfully presided over the modernisation of Lord's and the improvement of its facilities. He also displayed unswerving loyalty to the club, fighting zealously to protect its independence and that of Lord's from the ever-growing tentacles of the TCCB. In a report initiated almost a decade earlier by Raman Subba Row, then chairman of Surrey and later chairman of the TCCB from 1985 to 1990, the virtual demise of MCC's wider role had been recommended. This role still included responsibilities for the laws of the game, for providing the president and secretary to the International Cricket Council, and for the ownership of Lord's, on whose property the TCCB still resided as uneasy tenants. In 1982 a further shift of power within the Cricket Council in favour of the TCCB, in recognition of its growing commercial responsibilities, gave Bailey further cause to dig in his heels. At issue was who had absolute control over matches at Lord's. MCC had never questioned the Board's ultimate responsibility for the running of Test matches and the Board, in turn, relied upon each Test Match Ground Authority for the staging of these major fixtures. The sticking point came over the Board's insistence that, in the event of a serious disagreement between them and the Ground Authorities for the promotion of a match, they should have ultimate responsibility for its resolution.

Confronted by these demands, Bailey saw red. Unhappy about the way that the TCCB were using their facilities at Lord's to interfere in responsibilities which he felt weren't their concern, such as whether sponsors should be allowed a guaranteed (though paid for) box, he vigorously upheld MCC's control of the premises. Because of the club's still important role in harmonising international cricket and its responsibility to its own members, he maintained that arrangements with the TCCB should be different from

other grounds. A number of his colleagues on the committee, most
notably a powerful faction with strong TCCB links, were more
conciliatory. They recognised that since 1968 the Board had overall
responsibility for the running of the game in England and provided
that the rights of MCC members were respected it was in everyone's interests that the two bodies should co-operate. This view
was to gain currency the longer time went on and the more
unpleasant the bickering became.

As the secretary fought his dogged rearguard action, his relationship with a number of presidents – one of whom, George Mann,
president in 1984–85, had been chairman of the TCCB from 1978 to
1983 – deteriorated to the point where he felt his influence seriously
diminished. The die was thus cast when Jack Davies, president in
1985–86, nominated a former captain of his old school as his successor in the club's bicentenary year. To some insiders the choice of
Cowdrey in one sense was surprising, given his relatively low profile
in the councils of debate, although he was invariably incisive when
roused. Set against this, however, was a playing record second to
none, a history of undeviating loyalty to MCC and his immense
stature throughout the cricketing world. He also had friends in high
places. David Clark, the MCC treasurer, had been his first captain at
Kent; Sir Anthony Tuke, the chairman of finance, as chairman of
Barclays had been his employer; and Gubby Allen, the doyen of
Lord's officialdom, had been the chairman of selectors when
Cowdrey was first made England captain.

Although the presidency was less of a ceremonial position than
hitherto, the problem which Cowdrey, along with his predecessors,
faced was that there was a limited time to leave his mark. With a foot
in both camps on account of his work for the TCCB between 1983
and 1986, Cowdrey came in desperate to end the feuding so that
MCC's bicentenary celebrations could pass off without a hitch. It was
in this context that on the one occasion he met Bailey before taking
up office, he told him to lie low for a while so that the breach with
the TCCB could be healed.

Bailey replied that they must consult the members, something
which his committee was reluctant to do for fear of exposing their
problems in public. By the summer of 1986 they felt that they had

reached the point of no return. Unwilling to follow their secretary into the trenches any longer, powerful voices on the committee looked to their new president to assert his authority and bring him to heel. He obliged with surprising alacrity.

When Bailey returned from holiday in October, he found that the management of the club's affairs had virtually been taken over by Cowdrey and Tuke. On the third Wednesday of October, during a regular meeting of the full MCC committee, Cowdrey astounded Bailey by requesting him and his assistants to leave the room. During Bailey's absence from the fateful meeting, the committee drew up guidelines about their relationship with the TCCB, accepting that the latter had the ultimate right to organise matters at Lord's. Bailey welcomed them while reserving the right to seek clarification of any areas which might be difficult. A further meeting with Cowdrey and other officers of the club at which Bailey sought answers to potentially difficult questions degenerated into acrimony. It was now that Cowdrey's patience began to wear thin and he later produced a letter, carefully drafted by outside solicitors, warning Bailey that, because of what he, Cowdrey, had told them the committee had lost confidence. Faced with this inexorable incoming tide Bailey decided now to resign – before heading off to Australia for a New Year holiday. He was replaced by one of his assistants, John Stephenson, in a temporary capacity but so adept was Stephenson at rising to the challenge that in April 1987 he was, with Cowdrey's blessing, confirmed in his position.

Getting rid of his turbulent priest did not end Cowdrey's difficulties. If Bailey, in the eyes of his detractors, had been the author of his own undoing, the same could not be said of the treasurer, David Clark. A man of great experience and integrity, Clark had given thirty years of stalwart service to MCC in various guises, including the presidency, when he had formed a close and effective liaison with Bailey. He did not always agree with the secretary's uncompromising style in relation to the TCCB, but admired his commitment to the club and felt that he had been poorly rewarded for his sturdy defence of their interests. He also felt that MCC's membership should have been consulted about any change in arrangements with the TCCB over the staging of important matches at Lord's.

Unable to win support from his fellow committee men, Clark walked out of the meeting in December, never to return – the first treasurer to resign in the club's history. Michael Melluish, MCC president in 1991–92, recalls Cowdrey putting his hand on his shoulder and informing him that the treasurer was about to resign and to stay still, so that the meeting did not break up. Clark meanwhile went home and thought nothing more about it until rung up by a newspaper weeks later seeking his reaction to Bailey's early retirement once it was publicly announced in January. It was only then that he confessed to no longer being treasurer, giving the journalist in question a considerable scoop. Later, an interview Clark gave to the *Sunday Telegraph* in April formed the basis of several articles hinting at a TCCB takeover of MCC. The paper was strongly critical of a letter which Cowdrey had sent in February to MCC members explaining the club's position and the circumstances which had led to the secretary and treasurer's resignation. They also reported that the club's solicitors, Halsey, Lightly and Hemsley, were unhappy about the letter and the contents of the annual report. The solicitors advised their clients to consult with their membership before agreeing to the TCCB demands.

These embarrassing allegations formed the backdrop to a crowded AGM held in the Lord's banqueting suite on 6 May, where discontented members had gathered to ambush club officials. Despite a reasoned defence of the committee's position by Sir Oliver Popplewell, the membership, true to the spirit of Bailey and Clark, were in no mood to cede any further ground to the TCCB. After a rancorous meeting in which calls for Cowdrey's resignation were aired, the membership, for the first time in their history, refused to accept the club report and accounts. So bemused was Cowdrey by this mutinous reaction that he put the motion a second time, only to be rebuffed again. It said much for his resilience that he could put his shock to one side to play host to Prince Philip for the evening. After the Prince had officially opened the new Mound Stand he escorted him into the Long Room for the first of the club's two bicentenary dinners at which J. J. Warr, the president elect, spoke with his usual aplomb.

With their credibility badly undermined, president and committee now regrouped ready to launch a fightback. Aware of the need to regain the confidence of the members and procure their support for full co-operation with the TCCB – without which they feared Lord's could be isolated – they got to work on devising an effective strategy. First, they would call, on the same afternoon, an AGM to complete the unfinished business, and a special meeting, implicit in which was a postal vote. Second, they would circulate to members a summary of the relationship between MCC and the TCCB, which vigorously defended their recent stance. Third, they would dispense with their solicitors, since their legal advice had inspired little confidence, much to the detriment of the committee.

The strategy worked. At the special meeting held in the Central Hall, Westminster on 30 July, attended by nearly 2,000 members and tactfully handled by Hubert Doggart, the new treasurer, the mood was more sober than its predecessor three months earlier.

Having accepted some of the initiatives which the committee had instigated, notably their need to improve their public relations, the members now overwhelmingly accepted the accounts. Amidst palpable sighs of relief about the outcome, there was only unmitigated gloom about the enforced absence of Cowdrey, who was recuperating from his heart by-pass operation. Several weeks earlier, he had been forced to leave a golf course in Hong Kong, where he was present on ICC business, with symptoms of a heart attack. While the hullabaloo at Lord's, and the strain of travelling thousands of miles to defuse political problems which threatened to disrupt the pending World Cup, had undoubtedly taxed him, Cowdrey's surgeon dismissed these afflictions as mere irritants. More crucial was the history of heart trouble in the family which had caused the premature death of both his grandfather and father. Advised to have immediate surgery, Cowdrey told John Stephenson how reluctant he was to miss the special meeting, aware that his absence might be construed as failing in his responsibilities. Stephenson replied that his life was more important than the meeting. Once the proceedings were over and normality had been restored the secretary visited him in hospital to inform him of the good news, at which point Cowdrey was overcome with relief.

He was also forced to miss the climax of the bicentenary celebrations which were ably masterminded by Doggart with assistance from Bailey and Stephenson. Doggart presided over proceedings at the glittering banquet at the Guildhall, and the MCC versus Rest of the World match at Lord's. At the banquet he read out a message from Cowdrey to the assembled company urging them to 'keep cricket a happy game'. Being president had had its congenial side, not least acting as a gracious host at Lord's, but inevitably the year was marred by the ramifications of the Bailey and Clark resignations. By acting out of character, Cowdrey stilled the storm which had raged through the corridors of power for a decade.

But the personal cost had been a heavy one, not least the rupturing of two important friendships. In the face of such setbacks, it is perhaps surprising that within two years he was back for more, charged with an even more arduous mission.

24

Dynasty

On 1 December 1978 the *Daily Mail* caused something of a stir when it revealed that Colin Cowdrey was leaving his wife of twenty-two years for Lady Anne Herries, the eldest daughter of the Duke of Norfolk. The news left people nonplussed, since it had always been fondly imagined that the Cowdreys were a model of family propriety. The truth was rather more complex, given that Colin and Penny possessed very different temperaments, which ultimately, to their lasting regret, proved incompatible.

Cowdrey had first met Lady Anne Fitzalan Howard (as she then was) on the 1962–63 tour to Australia when her father, the Duke of Norfolk, head of the Roman Catholic Church in Britain and Earl Marshal of England, was the manager. He and Cowdrey were very good friends. But it was only in 1974, the last year of the Duke's life, when Cowdrey met Anne at Arundel Castle, the family seat in Sussex, that they became close. She was an outstanding National Hunt trainer and after a brief spell at Everingham Park in Yorkshire, an estate she inherited after her father's death, she returned to Arundel in 1978, to live and train in nearby Angmering Park. Her move south brought Cowdrey's domestic predicament to a head and in November of that year he finally left home.

He kept his counsel as the entrails of his marriage were duly picked over by reporters and news editors alike. Most sided with his wife, giving him the worst press of his life, although close family friends were more sympathetic to his predicament. Penny called her loss a living bereavement and, desperate for Cowdrey's return, refused to grant him a divorce, which meant that he was unable to marry Anne until September 1985. The children for their part – protective towards their mother – initially kept their distance from their father as he tried to rebuild his life. Gradually, as the years went by and adolescence gave way to adulthood, they adjusted to the new realities, placing their relationship with him on a new and firmer footing.

During the children's formative years, whatever problems lurked in the background, there was at least a mutual love of sport, and cricket in particular, to keep the family happy, successful and united. Following in their father's footsteps, all three boys soon succumbed to the game's manifold charms and, encouraged by his gentle guidance in their garden, first in Bickley, then in the Surrey village of Limpsfield, replete with a hard net and a bowling machine, they learnt the joys of batting from an early age. In contrast to his own strict cricketing education, Cowdrey was much more relaxed with his sons, allowing them to savour the thrill of hitting the ball in the air, and the fun of catching competitions. When they went away to prep school at Wellesley House, Broadstairs, recommended to the Cowdreys by Stuart Chiesman, rarely a match went by without a major contribution from Christopher, Jeremy or Graham. By the time they went on to Tonbridge, they were attracting the same kind of attention Colin had received thirty years earlier, with the difference that they were the sons of a world famous cricketer to whom they instinctively looked up.

Although Cowdrey's impeccable public standing and judicious avoidance of controversy shielded his family from the embarrassment of unwelcome publicity, he was under no illusion about the rod he had unwittingly laid for their back. From the moment Christopher arrived at Tonbridge in September 1970, he found the inevitable comparisons with his father a real burden to shoulder, as everyone from parents to visiting preachers claimed some kind of association with Colin. It is perhaps not surprising that Christopher disliked his father coming to watch him bat, for although Colin tried to adopt a low profile, his presence would soon be detected and relayed back to Christopher, who more often than not failed. It was fortunate that there were those in authority who divined his particular problem and helped him develop his own personality. In particular, there was his housemaster, David Kemp, at the sport-oriented Park House, who besides being in Christopher's estimation a first-rate schoolmaster was also his godfather. There was also his tutor and close friend Jonathan Smith, who later collaborated on his book *Good Enough?*, an honest self-appraisal of his ability and progress.

Despite lacking his father's flawless technique (which made it difficult for Colin to coach him), Christopher made the Tonbridge XI when he was 14, and after a difficult start progressed so rapidly that in his last summer at the school he scored 966 runs at an average of 80, as well as taking thirty wickets. These figures bore an uncanny resemblance to Colin's average of 79 in 1950, but in other ways their characters were markedly different both on and off the cricket field. Whereas Colin was diffident, diligent and conformist, Christopher was gregarious, academically workshy and impetuous, and scrapes with authority were not unknown. David Kemp recalls having to punish him after Christopher had absconded home on a field day without telling anyone, as well as having frequently to cajole him into working. His son's headstrong personality worried Colin, but although very supportive of Kemp, he was an indulgent father who, well aware of the pressures they faced, did not push his children too hard, least of all on the academic side. In any case, for all Christopher's foibles, there was no malice in him. He had a warm personality, recalled Kemp, and was soon as adept at holding his own in conversation with adults as he was at mixing with his peers. He was also a charismatic captain, one of the very best Tonbridge had had, combining tactical flair and aggression with the Cowdrey will to win.

While still at school, Christopher played for England's Young Cricketers against West Indies at Lord's, and two years later he captained a talented and unbeaten side to the West Indies, outscoring allcomers including David Gower and Mike Gatting. The next year, in 1977, he made his debut for Kent, aged nineteen, against the Australians at Canterbury. Again, the pressures of being a Cowdrey were evident, particularly in front of home crowds who were exacting in their judgement, although this was counterbalanced by the goodwill of his team-mates, many of whom had grown up under Colin's tutelage. They were now at the height of their powers, and if

Christopher was to survive in such illustrious company, he was going to have to show his mettle. The one-day game particularly suited him because of his lively athleticism in the field, his useful change bowling, his daring improvisation and strong running between the wickets. Within weeks of his début he scored a spectacular 114 against Sussex, winning Kent a crucial Benson and Hedges quarter-final, followed by a maiden championship hundred against Glamorgan, a feat which had eluded Colin. It was to be another six years before he made another, as years of bottom-hand hitting left him vulnerable outside the off stump. His failure to land the Kent captaincy on Asif Iqbal's retirement in 1982 was the occasion for some thorough soul-searching, including whether he would be better off at another county. His father, ever supportive, persuaded him to stay with Kent and, appreciating the need to become more prolific if he was one day to realise his leadership ambitions, Christopher set about ironing out a number of technical flaws. The hard graft in Australia that winter immediately paid dividends, for he arrived home a much more complete player, scoring 1000 runs for the first time and achieving an average of 56, placing him seventh in the national averages. He also proved a dependable vice-captain, leading Kent with flair when Chris Tavaré was away playing for England. Not least against the champions Essex when his superb undefeated 125 helped his side to a comprehensive ten wicket victory.

1984 was less spectacular, but a pugnacious 58 in the NatWest final against Middlesex helped him win a place on the England tour to India under his great friend David Gower, as the all-rounder in place of Ian Botham, who opted for a winter at home. The tour began against the traumatic backdrop of the assassinations of both the prime minister, Indira Gandhi, and the British deputy commissioner in Bombay, the night after he had entertained the team at his residence. This shocking news overshadowed Christopher's call-up for the first Test, after injuries had restricted his appearances hitherto. He failed in both innings in England's emphatic defeat, but managed to get a wicket in his first over, causing a moment of embarrassment for his father, who was driving up to London at the time. So preoccupied was he with the radio commentary from Bombay that, taking a wrong exit from a roundabout, he found himself being flagged down by a police officer as he went down a one-way street. As he was about to be booked, the policeman became so intrigued by the cricket that he started quizzing Colin about the state of the game. He explained that his son had just come on to bowl, at which point a huge roar signalled the downfall of Kapil Dev, bowled Christopher, 42. 'That's fantastic,' said the policeman, inclining now towards leniency. 'We'd better get you of of here.'

Unfortunate with a couple of poor decisons, Christopher struggled to make much headway during the series, but his *joie de vivre* made him an indispensable part of a tour of this kind. England won 2–1 and Christopher returned to a new challenge of captaining Kent. The circumstances of his accession were hardly propitious. Chris Tavaré, captain for the two previous years, had, much to Colin's embarrassment, been unceremoniously dismissed by the Kent committee after leading the county to two narrow NatWest final defeats in consecutive seasons. Their decision to ditch the popular, if unadventurous, Tavaré was resented by some of the senior players, and Christopher experienced several difficult years restoring unity to the dressing-room. His salvation came with the arrival of some younger players, and a dynamic new chairman of the cricket committee, Jim Woodhouse, in 1987, who quickly became a good friend. Together they worked closely to restore morale, not least by lending a friendly ear to the players. The catalyst came at Leicester after Kent had lost their first three matches in 1988. Woodhouse called the team together to mull over their dismal start, and invited all the players to contribute. Out of this discussion came a settlement of some grievances, and the decision to appoint a top coach, John Inverarity, the former Australian Test player who later briefly taught at Tonbridge, arrived from Perth at a moment's notice and helped Christopher to galvanise the team. Six victories in succession transformed an ordinary team into a winning one through positive outcricket and a special camaraderie – the best team spirit Christopher ever knew. By the end of June, Kent were top of the table, and as England slithered from one defeat to another against Viv Richards's West Indians, losing captains with alarming regularity, Christopher's name came into the reckoning.

When he was eventually appointed for the fourth and fifth Tests, the press, captivated by the romance of the Cowdrey name, unrealistically hailed him as England's Messiah, something which Colin privately foresaw, as he and Christopher followed F. T. and F. G. Mann, the first father and son to lead England. Christopher's daunting legacy soon became clear once proceedings began at Headingley. After three rain-affected days, the match was evenly poised until the West Indian fast bowlers ran amok on the fourth day. All out for 138, England lost by ten wickets with Cowdrey contributing a measly 0 and 5. He returned subdued to Canterbury for Kent's match against Sussex. A nasty blow on the foot, sustained in the first innings, was serious enough to compel his withdrawal from the fifth Test. Gooch took over the captaincy and kept it for the one-off Test against Sri Lanka, despite another heavy defeat at The Oval and Christopher's evident recovery from injury, confirmed by a century against Derbyshire. The decision upset Colin and shattered Christopher, and not only because Peter May, the chairman of selectors, and ironically his godfather, did not ring to tell him – he also had previously indicated that he was likely to take England to India that winter. When he gave vent to his frustration days later to the *Sun*, his outburst landed him in trouble with the TCCB for speaking out without official sanction. He was fined £500 for his pains, and to add insult to injury Kent missed out on the championship to Worcestershire by one point.

In retrospect 1988 was the high-water mark of Christopher's captaincy of Kent. The next year began with Colin helping with some pre-season coaching, an exhibition which Jim Woodhouse found riveting to watch, but Kent could not repeat their form of the previous summer, slipping alarmingly to penultimate position in the championship. In addition to their steep fall from grace, Christopher, in his benefit year, caused some ructions by signing on for Gatting's rebel tour to South Africa. Unlike Asif in 1977, he retained the captaincy, but was disconcerted by the failure of the committee to renew Woodhouse's contract as Chief Executive, a post he held in addition to his duties as chairman of the cricket committee. The decision of his fellow committee men in October 1989 left Colin isolated and affronted. He had been grateful to Woodhouse for all the support that he had given Christopher, and now, in a show of solidarity, he walked out of the committee meeting in protest.

Things went from bad to worse. Kent's fortunes in 1990 showed no upturn as once again they finished sixteenth; Christopher, finding the captaincy an increasingly strenuous business, had handed over the reins in August to Mark Benson. Then, with his fitness becoming less reliable, and much to his parents' consternation, he was released at the end of the following season. After a year turning out for Glamorgan, Christopher retreated into the media, disappointed that his efforts for Kent had never been rewarded with a trophy.

For Jeremy Cowdrey there was the additional problem of living in the shadow not only of his father, but also of his older brother, from whom he received his first XI colours. Under normal circumstances, his school record of three years in the cricket team, two years in the racquets team and a year as full-back in the rugby XV (the same position which Christopher played, Graham was later to play on the wing) would have spoken for itself, but it did not match those of his father or his brother. Fortunately, this did not worry him. The most academic of the three brothers, Jeremy had a well-rounded temperament and once it became clear that professional cricket was not for him he went to Durham University, on his way to a successful career in the City.

For Graham, the pressures of being a Cowdrey were less intense at Tonbridge than they had been for Christopher, despite arriving there with an even more glowing reputation after averaging 85 in his last year for Wellesley. He did, though, have to contend with the break-up of his parents' marriage at a particularly impressionable age, which may have contributed to a rather introspective, capricious temperament.

He, like his father, made the school cricket XI at 13, but his strengths corresponded to Christopher's, with a razor-sharp eye and powerful bottom-hand technique which brought him a feast of runs on Tonbridge's plumb surfaces. In 1982, his final summer, Graham was captain of an unbeaten team, and although not quite as prolific as expected – Colin thought him the best of the three boys – he still had the class to succeed at a higher level. The question was whether he had the inclination to follow the family tradition. He certainly faced no pressure from his father, who was keen that Graham, like Jeremy, should enjoy the benefit of a university education. In 1982 he duly followed his brother to Durham, but dropped out after a year and decided to throw in his lot with Kent. He immediately came face to face with the problems of being a Cowdrey, finding the media an unwelcome intrusion, particularly when the inevitable comparisons were made.

Having his brother as captain when he made his championship debut in 1985 was a mixed blessing too, as Christopher bent over backwards not to discriminate in his favour. The result was that Graham became frustrated at not getting more first XI cricket and, when he was playing, being expected to score quick runs in the middle of the order, something he was adept at doing, particularly in the one-day game. Another problem he had to overcome was an uncertain technique against quick bowling, particularly after a nasty crack on the jaw from Michael Holding, the West Indian fast-bowler, at Derby in 1987, which did little for his confidence. More than ever he sought out Colin for technical advice. His father tried to get him to play straighter.

1988 saw Graham contribute significantly to Kent's success, making his maiden hundred and winning his county cap from a delighted Christopher, and over the next three years he really came into his own. His form in the championship thereafter blew rather hot and cold, until the arrival of Aravinda de Silva in 1995 inspired him to new heights. He struck up a firm friendship with the charming Sri Lankan, and they shared several notable partnerships, the highlight being a mammoth 368 against Derbyshire at Maidstone, the all-time Kent record for any wicket. Graham's métier, however, had always been the one-day game, where his aggressive hitting could be devastating, and in 1995 he did as much as anyone to help Kent win the AXA Sunday League, their first trophy for seventeen years. When he retired in 1998, he had successfully cast off the inhibitions of his youth and developed into a fun-loving and popular cricketer who fully merited the rich pickings his benefit year had served up. Had he been more consistent at crucial stages in his career, he might have attained his ambition of captaining Kent, a responsibility he had enjoyed at Tonbridge and with the county second XI and a position for which his tactical ingenuity suggested he was eminently qualified. As it was, he could be satisfied that after fifteen years of spirited service, he and Christopher had done their father proud. Kent in 1999 will seem a strange place when for the first time since 1950 there will be no Cowdrey on their books. The era of Camelot was finally over.

25

Peacemaking

For all his public appearances, Colin Cowdrey has remained a very private man, who is extremely guarded in revealing his true feelings. In a less intrusive age which put less store on interviews and quotes, this was nothing exceptional so that even when wounded by press criticism or buffeted by selectorial whim, he simply conformed to the adage of never explain, never complain. Such an approach not only spared him further controversy, it also kept him in good odour with his superiors at Lord's.

In private, however, Cowdrey could be more forthcoming with his strong views about the game, particularly as the passing years ushered in an erosion of standards. Always the most decorous of men, he deplored the meaner, brasher trends which emanated from the Packer era, and it was partially his determination to contain the Gadarene stampede which kept him active in administration.

As with many leading figures in authority, he liked to get his own way, but he worked long and hard to achieve it by painstakingly taking people with him rather than going out on a limb. Graeme Wright, in his book *Betrayal*, reckoned that because Cowdrey was not a businessman like the power players at the TCCB, he was less drawn to the prolonged conflict of wills that carried such men as Gubby Allen through interminable hours of committee room deliberation. 'His strength,' Wright wrote, 'lay outside the committee room where the full force of his personality was brought into play.' Be it at his London club, Boodles, his home at Angmering, or the many hours spent on his mobile phone, he would weigh up options, bounce ideas and try to disarm opposition with sweet reason.

These tactics became his stock in trade during his years as chairman of the ICC when he formed a very close relationship with its secretary, John Stephenson, a post he held in addition to being Secretary of MCC.

Originally founded in 1909 by England, Australia and South Africa, the ICC developed into cricket's international governing body, composed of representatives from all the Test-playing countries and, since 1965, associate members. Traditionally it met annually at Lord's, presided over by the President and Secretary of MCC, to discuss topical matters and suggest amendments to the laws of the game. For the most part, the deliberations had been leisurely and informal until the advent of political boycotts, the World Cup and World Series Cricket took them into rougher, uncharted waters. Faced with a profusion of unwelcome developments, as well as growing commercial opportunities, the ramshackle ICC proved unequal to the task. It was to help equip it for a more professional era that, following a review of its machinery and methods between 1986 and 1989, a new constitution was established. At the heart of it was the proposal that the new ICC chairman would be an elected four-year appointee, with time at his disposal to deal with the increasingly complex issues. When Cowdrey was nominated by his predecessor, Field Marshal the Lord Bramall, in 1989, he was the obvious candidate for this new role, not only because of his stature as a player but also for his much admired diplomatic skills throughout the cricketing world. He faced an uneasy inheritance with any number of contentious issues needing resolution, not least the deterioration in players' behaviour, the pressure on umpires, the surfeit of short-pitch bowling, declining over rates and the future of South Africa. Such was the mood of desperation which prevailed among cricket lovers that Cowdrey carried the hopes of many on his shoulders as he attempted to build a new world order. 'Gentle, considerate and sensitive, he is also by nature a conciliatory man and here lies the danger,' wrote David Frith, the former editor of *Wisden Cricket Monthly*. 'He knows what medicine is needed, but there will be those at the table whose needs and motives will be cloaked selfishly. Most threatening there will be political allegations.'

From the very beginning of his tenure, following comments to him from Lord Bramall, Cowdrey had earmarked discipline on the field as his greatest priority. It was felt that a code of conduct was needed to rigorously reinforce the traditionally accepted standards of behaviour. At the 1989 meeting England and Australia outlined their own codes, which provided the model for what Cowdrey was looking for. Determined not to lose the momentum, he spent the next six months travelling to each cricket country to explain his aim to their officials. After viewing various codes of conduct, he realised that on their own they were not enough. A match referee was needed, who would endorse the authority of the umpire, a conviction only strengthened by the shenanigans he witnessed in the Caribbean during England's visit in 1990. The unseemly episode in Barbados when the West Indian captain, Viv Richards, appeared to influence the umpire's decision by a display of gratuitous exuberance was a particular cause for concern. Armed with this latest amunition, Cowdrey, with great support from Alan Smith of the TCCB, Graham Dowling of New Zealand, Dave Richards of Australia and Steve Camacho of the West Indies, chipped away at resistance until it disappeared.

At Melbourne in January 1991, at the first ICC meeting to be held away from Lord's, there was unanimous agreement to introduce from October of that year an international code and paid referees for Tests and one-day internationals. They would wield wide disciplinary powers, including the fining and suspension of players, either from their own observation or from what they were told by umpires. Once the code had been finalised, Cowdrey called it a message of hope, reviving Lord Harris's appeal to cricketers everywhere to play the game keenly, honestly, generously and self-sacrificingly. He himself wrote one paragraph, the most important of the eight points dealing with unbecoming conduct, dissent, intimidation and crude language. It stated that the captains were responsible at all times for ensuring that play was conducted within the spirit of the game as well as within the laws.

As for the referees, they were chosen by Cowdrey and John Stephenson for the first year. Not only did they want them to be former players but good ambassadors. The panel of M. J. K. Smith, Peter May, Raman Subba Row and Donald Carr, all good friends of Cowdrey, generated some adverse comment but Cowdrey needed men he could trust who were available at short notice. Thereafter each cricket country put forward two or three candidates. The quality varied somewhat at first and a couple of referees were soon replaced, while other candidates proved unacceptable because of past indiscretions. Tom Graveney recalls Cowdrey ringing him up in some embarrassment when the Pakistan authorities, citing some previous unflattering comments of his about their sporting ethics, objected to him standing. 'You don't mind if you don't go?' he said. 'We'll find you somewhere else to go', though Graveney heard nothing from him on the subject again.

The final part of the jigsaw was the question of international umpires, an innovation long favoured by Pakistan, who had seen their growing success at Test level somewhat overshadowed by the seemingly endless wrangling over the integrity of their officials. In July 1989 the ICC tentatively targeted 1991 as the year when an international panel would be set up. The principle was re-endorsed at Melbourne in January 1991 but given the practical problem of funding a project likely to cost half a million pounds per year, it was considered unviable without commercial sponsorship. There it might have remained without the work of Cowdrey, Mike Denness and others. It so happened that Denness, then working for the consultancy firm of K.B.M.D. PR sat next to Cowdrey at the Edgbaston Test that summer and was informed of his plans. He doubted whether any company would come up with the kind of money Cowdrey needed for an enterprise with no proven record behind it but felt that there might be ones which would assist.

In early 1992 Denness informed Cowdrey that he had met John Hatch, a non-executive director of the National Grid, on a supporters' tour of New Zealand. He was attracted to the idea of his firm becoming involved in the sponsorship of umpiring. A pilot scheme was formulated in October 1992 for India's tour of Zimbabwe, and worked sufficiently well to justify its continuation in 1993. 'Dickie' Bird, the umpire, and Subba Row, the match referee, were sponsored in two Tests between West Indies and Pakistan in April, and the inaugural Test Umpires Conference at Coventry, attended by Cowdrey, was deemed a great success. In this inaugural year Hatch was asked by Cowdrey to chair the meeting, a shrewd move according to

Denness, the conference organiser, since it helped encourage over-seas umpires to speak their mind to an independent figure. Because of Hatch's love for the game and the company's substantial overseas interests in cricket-playing countries, National Grid were now will-ing to be fully committed. In January 1994 they signed a £1.1 million sponsorship agreement with the ICC for the next three years, to fund the cost of the umpiring and match referees. Without this generous assistance a major part of Cowdrey's programme to clean up the game would never have seen the light of day.

There was mixed success on two other fronts. In July 1989 the ICC had set a target of fifteen overs an hour to try to solve a problem which had become increasingly serious over the years. Not only did slow over rates deprive spectators of value for money at a time when admission charges had escalated, it also gave an unfair advantage to teams such as West Indies with their all-pace attack. The cynical way which both West Indies and England respectively slowed down the over rate to little more than ten an hour in the Trinidad and Barbados Tests in 1990 only strengthened Cowdrey's determination to act. After overcoming a rearguard campaign by the West Indies, Cowdrey managed in July 1991 to secure universal agreement for a minimum of fifteen overs an hour, with fines for failure to uphold this; an undoubted step in the right direction.

On short-pitched bowling, progress was less spectacular. Although the bravest and most skilful player of genuine pace himself, Cowdrey felt that the fast men had always had too great a licence to fire their missiles down on unsuspecting batsmen. He always rued the failure to use a softer ball, and deplored the increas-ing number of bouncers and the moves towards greater protection for batsmen, especially since the unaesthetic helmet destroyed much of the game's individuality. The nasty accident sustained by his son Graham, facing Michael Holding in 1987, would only have accentu-ated his belief that action by the ICC was long overdue.

Again the West Indians, with their quartet of quick bowlers, and Pakistan proved less than amenable to restricting the number of bouncers an over, arguing that it gave undue protection to the bats-men. For a number of years they were able to block proposals before Cowdrey effected a breakthrough at the ICC in 1991 when a limit of one short-pitched ball an over was introduced for a three-year trial period. Infringements were to be penalised first by a no ball, then by a caution and lastly by a ban from bowling for the remainder of the innings. Cowdrey called it an end to the 'throat' ball, but it was not only the West Indians and Pakistanis who were unhappy with the ruling. In 1994 ICC extended the experiment for one more year, opting in 1995 for a limit of two short balls an over.

And then there was South Africa, the issue which more than any had inflamed passions in the ICC over the previous decade and exposed the stark divisions within the family of cricketing nations as their sport increasingly fell victim to raw politics. Once South Africa left the Commonwealth in 1961 they effectively signed their own death warrant as far as international cricket was concerned because at the time, in accordance with Rule 5 of the ICC, membership of its organisation ended should a country cease to be part of the British Commonwealth.

In 1977 the all-white South African cricket board dissolved itself in favour of a multiracial South African Cricket Union, and from then on big steps were taken towards integration within the sport. Unfortunately, this initiative occurred in the same year as the Gleneagles Declaration – under which sporting participation with South Africa had been outlawed – so that the politics of exclusion predominated over those of reconciliation, particularly since the majority of the ICC officially represented non-white countries much beholden to their governments. In 1986–87, when president of MCC, Cowdrey had fought hard to avert a major split as these countries tried to impose a ban on anyone playing or coaching in South Africa. His success was merely a holding operation, for in 1988 the England tour to India that winter was cancelled after the Indian government had refused to grant visas to Graham Gooch, the captain, and seven other cricketers who had cricket links with the Republic.

Increasingly shunned by the international community, the South Africans turned in desperation to financing rebel tours from England, Australia and West Indies during the 1980s in order to keep interest in the game alive and fund their cricket programme in the black townships. It was the second of these English tours under Mike Gatting, when the sixteen-strong party included Christopher, which confronted Cowdrey on taking up office at the ICC on 1 October 1989. The announcement of its existence two months earlier had caused a great outcry and one of Cowdrey's first tasks had been to write his son's name in the new register of players ineligible for international cricket. The tour in early 1990 proved to be a total failure as Gatting's men fell prey to the political tornado then engulfing South Africa which culminated in Nelson Mandela's release from imprisonment and the legalisation by F. W. de Klerk's government of the African National Congress.

The tour was ignominiously cancelled, but at once disaster turned to opportunity. For the SACU, sensing that there was much common ground to build on, looked to the ANC as a potential ally not only in legitimising the township programme but also in ending South Africa's long period in exile. With the committed support of one of Mandela's closest comrades, the sports-loving Steve Tshwete, who recognised the genuine developments towards integration so far, talks began between the two rival boards to create a new united non-racial one. Within three months an agreement had been reached in principle and the news was communicated to the ICC meeting in Melbourne in January 1991. Cowdrey, in a prepared statement, confirmed that a letter had been received from the presidents of the South African Cricket Union and Board recording their progress and that the ICC meeting had noted its contents. Beyond that, at this stage, he was not prepared to go. For whatever his own personal inclinations might have been towards South Africa, his position as head of an organisation where dislike of apartheid was deep-rooted, forced him to tread very carefully. He could, however, count on the support of Britain's new prime minister, John Major, a fervent cricket enthusiast and a great admirer, ever since as a teenager he listened to Cowdrey's record-breaking stand with May in 1957.

Apart from sharing a similar outlook on life, their mutual love of the game and desire to see sport triumph over politics brought them together, and they soon developed a close friendship. Major recalls that rarely an encounter goes by when they don't try to outwit each other with searching questions about the game. Much more than most cricketers, Cowdrey has always had a deep appreciation of cricket's history and is well acquainted with its intricate details, but

216

was stumped when Major asked him which great author had taken one first-class wicket. The answer was Sir Arthur Conan Doyle and his victim, surprisingly enough, was W. G. Grace.

Believing that the time was now ripe for South Africa to return to Test cricket, Major raised the matter with Commonwealth leaders, and, according to Cowdrey, was brilliant at opening doors to progress when previously they had remained closed and bolted. In May 1991, Ali Bacher, managing director of the newly formed United Cricket Board of South Africa, accompanied by Steve Tshwete, went to England to lobby for South Africa's return to the ICC. The response was much warmer than any Bacher had previously experienced. Cowdrey met him at the airport and they received encouraging noises from the High Commissioners of the Caribbean states and from Sri Lanka, all clearly impressed by the warm breezes of change blowing through South Africa. Their cause was further enhanced by the celebrations in Johannesburg a month later to mark the official formation of the United Cricket Board of South Africa (UCBSA), with Sir Garfield Sobers and Sunil Gavaskar among the illustrious guests. In a meeting with Gavaskar and Indian journalists at his Soweto residence, Mandela indicated his desire to see South Africa's return to world cricket, a significant intervention which was conveyed back to the Indian government. When the final apartheid restrictions were lifted on 28 June, the stage was now clear for a historic breakthrough at the forthcoming ICC meeting at Lord's, provided that reservations from the West Indies were overcome.

Their opposition at this point stemmed as much from procedure as principle; they felt that South Africa's readmission was being rushed through without going through the proper channels. They argued that it wasn't on the agenda from the previous ICC meeting but Cowdrey ruled that they should be heard. Keen to do his bit to resolve these tensions, Major invited all the ICC delegates and their wives to Downing Street to a pre-conference reception at which both he and Cowdrey addressed them from a table in the main reception room. Having welcomed his guests, Major spoke of cricket's appeal as a unifying force among nations and his hope that South Africa's spell in exile would soon be over. The next day it seemed that his words had failed to stir the sceptics as West Indies, in particular,

remained unmoved. It needed some arduous pre-conference negoti-
ations, which left Cowdrey at times close to despair, before he and
John Stephenson managed to persuade the West Indians to abstain
on the issue rather than vote against. Their retreat was a very reluctant one, but it was enough to allow matters to proceed without a
hitch. On 10 July a motion to readmit South Africa to the ICC,
proposed by India and seconded by Australia, was carried unanimously by the twenty-six members who actually voted. Cowdrey
announced the news in a written statement from the Lord's pavilion, and as the South African mixed delegation celebrated with
unrestrained joy, he contacted their High Commissioner in London.
'You wouldn't believe it,' he said. 'We've had a breakthrough.' Later
that evening he attended, on Cowdrey's invitation, a drinks party at
John and Caren Stephenson's for all ICC delegates and their wives.
Then after a dinner hosted by MCC at Lord's, Cowdrey and
Stephenson took a taxi to Downing Street where they celebrated the
day's historic breakthrough with the Prime Minister over a glass of
beer. All three had cause for great satisfaction. 'Cowdrey's ambas-
sadorial role has been influential in the acknowledgment of South
Africa's advances by countries who could not, until recently, have
contemplated yesterday's events,' wrote Alan Lee, the *Times* cricket
correspondent, the next day. 'His work on the matter has been
considered, yet always discreet.'

Following the heady atmosphere of the night before, the celebrations gave way to a hangover on the morning after when the ICC
resumed their deliberations. With South Africa now back in the
international fold, delegates were exercised by the question of
whether they should participate in the World Cup due to take place
in Australia and New Zealand the following February. The two host
countries, aware of South Africa's marketing value, were keen to
admit them and were unhappy about Cowdrey using his preroga-
tive powers as chairman to prevent any discussion of their participation. His rationale was twofold. First, with all the arrangements
already in place, Cowdrey thought that it was not practical to
include them. Second and more important, he was loathe to alien-
ate those countries such as West Indies and Pakistan who still
needed further proof of South Africa's renaissance before giving

them a further seal of approval. Cowdrey however hadn't reckoned on the determination of Malcolm Gray, Chairman of both the Australian Cricket Board and the World Cup sub-committee and a shrewd businessman, to achieve his goal. A meeting of the World Cup sub-committee took place in late August in Melbourne in the presence of John Stephenson which ruled that South Africa could still participate provided that the formalities were concluded by mid-October. The West Indian Board remained resolutely opposed to South Africa's inclusion at their annual meeting in September, and Pakistan thought along similar lines although the same couldn't be said of India. More important was the attitude of Nelson Mandela. He gave Cowdrey much food for thought when he wrote to him in late September supporting South Africa's admission to the World Cup. Not only did the cricket-loving leader of the ANC wish to reward the cricketers for the steps taken towards racial integration, he felt that participation in the World Cup would help the reconciliation process in the country.

Appraised of Mandela's views, Cowdrey made endless telephone calls and went to South Africa to meet officials before calling an emergency ICC meeting in Sharjah on 23 October. Thirty-six hours earlier the Commonwealth Conference had met in Harare and had not only endorsed South Africa's return to international sport, but had expressed the hope that they would appear in the World Cup. Before he left for Sharjah, Cowdrey agreed that the Commonwealth had clearly marked the ICC card, especially now that Pakistan had changed its mind. The meeting, despite the West Indies' lingering reluctance, was unanimous and Cowdrey informed the jubilant South African delegation of the verdict. Their rehabilitation was now well and truly complete. In 1994 the South Africans made their first tour of England for twenty-nine years, and it must have given Cowdrey immense satisfaction to organise Test match tickets for his old friend, David Sheppard, by then Bishop of Liverpool, whose stance on the apartheid issue had been markedly different from his own.

South Africa was not the only country under the spotlight during Cowdrey's chairmanship, since Zimbabwe were pressing for full

219

member status in the ICC and the opportunity to play Test cricket. In 1989 the ICC had deferred a decision for five years, during which Zimbabwe's performances in a series of 'A' tours with all the major cricket countries would be closely scrutinised. The return of South Africa from the wilderness gave added urgency to the situation and at that same meeting in 1991, the ICC agreed to consider Zimbabwe's full membership two years earlier than originally planned. With a lack of depth in their first-class cricket, particularly among the majority black population, and scarce financial resources, the case for entry seemed tenuous. At the same time, Zimbabwe, who as Rhodesia used to play in South Africa's Currie Cup, was by some way the strongest of the associated members, on a par with Sri Lanka when that country had gained entry to ICC a decade earlier. Just when the World Cup was taking the game to the far corners of Africa and Asia, an invitation to partake at the top table would carry an enormous symbolic significance. Now that South Africa's readmission was imminent, this was the moment of no return. Continued rejection would encourage Zimbabwe's most talented performers to move south across the Limpopo, reducing their resources to a trickle.

When these arguments – supported by Cowdrey – were aired at the ICC in 1992 they received a sympathetic hearing from everyone except England, who ironically had just lost to Zimbabwe in the World Cup. Their concern was that they stood to lose substantial revenue from sponsorship and television because of Zimbabwean cricket's limited appeal, but they eventually saw the larger picture and fell in with the general view. The decision at first seemed a foolhardy one, as Zimbabwe had looked out of their depth in the international arena; but recently their game has undergone a significant improvement. Provided that current threats to white property owners in Zimbabwe do not lead to a massive exodus by this important section of the cricketing population, the outlook for further progress looks encouraging.

*

No sooner had the South African question been settled than Cowdrey had his hands full with another of the spats which developed periodically between England and Pakistan. Because of the bad blood between the two countries, stretching back over the previous decade, the Pakistan tour of England in 1992 under their controversial captain Javed Miandad, was always going to be a frayed affair. Sadly the worst forebodings of the doom-mongers were amply vindicated. After a rain-ruined first Test, and a classic second Test at Lord's when Pakistan won by the narrowest of margins, trouble flared at Old Trafford when Aqib Javed, the visitors' volatile young quick bowler, peppered England's no. 11, Devon Malcolm, with a series of bouncers. Warned by umpire Roy Palmer for intimidating bowling, Aqib became abusive and was supported by his captain in an unseemly exchange of inflammatory gestures.

The Pakistan behaviour was universally condemned, and Aqib was fined half his match fee by the international referee, Conrad Hunte, deputising for Clyde Walcott, who had been called to Lord's for an ICC meeting. Hunte, however, managed to infuriate England's captain, Graham Gooch, with a statement reminding both captains of their obligation to the game's true spirit, the implication being that England were just as culpable as Pakistan for the histrionics. With feeling remaining high after the Pakistan manager, Intikhab Alam, publicly criticised Roy Palmer, Cowdrey had his work cut out. Unhappy with Pakistan's antics, he had discussions with their officials at Chester-le-Street during their match with Durham. Then, after a fractious meeting between the respective sides before the Headingley Test, Cowdrey urged both captains to bind up old wounds and start again.

His words fell on deaf ears. Another ill-tempered Test, in which Pakistan took exception to some dubious umpiring decisions, saw England winning by six wickets. Their joy, however, proved ephemeral. Awesome swing bowling by Wasim Akram and Waqar Younis in the final Test at The Oval gave the visitors an easy victory and the series two-one. All Gooch's men could hope for now was to win the one-day Texaco Trophy, which resumed from earlier in the summer with England already two up. Much now depended on the third match at Lord's on 22 August. Bad weather forced the match into a second day when England, chasing 204 for victory, reached 140 for five at lunch. At the crease was Alan Lamb who, just before the interval, picked up the ball and showed it to umpire Ken Palmer. On

221

one side there were big scuff marks caused, in Lamb's eyes, by tampering by Wasim Akram and Waqar Younis, who had suddenly begun to swing the ball prodigiously.

This practice of roughing up the ball so that bowlers could obtain greater movement had become a cause of sufficient concern in the county game for the TCCB in 1990 to increase the umpire's powers with respect to Law 42 – Unfair Play: Changing the Condition of the Ball. Thereafter several cases of suspected ball-tampering between 1990 and 1992, which led to Surrey, Waqar's team, being fined £1000, and alleged malpractice in the Pakistan–New Zealand series of 1990–91, fuelled rumours in the English dressing-room during the summer of 1992. Their suspicions were only accentuated by the way their middle and lower order continued to be blown away by an old ball which uncannily began to swing more sharply as the innings progressed.

At lunch in the Lord's match Lamb told Micky Stewart, the manager, of his suspicions. Stewart went to see the umpires and they changed the ball on the approval of the match referee, Deryck Murray, the former West Indian wicket-keeper. This change was later made public, but on Murray's insistence the reasons for it were not, leaving John Stephenson in an impossible situation as the players' version of events leaked to the press box. As rumours of ball-tampering and an official cover-up flew around Lord's that evening, Stephenson found that he could not reveal the real reason why drastic action had been taken because that would have let down the match referee. After several days of stalling and consultation, he exposed himself to public derision by issuing a statement refusing to explain why the ball had been changed, claiming that umpire's reports were alway confidential. The next day Lamb stirred the pot further by going public with his allegations about ball-tampering in the *Daily Mirror*, which landed him with a heavy fine.

While all this drama was being played out, Cowdrey was in India and out of reach when Stephenson tried to get hold of him. When they did make contact he agreed that, following legal advice, there should be no comment on the match referee's report. In his book *Tampering With Cricket*, Jack Bannister recalls how Cowdrey, on his

222

return home on 1 September, found the report of Don Oslear, the reserve umpire at the match, awaiting him. Having read it, he invited Oslear to stay at Angmering, where they talked about it for hours. Cowdrey was deeply troubled by the affair, and wanted to get everything into the open. On 10 September he spoke to most of the ICC representatives and was particularly heartened by support from Ali Bacher, and the next day Oslear, in his role as chairman of the first-class umpires, assured him of their support.

He was all set to make a statement but was frustrated by lawyers who feared the legal consequences. For even though the umpires would confirm why they changed the ball, a court of law would require proof. Cowdrey's predicament was that Murray's unilateral backtracking on the day, when a misreading of the Texaco Trophy playing conditions gave Pakistan a substitute ball of equal rather than inferior quality, had handed ammunition to the Pakistani management they might not otherwise have had. Given these uncertainties and the high costs likely to accrue from court proceedings, should their views be challenged, Cowdrey and Stephenson decided that refraining from saying anything of substance was the wisest course to take. All Cowdrey did allow himself was an anodyne statement on 10 October affirming his intention to stamp out ball-tampering in future, with no reference to past misdemeanours. His hopes might have seemed somewhat far-fetched at the time but the introduction, at Cowdrey's last ICC conference in July 1993, of the third umpire as an extra pair of eyes, and the new rule requiring the ball to be returned to the umpire at the end of each over, have gone a long way towards achieving them.

There was more trouble with the subcontinent when the ICC met at Lord's in February 1993 to determine the location of the next World Cup. It was only five years before this that India and Pakistan had proved their detractors wrong with their successful staging of the Cup, and had benefited accordingly. With Australia and New Zealand having derived similar financial rewards in 1992, the quest to host such a prestigious event intensified, leading to an ill-tempered showdown at Lord's. The venues of previous World Cups had been decided in accordance with the principle of a binding resolution requiring a simple majority of all ICC members, with each of the associate members having one vote and the nine Test-playing countries having two.

At the time of Australia's award of the previous competition, it was felt that the destination of the World Cup should not simply be in the hands of the associate members *en bloc*. The rules were therefore amended in 1989, without any dissension, so that any future decision needed the support of a two-thirds majority of members and one of the founder members. Under this scheme, the Indian hopes of winning over the full members for their bid seemed to have been scuppered. They were in no mood, however, to abide by the time-honoured traditions of the ICC. Their delegation, under Madhavrao Scindia, a former Minister for Civic Aviation and Tourism, and Jagmohan Dalmiya, the President of the Indian Cricket Board, betraying a strong political agenda, looked to shift the balance of power within the organisation towards the developing world. With government resources behind their bid, they held out the attraction of more money from the competition to the other Asian ICC countries should India and Pakistan be granted the World Cup.

Lured by this promise, Sri Lanka and Zimbabwe lined up behind India and Pakistan, thereby preventing the England bid from gaining the necessary two-thirds majority among Test-playing countries. When the Indians tried to get a simple majority verdict of all those present, Cowdrey, advised by John Stephenson, insisted on sticking to the previously agreed formula, since under the constitution such a vote only had the force of a recommendation. His reward for his pains was a vitriolic outburst from Scindia, who accused him of abusing his position to England's advantage.

With the meeting becoming increasingly fractious as the Indians sought frequent adjournments to seek the support of the Indian High Chief Justice in Delhi for their legal position, the day's procedural wrangling took its toll on Cowdrey. Michael Melluish recalls him becoming so exhausted that Clyde Walcott took the chair for the final session. In the end, after thirteen hours of unpleasant wrangling, Walcott helped persuade the English representatives, in the wider interests of the game, to back down on the express condition that they would have the right to host the 1999 World Cup. Recalling the meeting as 'rather fierce and very tough', Cowdrey felt that the old spirit of trust had been violated and there were lessons to be learnt for future meetings.

When Cowdrey had taken over as chairman in 1989, it had been widely recognised that the ICC should evolve away from the patrician clutches of the MCC, who lacked the time and resources to deal with the increasingly global agenda of the modern game. It said much for Cowdrey, John Stephenson and his assistant Stephanie Lawrence, that they coped as effectively as they did with the countless demands placed upon them. 'What Cowdrey's role as a roving ambassador illustrated,' declared Graeme Wright, 'was the way an international body could function given finance and organisation.'

In February 1993 a major step was taken towards creating a more administrative ICC with the appointment of Dave Richards, of the Australian Cricket Board, as chief executive to do professionally what Cowdrey had done as an unpaid amateur. When England and Australia, in response to pressure from other countries, agreed to give up their ICC veto in August 1993 and Clyde Walcott was appointed as Cowdrey's successor, a major watershed in the game's evolution had been reached. As MCC finally relinquished their control over the game to the international community, Cowdrey could look back at his tenure at the ICC with considerable satisfaction. Not only was South Africa back in international cricket and Zimbabwe in, but the new system of neutral umpires and match referees was beginning to curb the worst excesses of misbehaviour on the field, even though much still needed to be done. 'He has never been the type,' commented Alan Lee, 'to bang the table in order to make a point. Bristling dogma is not a Cowdrey trait, nor, some would say, is decisiveness. If this led to occasional dissatisfaction over the handling of the most basic point of the job – chairing the annual meeting – it was more than compensated for by his broader, less obvious input as a global ambassador for the good and progressive things in cricket.'

'Often referred to as indecisive,' wrote Jack Bannister, 'the first ICC chairman to hold office over four years accomplished as much for the game in that period as he did as one of the most elegant batsmen of his time.' It had been an unpaid labour of love, but his efforts and achievements had not gone unnoticed in Downing Street.

26

Pavilioned in Splendour

After the trauma of his failed marriage, Cowdrey's new life in the West Sussex countryside has been an oasis of tranquillity. When the sixteenth Duke died in 1975, his estate was divided between his wife, Lavinia, and his cousin, Miles, the heir to the title, with the former inheriting the stables and gallops at Angmering. On her demise, they passed to Lady Anne Herries, her eldest daughter. According to Paul Normand, sometime agent to the Duke of Norfolk, Cowdrey knows a lot about the estate and plays an important part in its upkeep. With dogs invariably in tow, he has taken to the life of a country gentleman as he indulges in a little shooting in the winter or potters up to the gallops to watch the horses exercise. Never a racing enthusiast by upbringing, he has come to take an interest in the sport and follows Anne's success with justifiable pride. She is an accomplished trainer whose burgeoning stud at Angmering has turned out some prize fillies, the pick of which has been Celtic Swing, who won the French Derby, and Taufan's Melody, who in 1998 became the first overseas horse for 122 years to win Melbourne's prestigious Caulfield Cup.

In the midst of Angmering Park there stands the Cowdrey home, a delightful manor house converted out of two former cottages, which is comfortable without being aggressively grand. At either end of the house Anne and Colin have their respective studies, Colin's adorned with cricketing portraits and photographs, and housing a set of *Wisden*. Here too he has his television, which enables him to follow cricket through summer and winter, thinking nothing of rising early (he is a poor sleeper) to watch the final session live from Australia.

Like Penny, Anne is quiet and shy, with little time for formal gatherings, but she can sparkle in select company, particularly when the conversation turns to racing. She is also a consummate hostess, either at a formal black-tie dinner or at more casual house parties, when fine wines and good homely food abound. She is also very good with Colin's children and they appreciate the care she takes with their own children when they come to visit. A further bond has come through Graham's wife Maxine's love of horses, which had much to do with her move to Angmering in 1993 to become assistant trainer to Anne.

It is a measure of Colin and Anne's secure relationship that they get on so well, despite leading very different lives. With no interest in the game, and preoccupied with her own equestrian pursuits, Anne leaves Colin to his cricket, rarely attending any of his engagements. If in need of female company he tends to lean on his daughter, Carol, who with her ebullient personality is adept at helping her reticent father through some of the more laborious small talk. A popular figure in her own right, as well as being an excellent tennis player, Carol has learnt to cope with being the only girl in a cricket-loving household and has unfailingly supported her brothers through all weathers. All four children remain in close contact with their mother and ensure that she is not neglected, while Penny, for her part, does sterling work in looking after her eight grandchildren. Day-to-day practicalities were never Colin's forté but he is kindness personified with them and he remains very much on call whenever his children need a helping hand. In 1997 he was invaluable to Graham and his benefit not only by gracing a number of events with his presence, but appearing also with Christopher and Graham on a special family video to look back on their careers with Cliff Morgan, the radio sports presenter. It made for compelling viewing as all three Cowdreys spoke openly and engagingly about their various triumphs and setbacks.

One problem which Cowdrey has increasingly had to contend with has been poor health. There was his serious heart by-pass operation in 1987 and painful attacks of gout now restrict his appearances on the golf course. He has also sufered a number of chest infections which have kept him under close medical supervision. Their origins date back to childhood when, as a fourteen-year-old on holiday in Croydon, he suffered a severe attack of pneumonia which at one point was thought to be life-threatening. He recovered quickly enough, but the illness returned to haunt him in June 1971, abruptly terminating his cricketing activities for the summer. His more recent troubles date from October 1991, after he developed a chill during a shoot close to home, which saw him spend time in hospital after returning from ICC business in Sharjah. Two months later, just before Christmas, when Christopher and his wife Christel were visiting him at Angmering, he suffered a relapse, prompting a speedy readmission to hospital. Christopher recalls driving his father to the intensive care unit at King Edward VII Hospital in Midhurst, over half an hour's drive away, and relying on him for directions. Little was said *en route*. Eventually, following Colin's instructions, they turned down a small country lane which Christopher desperately hoped would lead to the hospital. To his dismay it led instead to the private grounds of Lord Cowdray (no relation). 'I just wanted to show you this beautiful drive,' declared Colin. 'It's the most lovely picture of England. Don't worry,' he reassured his flabbergasted son and daughter-in-law, 'it's only a few minutes out of the way.'

Cowdrey remained in hospital over Christmas and New Year. On New Year's Eve he telephoned John Stephenson, requesting him to get the press off the backs of the hospital. News had leaked out that he was to receive a knighthood, making him the thirteenth cricketer in history and the ninth English player to be so honoured. 'It could well be argued,' wrote E. W. Swanton, 'that the breadth of his service to cricket can have been exceeded only by Sir George Allen and Sir Pelham Warner.' 'No one of Cowdrey's generation,' commented John Woodcock, 'has championed more devoutly the ethos of the game.'

Another honour came his way in August 1992, when in the presence of his eighty-nine-year-old mother (she died in 1997) he saw the North Stand at Canterbury, originally built in 1986, renamed the Colin Cowdrey Stand by his good friend Robin Leigh-Pemberton, the lord lieutenant of Kent.

In October 1993 Cowdrey relinquished his chairmanship of the ICC, but his service to cricket had by no means ended. Apart from joining the new ICC sub-committee of former top-class players to give advice on complex cricketing matters, he continued to be a conscientious president of the Umpires Association, a post he had inherited from 'Gubby' Allen on his death in 1989. He also took on a second five-year spell as Chairman of the MCC Cricket Committee, proving more active in the job than his predecessor, Peter May. This committee retains responsibility for the laws of cricket, and with declining standards still a problem Cowdrey's main priority for the game was to root out the bad soil and plant seeds of hope. In a document due out in 1999 called 'The Spirit of the Game', and produced largely as a result of his own efforts, the emphasis is not only on supporting umpires against all forms of abuse, but on firmly restoring the authority of the captain and charging him with the responsibility of setting the right tone for the way in which a match is played. The document is very much a personal mission statement, and if its principles help restore cricket's tarnished image in certain quarters Cowdrey will have performed another valuable service to the game.

In September 1994 Cowdrey teamed up with Rob Andrew, the rugby player, Bobby Charlton, the sometime World Cup footballer, Judy Simpson, the Olympic athlete, and Alec Stewart, the Surrey and England cricketer, to accompany John Major on a tour of South Africa. The prime minister addressed both houses of Parliament and, in one of the most successful trips of his premiership, he presented Nelson Mandela with a bat autographed by both the England and South African teams. At a reception hosted by Mandela, Cowdrey overheard the South African president ask one of the sixty-strong English delegation where Colin Cowdrey was, afraid that he might miss the opportunity of meeting him. It was then that Cowdrey was introduced to him, thus beginning a cordial relationship which has seen him put Mandela in touch with Sir Donald Bradman. After the political formalities, Major moved on to Alexandra township, where he and Cowdrey launched a major sporting initiative designed to promote coaching. Touring the local Oval, which had been trans-formed from a rubbish dump with British funds, the prime minister rolled up his sleeves and bowled Steve Tshwete, South Africa's Minister of Sport, first ball.

Buoyed by his trip to South Africa, Cowdrey returned to be

presented with a new challenge. The Lord's Taverners charity had been founded in 1950 by a group of actors with a love of cricket, keen to put something back into the game. With a host of celebrities from the world of sport and entertainment to the fore, the charity has developed an ever higher profile over the years with a mixture of cricket matches, dinners and galas and other fundraising activities. In addition to a chairman in charge of the eighteen elected trustees and a chief executive known as the director to oversee the day-to-day business, it has a president appointed as a figurehead. Throughout the 1990s they were fortunate with their presidents, with Tim Rice, Leslie Crowther and Prince Edward all serving with distinction. When the question of the Prince's successor loomed, Brian Baldock, the chairman, and Patrick Shervington, the director, decided it was time for a prominent cricketer to be appointed. Their choice fell on Cowdrey, already a former chairman of the charity's City of London region. His acceptance was endorsed by The Duke of Edinburgh as Patron and Twelfth Man and Prince Edward, and announced to public acclaim.

'What wonderful news that Colin Cowdrey is to be the new President of the Lord's Taverners,' wrote Ben Brocklehurst, the Managing Director of *The Cricketer* magazine in a letter to Shervington. 'When he was President of MCC he came up to the Lord's Taverners Cricketer Colts Trophy at Trent Bridge. When the President of Nottinghamshire, as is his wont, asked us all up to his box for drinks, Colin was nowhere to be found. He was later discovered huddled with one of the teams on a bench as if he was a member of their side. The boys as you can imagine were absolutely thrilled and he made a lasting impression on them.'

Cowdrey began his presidency by writing to many former colleagues who belonged to the Taverners, requesting their attendance at as many functions as possible. He himself led by example, and when he could not be present he sent one of his 'night watchmen', such as Ted Dexter, Tom Graveney or Godfrey Evans, who proved to be very able deputies. Nothing was too much trouble. A stickler for detail, Cowdrey liked to know everything there was to know about his hosts, other likely guests and sponsors. Long dinners could visibly tire him, but whatever the strains of sustaining general conversation he could rouse himself for his key speech, which was invariably polished. So respected was he in his role that his tenure was extended by a year. There were also the personal acts of kindness. Patrick Shervington recalls being telephoned by the cricket master at one school and told how one of the boys in the eleven was extremely depressed. His one abiding love was cricket, and when Shervington appraised Cowdrey of the situation, he wrote a charming letter to the boy and his parents, enclosing a copy of his autobiography. The gesture worked wonders, and once the boy had recovered he sent Cowdrey a grateful note of thanks. Another generous touch was inviting all the Taverners staff down to Angmering and presenting Shervington with a print of Bryan Organ's portrait of him – only thirty were made – in gratitude for all his support.

Cowdrey's appreciation of Shervington was apparently not shared by others because in 1997 he was suddenly and unaccountably dismissed. The news appalled Cowdrey, who organised a meeting of all the past Taverners' presidents to find out why the trustees and their new chairman, over whom he had no control, had come to such a decision. The ruse of redundancy was never satisfactorily explained and for the last several months of Cowdrey's presidency the charity was in a state of turmoil. Although after some agonising he resisted the temptation to resign, an example set by former president Lord Rix and Leslie Crowther's widow, Jean, his harmonious association with the Taverners ended in unfortunate circumstances.

During his time with the Taverners he remained active on other fronts as his relationship with John Major continued to prosper. For some time they had both been so concerned about the lack of opportunity for team sports in so many of Britain's schools that they agreed that something would have to be done. It was thus that the prime minister announced at the 1996 Conservative Party conference that Cowdrey (who was in the audience) would lead a team of sporting ambassadors to promote more competitive sport in schools. The cause was a commendable one, but its genesis coincided with the dying fall of the Major government. On 1 May 1997, Cowdrey's great friend was heavily defeated in the general election, and although the scheme continued under new management, the commitment to it seemed tame in comparison, leading to an amicable parting of the ways between Cowdrey and his new masters. That was not the end, however, of his quasi-political role, for in June, in the Queen's Birthday Honours list, he became the first British life peer enobled exclusively for his contribution to sport, and the first cricketing peer since Learie Constantine in 1969. Rory Bremner (who does a brilliant impersonation of Cowdrey) recalls having dinner with him at Angmering on the night the announcement was made. The phone never stopped ringing, and each time he returned from taking a call he would refer to irreverent mickey-takers before changing the subject.

The news certainly astounded many, causing some consternation either among those who felt that he had already been adequately rewarded, or those who objected to cricketers being installed in the House of Lords. What many failed to recognise was that the 1958 Life Peerages Act enabled the Lords to be represented by people from all walks of life with a view to providing expertise on a whole range of issues. The fact that sport had been broadly neglected throughout this time, to the obvious detriment of team games in schools, was a deficiency which needed rectifying and Cowdrey, with a life of service in cricket, was as eminently qualified as anyone to act as a standard-bearer.

On 26 November 1997, with John Major watching, a nervous Cowdrey rose from the Conservative benches to make his maiden speech in the Lord's. Not surprisingly it was an impassioned plea for more sport in schools since sport, Cowdrey contended, helped to restore the troublesome fringe to the straight and narrow. His speech impressed Lord Runcie, the former Archbishop of Canterbury, who was surprised by its power and confidence, while John Major was ecstatic. 'Wonderful,' he wrote to Cowdrey. 'A debut century that had class written all over it.' The letter was framed and remains one of Cowdrey's prize possessions in his study at Angmering.

Since then Cowdrey has taken his new responsibilities very seriously, commuting up from Sussex most days when the Lords are sitting. He likes the stately ambience of the place, is a regular attender at prayers, and rarely misses a vote.

Away from Westminster, Cowdrey continues to be active on the public stage, going to speech day at Tonbridge, Canterbury Week and Lord's, where he is now one of the three trustees of the MCC. He is an assiduous attender at funerals of former friends or team-mates, and remains a sought-after speaker, not least in Australia where the special rapport established by his six tours continues to hold good. In October 1998 he held a large audience at the Melbourne Cricket Ground spellbound as he recalled some of those special moments of his cricket career and took issue against contemporary blights such as 'sledging', boorishness and financial greed. These opinions are strongly held, but they do not diminish the deep affection Colin Cowdrey continues to harbour for the game, an affection which first caused a little boy to dream dreams on an Indian hillside over sixty years ago.

Epilogue
The Last Roman

From the manner in which he batted to the way he conducted himself, Colin Cowdrey appeared to be the model of orthodoxy, his modest demeanour and his attention to form in line with his austere upbringing. As a child of the Empire and as a Christian gentleman with a reverence for its institutions, there has always been something reassuredly British about Cowdrey. Had he not become a cricketer, he would have excelled as a public schoolmaster or a cleric, in a life which combined order and discipline with a concern for others. The choice, in reality, barely existed, because as the famous initials implied Cowdrey was destined for a life of cricketing eminence. Imbued with a deep love of the game from an early age, his supreme gifts set him out from the crowd. At Tonbridge, a boy broke into a man's world and conquered by sheer weight of runs and wickets, a prelude to his cult status at Oxford and for Kent and England, when he remained the prize scalp for any opposition. His aura of mystique was compounded by a reclusive personality and, although he could cope well with public formalities, he was never fully at ease with his fellow players, especially at enforced socialising. His character remained elusive and the paradoxes in his career, not least the periodic uncertainties in his batting and captaincy, remain largely unexplained.

There is no doubting that Cowdrey was a consummate batsman who, technically, could cope with all types of bowlers on all kinds of wickets better than any post-war England batsman, with the exception of May. 'On his day,' remarked Tony Lewis, 'he could be cruelly destructive without jerking a single muscle – a beautiful but fruitful exercise.' A quick glance at his record – 42,719 runs, 7,624 in Tests (average 44.06), and 107 first-class centuries – would go far to support this. The fact that he was such a leading force in cricket for twenty-five years is a testament to his fitness which, despite a number of setbacks, most notably in the summers of 1963, 1969 and 1971, remained impressive for a man of heavy gait. It is also a tribute to his enthusiasm and dedication. In a television interview in 1998 he recalled meeting Sir Jack Hobbs at The Oval in August 1956 during the Test against Australia. At the end of a long conversation about the game on the pavilion balcony, Hobbs hit him firmly on the knee and said, 'You've had a good season, but each year mull over the weaknesses and rectify them by April. Each year keep ahead of the game.' It was advice he never forgot. Years later, in Australia, Jack Simmons recalls his surprise when Cowdrey, a veteran of over a hundred Tests, went to a position behind the bowler's arm to watch Ian Redpath play the short ball, thinking he could learn from the experience. The fact that Cowdrey continued to be a prolific batsman for Kent in his later years, and was recalled to the England side at forty-two, suggests that his efforts were not in vain.

Any quibbles about his outstanding record, which would stand comparison with any batsman in any era, would surely centre on two main deficiencies. First, his increasing tendency to become prone to introspection, so that his batting lacked the will to dominate. 'The proudest thing for me in my career was that I kept surviving,' Cowdrey is quoted as saying in Pat Murphy's *The Centurions*. It seems a curious self-assessment from someone of his ability, for although the changing nature of the game made batting a more prosaic business, he was surely a great enough player – like Dexter – to defy the spirit of the age, rather than to be conquered by it. Second, his record against Australia, which compared to his princely average of 51.50 against West Indies, was a modest 34.26, with four home series yielding only one century and four half-centuries in twenty-seven innings. This inability to perform at his best in the game's toughest arena was one reason why England failed to hold the Ashes throughout the 1960s when he was at his peak. In contrast, among his contemporaries, Barrington averaged 63.97 against Australia, Edrich 48.96, Boycott 47.50, May 46.06 and Dexter 38.80. In fairness to

Cowdrey, none of the others, except May, had his rough baptism at the beginning of his career against Lindwall and Miller. Further, only Edrich among them endured Lillee and Thomson at their most ferocious in 1974–75 when Cowdrey's best days were behind him. Equally, some of the Australian attacks during the 1960s lacked real bite, and they must have felt that against someone of Cowdrey's pedigree they got off rather lightly.

Cowdrey's instinct for survival seemed more appropriate when applied to his captaincy. Only Close at Yorkshire came close to emulating his fifteen years in charge of Kent, which maade him the longest-serving post-war county captain. Some, such as May, Dexter or Illingworth, captained England in more Tests, but no one over such a long time-span. The reasons he never made the crown his own by right, which shattered his dream of captaining in Australia, have been documented in this book. Some of them relate to the absence of a natural assertiveness, essential to great leadership; but if he lacked this fundamental quality his tactical insight and benign paternalism went some way towards compensating. Indeed, judged by his record for both Kent and England, his captaincy merits greater praise than has often been given. At Kent, little went right in the first few years as Cowdrey inherited a side shorn of depth, particularly in its bowling, but gradually, in partnership with Ames, his patience paid off. By 1963 they had turned the corner and thereafter a team of young cubs, inspired by Cowdrey's guidance, grew steadily into a pride of prowling lions able to devour all-comers. When he handed over to Denness in 1971, the outlook could not have been brighter. Before the decade was out, Kent had won the county championship three times (once shared), the Benson and Hedges Cup three times, the John Player League three times, and the Gillette Cup once, not to mention experiencing a number of other near misses.

Cowdrey's growing success at Kent enhanced his confidence, and by the time he returned to the England captaincy at the end of the 1960s, he looked more at ease in the role. His triumph in the West Indies in 1967–68 gave him greater confidence, and if still rather too defensive on occasions, notably against Australia at Old Trafford in 1968, he did enough in that series thereafter to win back the Ashes. Three times bad weather intervened when England were in the ascendancy, but having been frustrated twice, he won through with Underwood's bowling at The Oval as the minutes ticked by. Had fate not intervened in May 1969, the chances are that Cowdrey would have gone on to even greater things, including the likelihood of winning in Australia in 1970-71. As it was, his record of eight victories and only four defeats in twenty-seven Tests as captain, although not in the league of Hutton, May, Illingworth or Brearley, compared more than favourably with his contemporaries, Dexter and Smith, and greatly exceeded that of more recent incumbents such as Willis, Botham, Gooch, Gatting, Gower and Atherton. While it is undeniable that teams such as India, Pakistan and New Zealand now provide much stiffer oppposition than in Cowdrey's day, we should not forget that ten of his twenty-seven Tests in charge were against West Indies when Sobers was in his prime. The fact that only two England sides have ever won in the Caribbean, and that both were under Cowdrey for all or part of that time, is an achievement which speaks for itself.

It says much for Cowdrey's love of the game and his keen ambition that even after all the troubles afflicting his captaincy he continued to hanker after high office. Although still a conciliator rather than a confrontationalist by temperament, he marked his time as an administrator with a decisiveness not always evident hitherto. Nobody, least of all he, would look back at the events surrounding his presidency of the MCC with pleasure, but Cowdrey's willingness to lay down the law did at last go some way towards restoring sanity within cricket's tottering edifice.

Two years after this, and following his heart operation, he returned to the fray, this time as the first elected chairman of the newly constituted ICC. As the game became increasingly influenced by finance and professionalism, the old conventions were no longer adequate to deal with player power. It is much to Cowdrey's credit that he overcame the traditional faction-ridden inertia of the ICC and made it a much more effective body in addressing fundamental flaws, most notably the erosion of standards on the field. It is a battle still to be finally won, and until it is won Cowdrey will not cease from mental fight. His homilies to this effect play well with the large audiences he still attracts throughout the world. A number of them, seeing him from a distance, may not appreciate that the debonair charm and old-world finesse mask a complex personality with a more turbulent history than first meets the eye. That Colin Cowdrey has triumphed over so many doubts and setbacks is testament to his fortitude which, in conjunction with his manifold talent, places him among the cricketing giants of the twentieth century, the like of which we will not see again.

LORD COWDREY OF TONBRIDGE
his career in facts and figures

A STATISTICAL APPENDIX BY PAUL E. DYSON
Brief Chronology and Highlights

24 December 1932: Born Putumala, Ootacamund, India

29 July 1946: Made first appearance at Lord's – Tonbridge v Clifton

19 August 1950: First-class début – Kent v Derbyshire, Derby

2 June 1951: Scored maiden first-class century – 143, Free Foresters v Oxford University, The Parks

6 August 1951: Awarded Kent county cap

1953: Elected Best Young Cricketer of the Year

26 November 1954: Test match début – England v Australia, Brisbane

31 December 1954: Scored first Test match century – 102, England v Australia, Melbourne

1955: Elected one of *Wisden*'s Five Cricketers of the Year

20 August 1956: Passed 10,000 runs in first-class cricket – Kent v Cheltenham

1957: Appointed Kent county captain

23 July 1959: Took the field for the first time as England captain – v India, Old Trafford

10 May 1961: Passed 20,000 runs in first-class cricket – Kent v Derbyshire, Derby

16 August 1962: Made highest Test innings – 182, England v Pakistan, The Oval

24 December 1962: Completed highest first-class innings – 307, MCC v South Australia, Adelaide – on thirtieth birthday

17 August 1964: Passed 5000 runs in Test matches – England v Australia, The Oval

16 November 1965: Passed 30,000 runs in first-class cricket – MCC v South Australia, Adelaide

2 September 1967: Led Kent to victory in the Gillette Cup final

12 July 1968: Became first cricketer to play in 100 Test matches and scored a century on the third day – England v Australia, Edgbaston

1970: Led Kent to victory in the County Championship

29 November 1970: Became leading run-scorer in all Test cricket – England v Australia, Brisbane

5 January 1971: Played in the first one-day international – England v Australia, Melbourne

1 January 1972: Awarded CBE, in New Year's Honours List

29 April 1972: Scored the first century in the Benson and Hedges Cup – 107*, Kent v Middlesex, Lord's

17 July 1973: Completed 40,000 runs in first-class cricket – Kent v Middlesex, Dover

13 February 1975: Final day of Test cricket – England v Australia, Melbourne

13 August 1976: Final day of first-class cricket – Kent v Surrey, Canterbury

1986: Became President of MCC

1989: Became Chairman of International Cricket Council

1 January 1992: Received knighthood in New Year's List

13 June 1997: Received life peerage in Queen's Birthday Honours List

BATTING AND FIELDING

FIRST-CLASS MATCHES

Season-by-season

	M	I	NO	Runs	HS	Avge	100	50	Ct
1950	4	7	0	104	27	14.86	–	–	2
1951	20	36	0	1189	143	33.03	2	6	11
1952	25	45	3	1391	101	33.12	1	12	9
1953	28	50	6	1917	154	43.57	4	13	16
1954	27	47	3	1577	140	35.84	2	10	14
1954–55	17	31	1	1019	110	33.97	3	5	13
1955	14	25	4	1038	139	49.43	4	4	6
1955–56	4	8	0	271	50	33.88	–	1	5
1956	28	45	4	1569	204*	38.27	3	7	21
1956–57	18	27	1	1035	173	39.81	2	8	28
1957	27	43	6	1917	165	51.81	5	14	33
1958	28	41	4	1437	139	38.84	3	11	35
1958–59	20	31	5	1209	117	46.50	4	5	23
1959	26	44	4	2008	250	50.20	6	8	24
1959–60	11	18	2	1014	173	63.38	5	2	4
1960	23	37	1	1218	155	33.83	3	4	17
1961	19	34	1	1730	156	52.42	7	8	20
1961–62	2	4	1	146	83	48.66	–	1	1
1962	24	38	3	1839	182	52.54	6	8	29
1962–63	16	29	5	1380	307	57.50	3	8	10
1963	9	17	3	429	107*	30.64	1	–	11
1963–64	4	5	2	315	151	105.00	2	–	5
1964	23	37	5	1763	117	55.09	4	12	28
1964–65	5	10	2	300	95	37.50	–	3	1
1965	27	43	10	2093	196*	63.42	5	12	38
1965–66	16	26	6	1076	108	53.80	2	8	12
1966	25	40	6	1081	100*	31.79	1	7	32
1967	27	38	5	1281	150	38.82	3	3	41
1967–68	9	15	1	871	148	62.21	4	4	11
1968	20	28	2	1093	129	42.04	5	3	22
1968–69	7	8	1	228	100	32.57	1	–	2
1969	5	5	1	29	14	7.25	–	–	2
1969–70	4	6	1	239	83	47.80	–	3	2
1970	21	35	6	1254	126	43.24	3	8	19
1970–71	11	18	1	511	101	30.06	1	3	3
1971	10	16	1	655	132	43.66	1	5	12
1972	19	33	8	1080	107	43.20	2	8	12
1973	21	33	8	1183	123*	47.32	2	8	19
1973–74	1	2	1	102	88	102.00	–	1	1
1974	21	30	3	1027	122	38.04	5	3	24
1974–75	7	12	1	284	78	25.82	–	1	4
1975	18	31	6	777	151*	31.08	2	4	14
1976	1	2	0	40	25	20.00	–	–	2
TOTALS	692	1130	134	42719	307	42.89	107	231	638

For Each Team

	M	I	NO	Runs	HS	Avge	100	50	Ct
Kent (in County Championship)	367	594	76	21270	250	41.06	49	116	384
Kent (in other matches)	35	57	9	2509	204*	52.27	9	12	22
Oxford University	40	70	5	2848	154	43.81	5	20	16
England (Tests)	114	188	15	7624	182	44.06	22	38	120
England XI	9	13	0	511	100	39.31	1	5	7
MCC (in UK)	18	31	4	1136	130	42.07	3	5	7
MCC (overseas)	77	120	17	4855	307	47.14	14	24	66
Gentlemen	11	19	2	481	106	28.29	2	2	5
Cavaliers	5	10	2	240	95	30.00	–	2	2
E. W. Swanton's XI	4	8	0	271	50	33.88	–	1	5
Duke of Norfolk's XI	3	4	1	221	83	73.66	–	3	1
International XI	2	4	1	146	83	48.66	–	1	1
L. E. G. Ames's XI	1	2	0	147	143	73.50	1	–	–
A. E. R. Gilligan's XI	1	1	0	34	34	34.00	–	–	–
D. R. Jardine's XI	1	1	0	7	7	7.00	–	–	–
T. N. Pearce's XI	1	2	1	57	39*	57.00	–	–	1
Commonwealth XI	1	2	0	78	66	39.00	–	1	–
Free Foresters	1	2	0	182	143	91.00	1	–	–
World XI	1	2	1	102	88	51.00	–	1	1
TOTALS	692	1130	134	42719	307	42.89	107	231	638

Note: 'England XI' includes matches for England against Rest of the World in 1970.

Summary

	M	I	NO	Runs	HS	Avge	100	50	Ct
Kent	402	651	85	23779	250	42.01	58	128	406
Oxford University	40	70	5	2848	154	43.81	5	20	16
England (Tests)	114	188	15	7624	182	44.06	22	38	120
England XI	9	13	0	511	100	39.31	1	5	7
MCC	95	151	21	5991	307	46.08	17	29	73
Gentlemen	11	19	2	481	106	28.29	2	2	5
Other Teams	21	38	6	1485	143	46.41	2	9	11
TOTALS	692	1130	134	42719	307	42.89	107	231	638

Against Each Team
(*excluding Test matches*)

a) In United Kingdom

	M	I	NO	Runs	HS	Avge	100	50	Ct
Derbyshire	21	31	2	997	74	34.38	–	10	22
Essex	23	35	3	1496	250	46.75	5	5	30
Glamorgan	17	25	2	521	75	22.65	–	5	22
Gloucestershire	25	33	8	1731	148	57.70	5	12	21
Hampshire	43	75	9	2740	156	41.51	6	15	48
Kent	2	3	0	219	112	73.00	1	2	–
Lancashire	27	45	4	1655	198	40.37	4	9	27
Leicestershire	21	35	2	1252	132	37.94	1	11	25
Middlesex	36	58	10	2042	155	42.54	3	13	20
Northamptonshire	22	38	4	1194	139	35.12	2	9	25
Nottinghamshire	22	35	6	1511	196	52.10	5	4	27
Somerset	15	23	6	786	150	46.24	4	–	13
Surrey	31	52	6	1779	154	38.67	4	9	20
Sussex	31	50	4	1995	140	43.37	5	10	30
Warwickshire	15	27	4	934	152	40.61	2	5	10
Worcestershire	25	42	7	1607	197	45.91	4	6	30
Yorkshire	26	43	4	1353	122	34.69	2	8	28
Cambridge University	10	17	1	887	204*	55.44	3	6	13
Oxford University	7	11	2	668	143	74.22	4	–	–
Players	9	17	2	374	106	24.93	2	–	5
Free Foresters	3	3	1	84	82*	42.00	–	1	1
MCC	2	4	0	52	44	13.00	–	–	1
Ireland	1	2	0	50	42	25.00	–	–	3
Australians	14	23	2	1062	151*	50.57	4	6	2
Indians	5	8	0	356	101	44.50	1	2	3
New Zealanders	4	6	1	311	96	62.20	–	3	2
Pakistanis	6	10	2	366	105	45.75	2	1	4
South Africans	5	9	1	221	71	31.57	–	1	2
West Indians	9	15	4	441	143	40.09	1	2	2
Commonwealth	3	4	0	257	100	64.25	1	2	–
Rest of the World	5	8	0	241	73	30.13	–	3	7

b) Overseas

	M	I	NO	Runs	HS	Avge	100	50	Ct
New South Wales	6	10	1	443	110	49.22	2	2	5
Queensland	2	4	0	20	12	5.00	–	–	2
South Australia	11	20	4	736	307	46.00	1	4	7
Tasmania	4	7	0	298	108	42.57	1	1	–
Victoria	6	10	0	508	101	50.80	1	5	6

	M	I	NO	Runs	HS	Avge	100	50	Ct
Western Australia	5	10	3	215	65*	30.71	–	1	2
Australian XI	2	3	0	102	88	34.00	–	1	1
Combined XI	6	10	3	465	100*	66.43	1	4	3
Ceylon	1	0	0	–	–	–	–	–	1
East and Central Zones	1	1	1	6	6*	–	–	–	1
Bengal Chief Minister's XI	1	2	0	78	66	39.00	–	1	–
Cricket Club of India President's XI	1	2	0	30	21	15.00	–	–	1
Canterbury	1	2	0	17	17	8.50	–	–	–
Northern and Central Districts	1	1	0	0	0	0.00	–	–	–
Otago	1	1	0	115	115	115.00	1	–	2
Otago Invitation XI	1	1	0	60	60	60.00	–	1	–
Wellington	2	3	0	165	117	55.00	1	–	5
President's XI	1	1	1	46	46*	–	–	–	–
Central Zone	1	2	1	69	36*	69.00	–	–	1
Board of Control XI	1	2	0	26	17	13.00	–	–	1
Pakistan Cricket Board XI	1	2	1	116	83	116.00	–	1	–
Pakistan XI	1	2	1	102	88	102.00	–	1	1
West Pakistan Governor's XI	1	0	0	–	–	–	–	–	
Border	1	1	0	62	62	62.00	–	1	4
Eastern Province	1	1	0	33	33	33.00	–	–	2
Griqualand West	1	1	0	52	52	52.00	–	1	4
Natal	2	3	0	109	76	36.33	–	1	2
North-Eastern Transvaal	1	1	1	3	3*	–	–	–	1
Orange Free State	1	1	0	173	173	173.00	1	–	–
Rhodesia	1	1	0	20	20	20.00	–	–	1
Transvaal	1	2	0	85	84	42.50	–	1	–
Western Province	2	3	0	66	48	22.00	–	–	–
South Africa XI	1	2	0	29	16	14.50	–	–	–
Combined Universities	1	1	0	72	72	72.00	–	1	4
Barbados	6	11	0	423	95	38.45	–	3	3
British Guiana	1	1	0	139	139	139.00	1	–	–
Jamaica	4	7	2	256	107	51.20	1	1	4
Jamaica XI	1	2	0	8	4	4.00	–	–	–
Leeward Islands	1	1	0	115	115	115.00	1	–	2
Trinidad	4	7	1	300	173	50.00	1	1	1
Windward Islands	3	5	2	119	81	39.66	–	1	4
West Indies XI	1	2	0	93	48	46.50	–	–	3
President's XI	1	1	0	139	139	139.00	1	–	1

Summary

Against British teams	434	709	87	25927	250	41.68	62	140	421
Against Overseas teams	144	233	32	9168	307	45.61	23	53	97
Test Matches	114	188	15	7624	182	44.06	22	38	120
TOTALS	692	1130	134	42719	307	42.89	107	231	638

On Each Ground
(including Test matches)

a) In United Kingdom and Eire
(listed by county)

	M	I	NO	Runs	HS	Avge	100	50	Ct
Burton-on-Trent	1	2	0	58	39	29.00	–	–	–
Chesterfield	2	3	0	83	69	27.66	–	1	3
Derby	4	5	0	221	74	44.20	–	3	1
Derbyshire	7	10	0	362	74	36.20	–	4	4
Clacton	4	8	0	135	46	16.87	–	–	6
Colchester	1	0	0	–	–	–	–	–	–
Ilford	2	3	0	108	85	36.00	–	1	1
Leyton	1	2	0	32	30	16.00	–	–	2
Romford	2	3	0	139	129	46.33	1	–	1
Westcliff-on-Sea	1	1	0	7	7	7.00	–	–	4
Essex	11	17	0	421	129	24.76	1	1	14
Swansea	7	12	0	240	75	20.00	–	2	15
Bristol	6	9	3	515	148*	85.83	1	5	6
Cheltenham	2	4	2	245	119*	122.50	1	2	1
Gloucester	1	2	0	40	21	20.00	–	–	–
Gloucestershire	9	15	5	800	148*	80.00	2	7	7
Basingstoke	1	1	0	3	3	3.00	–	–	1
Bournemouth	1	1	1	73	73*	–	–	1	1
Portsmouth	1	2	1	42	32*	42.00	–	–	–
Southampton	16	28	2	1175	131	45.19	3	7	24
Hampshire	19	32	4	1293	131	46.18	3	8	26

	M	I	NO	Runs	HS	Avge	100	50	Ct
Blackheath	14	23	3	970	250	48.50	2	5	11
Canterbury	72	121	15	4401	156	41.52	12	23	48
Dartford	13	21	2	836	145	44.00	3	3	14
Dover	24	42	7	1043	119*	29.80	2	5	21
Folkestone	20	30	4	808	70	31.08	–	5	28
Gillingham	9	17	2	688	115*	45.86	3	3	17
Gravesend	22	35	4	1680	198	54.19	4	11	18
Maidstone	27	41	8	1046	123*	31.70	2	5	19
Tunbridge Wells	27	48	6	1806	139	43.00	7	8	30
Kent	228	378	51	13278	250	40.61	35	68	206
Blackpool	1	1	0	56	56	56.00	–	1	2
Old Trafford	15	26	2	622	80	25.92	–	5	12
Southport	1	1	0	11	11	11.00	–	–	3
Lancashire	17	28	2	689	80	26.50	–	6	17
Hinckley	1	2	0	38	23	19.00	–	–	1
Leicester	9	14	0	409	87	29.21	–	3	13
Loughborough	1	2	0	83	81	41.50	–	1	1
Leicestershire	11	18	0	530	87	29.44	–	4	15
Lord's	58	93	11	3104	155	37.85	8	15	42
Northampton	7	13	0	350	76	26.92		3	12
Peterborough	1	1	1	80	80*	–	–	1	–
Rushden	1	2	1	99	68	99.00	–	1	1
Wellingborough	1	2	0	68	66	34.00	–	1	3
Northamptonshire	10	18	2	597	80*	37.31	–	6	16
Trent Bridge	19	32	15	1585	196	58.70	4	8	23
Worksop	1	1	0	0	0	0.00	–	–	1
Nottinghamshire	20	33	5	1585	196	56.61	4	8	24
Glastonbury	1	2	2	113	101*	–	1	–	–
Taunton	2	3	0	14	8	4.66	–	–	1
Weston-super-Mare	3	4	0	59	30	14.75	–	–	5
Somerset	6	9	2	186	101*	26.57	1	–	6
Guildford	1	2	0	79	79	39.50	–	1	–
The Oval	22	35	3	1630	182	50.94	5	6	21
Surrey	23	37	3	1709	182	50.26	5	7	21

	M	I	NO	Runs	HS	Avge	100	50	Ct
Eastbourne	1	1	0	7	7	7.00	–	–	–
Hastings	15	24	3	1022	143	48.66	3	5	11
Hove	5	6	0	233	77	38.83	–	2	3
Worthing	1	2	0	171	92	85.50	–	2	–
Sussex	22	33	3	1433	143	47.76	3	9	14
Coventry	1	2	0	109	80	54.50	–	1	–
Edgbaston	14	24	2	1213	159	55.14	4	6	14
Warwickshire	15	26	2	1322	159	55.08	4	7	14
Kidderminster	1	2	0	38	38	19.00	–	–	3
Stourbridge	1	2	0	201	197	100.50	1	–	1
Worcester	11	18	3	783	113	52.20	2	4	15
Worcestershire	13	22	3	1022	197	53.79	3	4	19
Bradford	4	4	0	231	85	57.75	–	2	4
Harrogate	1	2	0	38	37	19.00	–	–	2
Headingley	11	14	0	586	160	41.86	2	3	22
Scarborough	10	17	4	628	106	48.31	3	2	9
Yorkshire	26	37	4	1483	160	44.94	5	7	37
Fenner's	5	7	1	481	204*	80.17	2	2	7
The Parks	32	53	5	2134	143	44.46	4	13	6
Dublin	1	2	0	50	42	25.00	–	–	3

b) Overseas

(listed by country)

	M	I	NO	Runs	HS	Avge	100	50	Ct
Adelaide	16	30	4	1058	307	40.69	1	6	12
Brisbane	6	11	0	169	40	15.36	–	–	7
Hobart	3	4	0	159	70	39.75	–	1	1
Launceston	4	7	1	371	108	61.83	1	3	–
Melbourne	16	27	2	1260	113	50.40	4	8	17
Perth	10	20	5	552	100*	36.80	1	2	4
Sydney	14	23	2	836	110	39.81	3	5	11
Australia	69	122	14	4405	307	40.79	10	25	52
Colombo	1	0	0	–	–	–	–	–	–

	M	I	NO	Runs	HS	Avge	100	50	Ct
Bombay	1	2	0	30	21	15.00	–	–	1
Calcutta	2	4	1	198	107	66.00	1	1	3
Delhi	1	1	0	151	151	151.00	1	–	–
Kanpur	1	1	0	38	38	38.00	–	–	1
Nagpur	1	1	1	6	6*	–	–	–	1
India	6	9	2	423	151	60.43	2	1	6
Auckland	5	8	0	298	86	37.25	–	3	1
Christchurch	4	7	1	131	43	21.83	–	–	3
Dunedin	4	5	2	306	115	102.00	1	2	3
Hamilton	1	1	0	0	0	0.00	–	–	–
Wellington	4	4	2	339	128*	169.50	2	–	6
New Zealand	18	25	5	1074	128*	53.70	3	5	13
Bahawalpur	1	2	0	26	17	13.00	–	–	1
Dacca	1	1	0	7	7	7.00	–	–	–
Karachi	2	3	1	130	83	65.00	–	1	–
Lahore	2	4	1	214	100	71.33	1	1	1
Lyallpur	1	2	1	69	36*	69.00	–	–	1
Sahiwal	1	0	0	–	–	–	–	–	–
Pakistan	8	12	3	446	100	49.55	1	2	3
Benoni	1	1	1	3	3*	–	–	–	1
Bloemfontein	1	1	0	173	173	173.00	1	–	–
Cape Town	4	6	0	300	101	50.00	1	2	6
Durban	2	4	0	63	32	15.75	–	–	4
East London	1	1	0	62	62	62.00	–	1	4
Johannesburg	3	6	0	213	84	35.50	–	3	6
Kimberley	1	1	0	52	52	52.00	–	1	4
Pietmaritzburg	1	1	0	76	76	76.00	–	1	–
Port Elizabeth	2	3	0	44	33	14.66	–	–	2
Pretoria	1	2	0	29	16	14.50	–	–	–
Salisbury	1	1	0	20	20	20.00	–	–	1
Southern Africa	18	27	1	1035	173	39.81	2	8	28
Bridgetown	9	15	1	609	139	43.50	1	3	5
Georegetown	3	5	0	372	139	74.40	1	3	1
Grenada	1	2	1	21	17*	21.00	–	–	1
Kingston	5	10	0	480	114	48.00	3	1	5
Melbourne Park	1	1	0	19	19	19.00	–	–	–
Montego Bay	1	2	2	77	77*	–	–	1	–
Point-a-Pierre	1	1	0	173	173	173.00	1	–	–
Port-of-Spain	8	15	1	653	148	46.64	2	3	6
St John's	1	1	0	115	115	115.00	1	–	2
St Lucia	2	3	1	98	81	49.00	–	1	3
West Indies	32	55	6	2617	173	53.41	9	12	23

Summary

In United Kingdom	540	880	103	32719	250	42.11	80	178	513
Overseas	152	250	31	10000	307	45.66	27	53	125
TOTALS	692	1130	134	42719	307	42.89	107	231	638

Note: Lord Cowdrey holds the following first-class records for grounds in Kent:

Blackheath   – highest score
Canterbury   – most centuries (shared with N. E. Taylor and F. E. Woolley)
Dartford   – most runs; most centuries (shared with R. A. Woolmer).

Highest Innings

307	MCC v South Australia	Adelaide	1962–63
250	Kent v Essex	Blackheath	1959
204*	Kent v Cambridge University	Fenner's	1956
198	Kent v Lancashire	Gravesend	1959
197	Kent v Worcestershire	Stourbridge	1956
196*	Kent v Nottinghamshire	Trent Bridge	1965
182	ENGLAND v PAKISTAN	THE OVAL	1962
173	MCC v Orange Free State	Bloemfontein	1956–57
173	MCC v Trinidad	Point-a-Pierre	1959–60
165	Kent v Nottinghamshire	Trent Bridge	1957
160	ENGLAND v INDIA	HEADINGLEY	1959
159	ENGLAND v PAKISTAN	EDGBASTON	1962
156	Kent v Hampshire	Canterbury	1961
155	ENGLAND v SOUTH AFRICA	THE OVAL	1960
155	Kent v Middlesex	Lord's	1962
154	Oxford University v Surrey	The Oval	1953
154	ENGLAND v WEST INDIES	EDGBASTON	1957
152*	Kent v Warwickshire	Edgbaston	1965
152	ENGLAND v WEST INDIES	LORD'S	1957
151*	Kent v Australians	Canterbury	1975
151	ENGLAND v INDIA	DELHI	1963–64
150	Kent v Somerset	Gravesend	1967

Two Centuries In a Match

110	103	MCC v New South Wales	Sydney	1954–55
115*	103*	Kent v Essex	Gillingham	1955
149	121	Kent v Australians	Canterbury	1961

Notes: At 21 years and 327 days, Lord Cowdrey remains the youngest English batsman to score two centuries in a match in Australia.

Lord Cowdrey was the first batsman from any country to score a century in each innings of a match (other than in a Test match) against a touring team from Australia. The feat has since been repeated in England only by P. E. Richardson (for Kent in 1964).

Three Centuries in Four Innings

114 and 97 (ENGLAND v WEST INDIES KINGSTON); 115 (MCC v Leeward Islands, St John's); 139 (MCC v British Guiana, Georgetown) – 1959–60

130 AND 10 (MCC v Oxford University, Lord's); 149 and 121 (Kent v Australians, Canterbury) – 1961

83 and 109 (Kent v Lancashire, Gillingham); 99 and 100* (Kent v Hampshire, Canterbury); 101 and 42 (Kent v Middlesex, Canterbury) – 1964

Six Consecutive Half-Centuries

76 (Kent v Gloucestershire, Bristol); 81 and 70 (ENGLAND v NEW ZEALAND, EDGBASTON); 116* (Kent v Gloucestershire, Tunbridge Wells); 139 (Kent v Nottinghamshire, Blackheath); 65 (ENGLAND v NEW ZEALAND, LORD'S) 1958

Century Before Lunch

Day 2	165	Kent v Nottinghamshire	Trent Bridge	1957
Day 3	100*	Kent v Hampshire	Canterbury	1964

Carrying Bat Through a Completed Innings

65* out of 169	Kent v Gloucestershire	Cheltenham	1956

Methods of Dismissal

Caught	642	64.46%
Bowled	205	20.58%
LBW	99	9.94%
Run out	28	2.81%
Stumped	18	1.81%
Hit wicket	2	0.20%
Total	996	100.00%

Bowlers with Most Dismissals of Cowdrey

14 G. D. McKenzie (Leicestershire, Western Australia and Australia)
13 A. K. Davidson (New South Wales and Australia)
    D. Shackleton (Hampshire)
12 G. St. A. Sobers (Nottinghamshire, Barbados, West Indies and Rest of the World)
11 R. Benaud (New South Wales and Australia)
    K. C. Preston (Essex)
10 L. R. Gibbs (Warwickshire and West Indies)
    J. B. Statham (Lancashire)

Double-Century Partnerships

411	4th	P. B. H. MAY	ENGLAND v WEST INDIES	EDGBASTON	1957
344	5th	T. W. Graveney	MCC v South Australia	Adelaide	1962–63
326	2nd	A. S. M. Oakman	MCC v Orange Free State	Bloemfontein	1956–57
290	1st	G. PULLAR	ENGLAND v SOUTH AFRICA	THE OVAL	1960
281	1st	G. Pullar	MCC v British Guiana	Georgetown	1959–60
249	2nd	G. Boycott	MCC v President's XI	Bridgetown	1967–68
248	2nd	E. R. DEXTER	ENGLAND v PAKISTAN	THE OVAL	1962
242	4th	I. F. Pretlove	Kent v Essex	Blackheath	1959
241	5th	M. H. Denness	Kent v Somerset	Maidstone	1973
233*	4th	B. W. Luckhurst	Kent v Gloucestershire	Bristol	1962
227	5th	R. C. Wilson	Kent v Northamptonshire	Tunbridge Wells	1955
218	3rd	A. G. E. Ealham	Kent v Leicestershire	Dartford	1971
212	3rd	T. M. Allan	Oxford University v Sussex	The Parks	1954
210	3rd	A. H. Phebey	Kent v Nottinghamshire	Blackheath	1958
210	1st	R. Subba Row	MCC v Leeward Islands	St John's	1959–60
205	4th	P. B. H. May	Gentlemen v Players	Scarborough	1953
202*	6th	Asif Iqbal	Kent v Surrey	Maidstone	1973
201	4th	S. E. Leary	Kent v Sussex	Tunbridge Wells	1960
201	2nd	J. H. Edrich	MCC v Jamaica	Kingston	1967–68

Note: The two instances in 1959–60, as well as the two in 1973, were in successive innings.

The stand of 242 is the record for the fourth wicket at Blackheath;
Lord Cowdrey also holds the record for the fifth wicket at Dartford 167 with S.E. Leary against Worcestershire in 1965.

Two Century Partnerships In Same Innings

190	3rd R. C. Wilson, 157* 4th J. Pettiford			
	Kent v Cambridge University		Fenner's	1956
139	4th J. F. Pretlove, 100 5th T. Pettiford			
	Kent v Lancashire		Gravesend	1959
165	3rd A. H. Phebey, 242 4th J.F. Pretlove			
	Kent v Essex		Blackheath	1959
135	3rd P. E. Richardson, 119 6th A.L. Dixon			
	Kent v Hampshire		Canterbury	1961
166	2nd E. R. DEXTER, 107 3rd T.W. GRAVENEY			
	ENGLAND v PAKISTAN		EDGBASTON	1962
117	1st REV. D. S. SHEPPARD, 248 2nd E. R. DEXTER			
	ENGLAND v PAKISTAN		THE OVAL	1962

105　3rd　Rev. D. S. Sheppard,　344　5th　T. W. Graveney
　　　　　　MCC v South Australia　　　　　　Adelaide　　　1962–63

129　2nd　J. H. EDRICH,　101　3rd　K. F. BARRINGTON
　　　　　　ENGLAND v WEST INDIES　　　KINGSTON　　1967–68

133　3rd K. F. BARRINGTON,　113　6th　A. P. E. KNOTT
　　　　　　ENGLAND v WEST INDIES,　　PORT-OF-SPAIN 1967–68

Two Century Partnerships in Same Match With Same Partner

128 & 103	3rd	M. J. K. Smith	MCC v Australians	Lord's	1961
152 & 164	4th	S. E. Leary	Kent v Australians	Canterbury	1961

Best Position in National Batting Averages

1st – 1965; 3rd – 1955, 1957

1000 Runs in a Season on Most Occasions
(including seasons overseas)

28　W. G. Grace, F. E.Woolley
27　M. C. COWDREY, C. P. Mead
26　G. Boycott, J. B. Hobbs

Youngest Batsmen to Score 10,000 Runs

G. A. Hick	22 years 237 days
L. Hutton	23 years 6 days
M. C. COWDREY	23 years 240 days

Youngest Batsmen to Score 20,000 Runs

G. A. Hick	27 years 20 days
W. R. Hammond	28 years 12 days
M. C. COWDREY	28 years 137 days

40,000 Runs

Lord Cowdrey was the twelfth batsman to score 40,000 runs and the second, after T. W. Graveney, to do so entirely in the post-1945 era. At the end of his career he stood in tenth position for highest number of runs but a further three batsmen have joined the list and Cowdrey is now placed thirteenth.

Batsmen with 20,000 Runs and 50 Centuries for Kent

		M	I	NO	Runs	HS	Avge	100
F. E. Woolley	1906–38	764	1213	67	47868	270	41.77	122
H. T. W. Hardinge	1902–33	606	990	98	32549	263*	36.48	73
L. E. G. Ames	1926–51	430	717	64	28951	295	44.33	78
I. Seymour	1902–26	536	881	60	26818	218*	32.62	53
A. E. Fagg	1932–57	414	767	44	26072	269*	36.06	55
M. C. COWDREY	1950–76	402	651	85	23779	250	42.01	58

Notes: Lord Cowdrey is the only entirely post-1945 player to score 20,000 runs for Kent. B.W. Luckhurst (1958–76, 19086, 36.92, 39) is next.

W.H. Ashdown has also scored over 20,000 runs, but made only 38 centuries.

Most Runs in Australia by English Batsmen

		M	I	NO	Runs	HS	Avge
J. B. Hobbs	1907/08–28/29	57	95	5	4570	187	51.34
M. C. COWDREY	1954/55–74/75	69	122	14	4405	307	40.78
W. R. Hammond	1928/29–46/47	47	70	4	4340	251	65.75

Highest Scores in Australia by English Batsmen

307	M. C. COWDREY	MCC v South Australia	Adelaide	1962–63
305*	F. E. Woolley	MCC v Tasmania	Hobart	1911–12

100 Centuries

Lord Cowdrey was the sixteenth batsman to score 100 centuries. He was the second, after T.W. Graveney, to do so in an entirely post-1945 career and a further seven have since completed the feat. He was the third Kent player and a comparison with the two others follows.

		100s	Inns	Inns per 100	Year	Inns	Age	
F. E. Woolley	1906–38	145	1532	10.157	1929	1031	42 years	93 days
L. E. G. Ames	1926–51	102	951	9.32	1950	915	44 years	251 days
M. C. COWDREY	1950–76	107	1130	10.56	1973	1035	40 years	193 days

Note: Lord Cowdrey was the first batsman to score his 99th and 100th centuries in successive innings; the feat has since been equalled only by G. Boycott.

Most Catches for Kent
(by non-regular wicketkeepers)

	M	Ct
F. E. Woolley	764	773
J. Seymour	536	659
A. E. Fagg	414	411
M. C. COWDREY	402	406

TEST CRICKET
Series-by-Series

Date	Opponents	M	I	NO	Runs	HS	Avge	100	50	Ct
1954–55	Australia	5	9	0	319	102	35.44	1	2	4
1954–55	New Zealand	2	3	1	64	42	32.00	–	–	1
1955	South Africa	1	2	0	51	50	25.50	–	1	0
1956	Australia	5	8	0	244	81	30.50	–	2	3
1956–57	South Africa	5	10	0	331	101	33.10	1	3	10
1957	West Indies	5	6	0	435	154	72.50	2	2	8
1958	New Zealand	4	4	0	241	81	60.25	–	3	7
1958–59	Australia	5	10	1	391	100*	43.44	1	1	6
1958–59	New Zealand	2	2	0	20	15	10.00	–	–	2
1959	India	5	7	1	344	160	57.33	1	2	7
1959–60	West Indies	5	10	1	491	119	54.55	2	2	1
1960	South Africa	5	9	0	312	155	34.66	1	1	7
1961	Australia	4	8	0	168	93	21.00	–	1	4
1962	Pakistan	4	5	0	409	182	81.80	2	–	9
1962–63	Australia	5	10	1	394	113	43.77	1	3	6
1962–63	New Zealand	3	4	2	292	128*	146.00	1	1	1
1963	West Indies	2	4	1	39	19*	13.00	–	–	6
1963–64	India	3	4	1	309	151	103.00	2	–	4
1964	Australia	3	5	1	188	93*	47.00	–	1	2
1965	New Zealand	3	4	1	221	119	73.66	1	1	2
1965	South Africa	3	6	1	327	105	65.40	1	2	5
1965–66	Australia	4	6	1	267	104	53.40	1	1	5
1965–66	New Zealand	3	5	1	196	89*	49.00	–	2	2
1966	West Indies	4	8	0	252	96	31.50	–	2	3
1967	Pakistan	2	4	1	41	16	13.66	–	–	1
1967–68	West Indies	5	8	0	534	148	66.75	2	4	3
1968	Australia	4	6	0	215	104	35.83	1	–	4
1968–69	Pakistan	3	4	0	133	100	33.25	1	–	0
1970–71	Australia	3	4	0	82	40	20.50	–	–	3
1970–71	New Zealand	1	2	0	99	54	49.50	–	1	0
1971	Pakistan	1	2	0	50	34	25.00	–	–	1
1974–75	Australia	5	9	0	165	41	18.33	–	–	3
TOTALS		114	188	15	7624	182	44.06	22	38	120

Against Each Opponent

	M	I	NO	Runs	HS	Avge	100	50	Ct
Australia	43	75	4	2433	113	34.26	5	11	40
New Zealand	18	24	5	1133	128*	59.63	2	8	15
South Africa	14	27	1	1021	155	39.26	3	7	22
West Indies	21	36	2	1751	154	51.50	6	10	121
India	8	11	2	653	160	72.55	3	2	11
Pakistan	10	15	1	633	182	45.21	3	–	11
TOTALS	114	188	15	7624	182	44.06	22	38	120

On Each Ground

	M	I	NO	Runs	HS	Avge	100	50	Ct
Edgbaston	8	13	0	737	159	56.69	3	3	7
Headingley	8	9	0	392	160	43.55	1	2	16
Lord's	13	21	3	733	152	40.72	2	2	20
Old Trafford	7	13	0	364	80	28.00	–	4	5
The Oval	11	18	2	717	182	44.81	2	3	14
Trent Bridge	8	14	1	594	105	45.69	1	4	8
In England	55	88	6	3537	182	43.13	9	18	70
Adelaide	5	10	0	322	84	32.20	–	2	5
Brisbane	4	7	0	149	40	21.29	–	–	5
Melbourne	9	15	2	661	113	50.85	3	2	10
Perth	2	4	0	104	41	26.00	–	–	–
Sydney	7	12	1	382	100*	34.73	1	3	6
In Australia	27	48	3	1618	113	35.96	4	7	26
Auckland	5	7	0	298	86	42.57	–	3	1
Christchurch	3	5	1	114	43	28.50	–	–	3
Dunedin	2	3	2	131	89*	131.00	–	1	1
Wellington	1	1	1	128	128*	–	1	–	1
In New Zealand	11	16	4	671	128*	55.92	1	4	6
Cape Town	1	2	0	162	101	81.00	1	1	2
Durban	1	2	0	30	24	15.00	–	–	2
Johannesburg	2	4	0	128	59	32.00	–	2	6
Port Elizabeth	1	2	0	11	8	5.50	–	–	–
In South Africa	5	10	0	331	101	33.10	1	3	10
Bridgetown	2	3	1	47	30	23.50	–	–	1
Georgetown	2	4	0	233	82	58.25	–	3	1
Kingston	2	4	0	312	114	78.00	2	1	–
Port-of-Spain	4	7	0	433	148	61.86	2	2	2
In West Indies	10	18	1	1025	148	60.29	4	6	4

Calcutta	1	2	1	120	107	120.00	1	–	3
Delhi	1	1	0	151	151	151.00	1	–	–
Kanpur	1	1	0	38	38	38.00	–	–	1
In India	3	4	1	309	151	103.00	2	–	4
Dacca	1	1	0	7	7	7.00	–	–	–
Karachi	1	1	0	14	14	14.00	–	–	–
Lahore	1	2	0	112	100	56.00	1	–	–
In Pakistan	3	4	0	133	100	33.25	1	–	–

Summary

Overseas	59	100	9	4087	151	44.91	13	20	50
In England	55	88	6	3537	182	43.13	9	18	70
TOTALS	114	188	15	7624	182	44.06	221	38	120

In Each Batting Position

Pos	Inns	NO	Runs	HS	Avge	100	50
1	4	0	29	16	7.25	–	–
2	34	2	1498	182	46.81	5	5
3	36	1	1565	160	44.71	5	9
4	47	5	1608	119	38.29	4	8
5	54	6	2377	154	49.52	6	16
6	11	0	413	151	37.55	1	–
7	1	0	6	6	6.00	–	–
8	1	1	128	128*	–	1	–
TOTALS	188	15	7624	182	44.06	22	38

Note: Only three other players have batted in each of the top eight positions for England – A. C. MacLaren, G. Ulyett and F. E. Woolley.

Record with Opening Partners

As noted above, Lord Cowdrey opened the batting for England in 38 innings, and this was with nine different partners. His record with them is shown below.

	I	UP	Runs	HP	Avge	100	50
G. Pullar	15	1	906	290	64.71	2	3
P. E. Richardson	8	0	455	174	56.88	2	1
M. J. Stewart	3	0	102	59	34.00	–	1
R. Subba Row	4	0	112	57	28.00	–	1

Also: Rev. D.S. Sheppard 117, 5; G. Boycott 21, 3*; D. B. Close 16, 17; D. L. Amiss 4; D. Lloyd 62

UP = Undefeated Partnership   HD = Highest Partnership

Note: Of England pairs who have opened in at least ten innings together, only J. B. Hobbs and H. Sutcliffe have a better average than that of Lord Cowdrey and Pullar.

Under Each Captain
(in chronological order)

	M	I	NO	Runs	HS	Avge	100	50
L. Hutton	7	12	1	383	102	34.82	1	2
P. B. H. May	35	56	3	2373	160	44.77	6	15
M. C. COWDREY	27	45	0	1715	155	38.11	6	8
E. R. Dexter	16	27	5	1315	182	59.77	4	–
M. J. K. Smith	17	27	5	1401	151	63.68	5	7
D. B. Close	2	4	1	41	16	13.66	–	–
R. Illingworth	5	8	0	231	54	28.87	–	1
M. H. Denness	4	7	0	142	41	20.29	–	–
J. H. Edrich	1	2	0	23	22	11.50	–	–
TOTALS	114	188	15	7624	182	44.06	22	38

Notes: Lord Cowdrey was the first English batsman to score 2000 runs under one captain.

Lord Cowdrey is the only England captain to play under as many as eight other captains.

Centuries (22)

102	v	Australia	Melbourne	1954–55
101	v	South Africa	Cape Town	1956–57
154	v	West Indies	Edgbaston	1957
152	v	West Indies	Lord's	1957
100*	v	Australia	Sydney	1958–59
160	v	India	Headingley	1959
114	v	West Indies	Kingston	1959–60
119	v	West Indies	Port-of-Spain	1959–60
155	v	South Africa	The Oval	1960
159	v	Pakistan	Edgbaston	1962
182	v	Pakistan	The Oval	1962
113	v	Australia	Melbourne	1962–63
128*	v	New Zealand	Wellington	1962–63
107	v	India	Calcutta	1963–64
151	v	India	Delhi	1963–64
119	v	New Zealand	Lord's	1965
105	v	South Africa	Trent Bridge	1965
104	v	Australia	Melbourne	1965–66
101	v	West Indies	Kingston	1967–68
148	v	West Indies	Port-of-Spain	1967–68
104	v	Australia	Edgbaston	1968
100	v	Pakistan	Lahore	1968–69

258

Notes: Lord Cowdrey was the first batsman from any country to score at least one Test century against six different opponents. He remains the only English player to have completed the feat against each opponent at home *and* away.

Lord Cowdrey's six centuries against the West Indies are the most by an England batsman.

Lord Cowdrey reached his century at Edgbaston in 1957 in 434 minutes; at the time this was the third slowest for England.

Lord Cowdrey's 107 at Calcutta is the highest Test score by an England batsman at that venue. A similar record is 89* at Dunedin in 1965–66.

Seven Half-Centuries in Eight Consecutive Innings

154, 152, 55, 68, 2 v West Indies 1957; 81, 70, 65 v New Zealand 1958

Note: Lord Cowdrey also scored four consecutive half-centuries against the West Indies in 1967–68 – 148, 71, 59, 82.

Century Partnerships (42)

411	4th	P. B. H. May	West Indies	Edgbaston	1957
290	1st	G. Pullar	South Africa	The Oval	1960
248	2nd	E. R. Dexter	Pakistan	The Oval	1962
193	4th	K. F. Barrington	India	Headingley	1959
191	2nd	E. R. Dexter	West Indies	Port-of-Spain	1959–60
182	4th	P. B. H. May	Australia	Sydney	1958–59
177	1st	G. Pullar	West Indies	Kingston	1959–60
175	3rd	E. R. Dexter	Australia	Melbourne	1962–63
174	1st	P. E. Richardson	Australia	Old Trafford	1956
174	7th	T. G. Evans	West Indies	Lord's	1957
172	2nd	G. Boycott	West Indies	Georgetown	1967–68
169	4th	T. W. Graveney	West Indies	Trent Bridge	1966
166	2nd	E. R. Dexter	Pakistan	Edgbaston	1962
166	4th	K. F. Barrington	New Zealand	Auckland	1962–63
163*	9th	A. C. Smith	New Zealand	Wellington	1962–63
151	1st	P. E. Richardson	Australia	Trent Bridge	1956
138	6th	J. M. Parks	Australia	Melbourne	1965–66
136	4th	K. F. Barrington	New Zealand	Edgbaston	1965
135	4th	K. F. Barrington	South Africa	The Oval	1965
134	3rd	K. F. Barrington	West Indies	Port-of-Spain	1967–68
133	3rd	K. F. Barrington	West Indies	Port-of-Spain	1967–68
131	2nd	G. Pullar	India	Old Trafford	1959
129	2nd	J. H. Edrich	West Indies	Kingston	1967–68
127	6th	A. P. E. Knott	West Indies	Georgetown	1967–68
126*	5th	K. F. Barrington	Australia	The Oval	1964

121	4th	P. E. Richardson	South Africa	Johannesburg	1956–57
121	4th	P. B. H. May	New Zealand	Edgbaston	1953
118	5th	P. B. H. May	Australia	Melbourne	1958–59
118	2nd	W. E. Russell	New Zealand	Auckland	1965–66
118	2nd	G. Boycott	West Indies	Port-of-Spain	1967–68
117	1st	Rev. D. S. Sheppard	Pakistan	The Oval	1962
116	4th	P. B. H. May	Australia	Sydney	1954–55
115	5th	P. H. Parfitt	India	Delhi	1963–64
113	6th	A. P. E. Knott	West Indies	Port-of-Spain	1967–68
108	4th	P. B. H. May	South Africa	Old Trafford	1955
108	2nd	J. H. Edrich	Australia	Edgbaston	1968
107	3rd	T. W. Graveney	Pakistan	Edgbaston	1962
105	5th	M. J. K. Smith	New Zealand	Lord's	1965
105	4th	J. H. Edrich	Australia	Melbourne	1965–66
104	4th	P. E. Richardson	New Zealand	Edgbaston	1958
104	3rd	Rev. D. S. Sheppard	Australia	Brisbane	1962–63
101	3rd	K. F. Barrington	West Indies	Kingston	1967–68

Notes: The stand of 411 is still the world Test record for the fourth wicket.

The stand of 163* is England's ninth-wicket record.

The stand of 248 is England's second-wicket record against Pakistan.

The stand of 172 is England's best partnership for any wicket at Georgetown and this also applies to a stand at Dunedin of 81 with J. T. Murray for the sixth wicket in 1965–66.

Only G. Boycott (48) has taken part in more century partnerships for England than Lord Cowdrey.

Summary

13 for 4th wkt; 9 for 2nd; 6 for 3rd; 5 for 1st; 4 for 5th; 3 for 6th; 1 for each of 7th and 9th.

  8 with Barrington
  6 with May
  4 with Dexter and Richardson
  3 with Edrich and Pullar
  2 with Boycott, Graveney, Knott and Sheppard
  1 with Evans, Parfitt, Parks, Russell, A. C. Smith and M. J. K. Smith

13 against West Indies
10 against Australia
  8 against New Zealand
  4 against Pakistan and South Africa
  3 against India

20 in England (7 at Edgbaston, 5 at The Oval, 31 at Old Trafford, 2 at Lord's and
Trent Bridge and 1 at Headingley)
10 in West Indies (5 at Port-of-Spain, 3 at Kingston and 2 at Georgetown)
 7 in Australia (4 at Melbourne, 2 at Sydney and 1 at Brisbane)
 3 in New Zealand (2 at Auckland and 1 at Wellington)
 1 in India (Delhi) and South Africa (Johannesburg)

Methods of Dismissal

Caught	116	67.0%
Bowled	31	17.9%
Lbw	19	11.0%
Run Out	5	2.9%
Stumped	2	1.2%
TOTALS	173	100.0%

For the sake of comparison, the percentages for the main three methods of
dismissal for four of Lord Cowdrey's contemporaries are:

	Barrington	Dexter	Graveney	May
Caught	57.8%	56.4%	60.9%	67.0%
Bowled	18.1%	30.9%	23.6%	23.7%
Lbw	20.7%	5.3%	8.2%	8.2%

Note: Most batsmen are caught in 50–60% of their innings. A figure of 67% is
exceptional.

Bowlers with Most Dismissals

9 A. K. Davidson, G. D. McKenzie (both Aust)
8 N. A. T. Adcock (SA), R. Benaud (Aust), L.R. Gibbs (WI)
7 W. W. Hall (WI)
5 G. St. A. Sobers (WI), H. J. Tayfield (SA), J.R. Thomson (Aust)

Highest Run Aggregate by English Batsmen
(as at 31 March 1998)

		M	I	NO	Runs	HS	Avge	100	50
G. A. Gooch	1975–94/95	118	215	6	8900	333	42.58	20	46
D. I. Gower	1978–92	117	204	18	8231	215	44.25	18	39
G. Boycott	1964–81/82	108	193	23	8114	246*	47.72	22	42
M. C. COWDREY	1954/55–74/75	114	188	15	7624	182	44.06	22	38
W. R. Hammond	1927/28–46/47	85	140	16	7249	336*	58.45	22	24
L. Hutton	1937–54/55	79	138	15	6971	364	56.67	19	33
K. F. Barrington	1955–68	82	131	15	6806	256	58.67	20	35

Notes: Lord Cowdrey overtook Hammond on 29 November 1970 and remained the leading run-scorer in all Test cricket until overtaken by G. St. A. Sobers (West Indies) on 26 March 1972. Lord Cowdrey thus held the record for one year and 119 days.

The next two tables are designed to show the consistency of Lord Cowdrey's Test career.

Home and Away Records of English Batsmen with 6000 Test Runs

	Home		Away		Difference
	Runs	Avge	Runs	Avge	in average
Boycott	4356	48.40	3758	46.97	1.43
COWDREY	3537	43.13	4087	44.91	1.78
Hutton	3930	57.79	3041	55.29	2.50
Gower	4454	42.82	3777	46.06	3.24
Gooch	5917	46.23	2983	36.83	9.40
Hammond	3004	50.06	4245	66.32	16.26
Barrington	3347	50.71	3459	69.18	18.47

Records of English Batsmen with 6000 Test Runs Compared by Age

	Before 30		After 30		Difference
	Runs	Avge	Runs	Avge	in average
COWDREY	3850	42.31	3774	46.02	3.71
Gower	6553	45.50	1678	39.95	5.55
Boycott	2609	42.77	5505	50.50	7.73
Hutton	1352	64.38	5619	55.09	9.29
Gooch	2540	35.77	6360	46.09	10.32
Hammond	3731	66.63	3518	51.74	14.89
Barrington	1056	44.00	5750	62.50	18.50

It is interesting to note that Lord Cowdrey's average improved with age and this is clearly shown in the following table which outlines each 1000-run stage in his career.

Runs	Tests	Average
1000	18	32.55
2000	31	41.83
3000	47	42.11
4000	59	43.71
5000	73	45.84
6000	86	47.66
7000	100	46.96

Most Catches in Test Matches
(as at 31 March 1998)

			M	Ct
A. R. Border	Aust	1978/79–93/94	156	156
G. S. Chappell	Aust	1970/71–83/84	87	122
I. V. A. Richards	WI	1974/75–91	121	122
I. T. Botham	Eng	1977–92	102	120
M. C. COWDREY	Eng	1954/55–74/75	114	120
R. B. Simpson	Aust	1957/58–77/78	62	110
W. R. Hammond	Eng	1927/28–46/47	85	110

DOMESTIC LIMITED-OVERS MATCHES

Season-by-Season

	M	I	NO	Runs	HS	Avge	100	50	Ct
1963	1	1	0	31	31	31.00	–	–	–
1964	1	1	0	25	25	25.00	–	–	–
1965	1	1	0	3	3	3.00	–	–	2
1966	2	2	0	128	116	64.00	1	–	1
1967	4	4	0	145	78	36.25	–	2	1
1968	1	1	0	9	9	9.00	–	–	–
1969	4	3	1	124	67	62.00	–	1	1
1970	14	13	2	263	83*	23.91	–	1	11
1971	9	9	1	251	98	31.38	–	3	8
1972	9	6	1	175	107*	35.00	1	–	1
1973	8	5	1	64	29*	16.00	–	–	3
1974	16	15	4	369	115	33.55	1	1	6
1975	10	10	1	277	59	30.77	–	3	2
TOTALS	80	71	11	1864	116	31.07	3	11	36

In Each Competition

	M	I	NO	Runs	HS	Avge	100	50	Ct
Gillette Cup	22	21	2	729	116	38.37	2	4	12
John Player League	53	45	6	916	67	23.49	–	6	22
Benson and Hedges Cup	5	5	3	219	107*	109.50	1	1	2
TOTALS	80	71	11	1864	116	31.07	3	11	36

By Venue

	M	I	NO	Runs	HS	Avge	100	50	Ct
Home (in Kent)	37	34	6	1025	115	36.61	1	8	17
Away (incl. neutral)	43	37	5	839	116	26.22	2	3	19
TOTALS	80	71	11	1864	116	31.07	3	11	36

Centuries

116	Kent v Suffolk	Ipswich	GC	1966
107*	Kent v Middlesex	Lord's	BHC	1972
115	Kent v Durham	Canterbury	GC	1974

Note: The innings of 107* was the first century in the Benson and Hedges Cup; it came in the first such game to be played at Lord's.

Century Partnerships

204	2nd	B. W. Luckhurst	Kent v Durham	GC	1974
133	3rd	B. W. Luckhurst	Kent v Worcestershire	GC	1970
103	2nd	D. Nicholls	Kent v Gloucestershire	JPL	1971

Note: The stand of 204 is the record for Kent for any wicket in the Gillette Cup/NatWest Trophy *and* the record for the second wicket for Kent in any of the three competitions.

ONE-DAY INTERNATIONALS

Lord Cowdrey played in only one of these matches. It was the very first such game – for England agairst Australia at Melbourne on 5 January 1971. He scored one run and took no catches.

BOWLING

FIRST-CLASS MATCHES

Season-by-Season

	Balls	Runs	Wkts	Avge	BB
1950	96	57	1	57.00	1-37
1951	615	391	9	43.44	4-22
1952	1230	816	11	74.18	2-31
1953	677	447	11	40.64	4-30
1954	642	388	4	97.00	1-5
1954–55	68	71	1	71.00	1-25
1955	132	117	3	39.00	3-64
1955–56	18	6	0	–	–
1956	6	3	0	–	–
1957	232	186	8	23.25	4-109
1958	19	23	1	23.00	1-13
1958–59	51	42	1	42.00	1-17
1959	21	18	0	–	–
1959–60	18	36	0	–	–
1960	42	24	2	12.00	1-5
1961	8	7	0	–	–
1961–62	18	12	0	–	–
1962	30	24	1	24.00	1-23
1963–64	30	34	0	–	–
1964	39	45	0	–	–
1964–65	6	6	0	–	–
1965	5	12	0	–	–
1965–66	8	7	0	–	–
1966	12	13	0	–	–
1967	42	30	0	–	–
1967–68	6	1	0	–	–
1968	18	24	0	–	–
1968–69	6	6	0	–	–
1970	66	47	1	47.00	1-44
1970–71	192	127	3	42.33	2-46
1971	24	9	0	–	–
1972	18	18	0	–	–
1973	114	71	1	71.00	1-17
1973–74	42	66	2	33.00	2-34
1974	90	54	2	27.00	1-14
1974–75	32	27	2	13.50	2-27
1975	84	55	1	55.00	1-24
1976	18	9	0	–	–
TOTALS	4775	3329	65	51.22	4-22

For Each Team

	Balls	Runs	Wkts	Avge	BB
Kent	1834	1285	27	47.59	4-22
Oxford University	1691	1046	14	74.71	4-30
Others	1250	998	24	41.58	3-64
TOTALS	4775	3329	65	51.22	4-22

Best Performances

7.1-2-22-4	Kent v Surrey	Blackheath	1951
10.5-2-30-4	Oxford University v Derbyshire	The Parks	1953
17-0-109-4	England XI v Commonwealth XII	Hastings	1957

TEST CRICKET
Series-by-Series

		Balls	Runs	Wkts
1958–59	Australia	11	9	0
1959–60	West Indies	12	19	0
1960	South Africa	6	4	0
1962	Pakistan	6	1	0
1963–64	India	30	34	0
1967–68	West Indies	6	1	0
1970–71	Australia	48	36	0
TOTALS		119	104	0

LIMITED-OVERS MATCHES
(all in Gillette Cup)

Season-by-Season

	Balls	Runs	Wkts	Avge	BB
1964	6	0	1	0.00	1-0
1966	6	7	1	7.00	1-7
1974	23	19	1	19.00	1-19
TOTALS	35	26	3	8.66	1-0

CAPTAINCY

RECORD AS TEST CAPTAIN

Series-by-Series

		M	W	L	D
1959	India	2	2	–	–
1959–60	West Indies	2	–	–	2
1960	South Africa	5	3	–	2
1961	Australia	2	–	1	1
1962	Pakistan	1	1	–	–
1966	West Indies	3	–	2	1
1967–68	West Indies	5	1	–	4
1968	Australia	4	1	1	2
1968–69	Pakistan	3	–	–	3
TOTALS		27	8	4	15

Against Each Opponent

Australia	6	1	2	3
India	2	2	–	–
Pakistan	4	1	–	3
South Africa	5	3	–	2
West Indies	10	1	2	7
TOTALS	27	8	4	15

In Each Venue

England	17	7	4	6
Pakistan	3	–	–	3
West Indies	7	1	–	6
TOTALS	27	8	4	15

Tosses

1) Lord Cowdrey won 17 of his 27 tosses.

2) Lord Cowdrey won all five tosses against South Africa in 1960; he is only the second England captain (after F. S. Jackson against Australia in 1905) to win all five tosses in a five-match series although K. W. R. Fletcher won five successive tosses in a six-match series against India in 1981–82.

3) Lord Cowdrey won nine consecutive tosses from 1959/60 to 1961 – a Test record for any country.

267

Father and Son as England. Captains

F. T. Mann (5 Tests in 1922–23) and F. G. Mann (7 Tests 1948/49 – 1949)
M. C. COWDREY (27 Tests 1959–1968/69) and C. S. Cowdrey (1 Test in 1988)

RECORD AS COUNTY CAPTAIN

County Championship

Best positions under Lord Cowdrey's leadership:

Champions – 1970   Runners-up – 1967, 1968

Notes: In Lord Cowdrey's first seven seasons as captain, Kent finished only once in the top eight.

In Lord Cowdrey's last eight seasons as captain, Kent finished only once outside the top eight.

Limited-Overs Competitions

Gillette Cup: winners, 1967
John Player League runners-up, 1970

Note: Lord Cowdrey led Kent in 15 matches in the Gillette Cup/NatWest Trophy and this is a record for the county, shared with M.H. Denness.

Longest-Serving County Captains

28 seasons	W. G. Grace	Gloucestershire	1871–98
	Lord Hawke	Yorkshire	1883–1910
21 seasons	W. Clarke	Nottinghamshire	1835–55
17 seasons	C. E. de Trafford	Leicestershire	1890–1906
16 seasons	E. Napper	Sussex	1847–62
	A.W. Carr	Nottinghamshire	1919–34
15 seasons	M. C. COWDREY	Kent	1957–71
	Lord Harris	Kent	1875–89
	E. B. Rowley	Lancashire	1866–79
	G. Parr	Nottinghamshire	1856–70

Note: Lord Cowdrey is thus the longest-serving county captain since 1946. His nearest rival is D. B. Close (14 seasons – 8 with Yorkshire and 6 with Somerset). Two players each led one county in 13 seasons – K. J. Barnett (Derbyshire 1983–95) and K. W. R. Fletcher (Essex 1974–85 and 1988).

MISCELLANY

Most Test Appearances for England

			Tests missed during career	% played
118	G. A. Gooch	1975–1994/95	84	58.4%
117	D. I. Gower	1978–1992	33	78.0%
114	M. C. COWDREY	1954/55-1974/75	80	58.8%
108	G. Boycott	1964–1981/82	64	62.8%
102	I. T. Botham	1977–1992	54	65.40%

Note: Gooch received a three-year ban (32 Tests) for playing in South Africa.

G.A. Gooch is the only player, other than Lord Cowdrey, to captain England in his 100th Test.

Lord Cowdrey was the first batsman to score a century in his 100th Test. This feat has since been equalled by:

Javed Miandad	145	Pakistan v India	Lahore	1989–90
C. G. Greenidge	149	West Indies v England	St John's	1989-90

but neither of these players, unlike Lord Cowdrey, were captain in the relevant match.

There were only 9 years and 289 days between the last day of Lord Cowdrey's final Test and the Test début of his son, C. S. Cowdrey. In the entire history of Test cricket there has been only one such shorter interval – 3 years and 356 days between B. L. Cairns and C. L. Cairns of New Zealand.

Pat Pocock is the only player who played in England Test teams with both Lord Cowdrey and Chris Cowdrey.

In the 1953 Varsity match Lord Cowdrey scored a century (116) and a duck; the only other batsman to record this feat in the same fixture, for Oxford, was H. K. Foster in 1895 (0 and 121).

In 1946, at the age of 13, Lord Cowdrey became the youngest cricketer, by repute, to play at Lord's. Appearing, in a schools match, for Tonbridge v Clifton, he scored 75 and 44 and had bowling figures of 3-58 and 5-59, these being the major performances in his side's victory by two runs.

Limited-overs awards (all for Kent):

Gillette Cup (Man of the Match)			Benson and Hedges Cup (Gold Award)		
v Suffolk	Ipswich	1966	v Middlesex	Lord's	1972
v Essex	Brentwood	1967			
v Sussex	Canterbury	1967			
v Northamptonshire	Canterbury	1971			
v Durham	Canterbury	1974			

Note: Lord Cowdrey's five awards in the Gillette Cup/NatWest Trophy are a record for Kent in that competition (B. W. Luckhurst has four).

When Lord Cowdrey (a right-hander from Kent) opened the England innings with Geoff Pullar (a left-hander from Lancashire) against South Africa at The Oval in 1960, both batsmen scored centuries in the second innings. The next time that this happened for England was in 1983 against New Zealand, again at The Oval, again in the second innings, and the two batsman were Chris Tavaré (a right-hander from Kent) and Graeme Fowler (a left-hander from Lancashire)!

Bibliography

The following books were consulted, in addition to countless copies of *Wisden*:

Arlott, John and Trueman, Fred, *Arlott and Trueman on Cricket* (BBC, 1977)

Arlott, John, *100 Greatest Batsmen* (MacDonald Queen Anne Press, 1986)

Bailey, Jack, *Conflicts in Cricket* (The Kingswood Press, 1989)

Bailey, Trevor, *The Greatest of My Time* (Eyre and Spottiswoode, 1968)

Bannister, Jack, *The Innings of My Life* (Headline, 1993)

Bannister, Jack, *Tampering with Cricket* (Collins Willow, 1996)

Barker, J. S., *Summer Spectacular* (Collins, 1963)

Barker, J. S., *In the Main* (Pelham Books, 1968)

Barrington, Ken, *Running into 100s* (Stanley Paul, 1963)

Bedser, Alec, *The Fight for The Ashes 1958–9* (George G. Harrap and Co, 1959)

Bedser, Alec, *Twin Ambitions* (Stanley Paul, 1986)

Benaud, Richie, *On Reflection* (Willow Books, 1984)

Boycott, Geoff, *Boycott: The Autobiography* (Corgi Books, 1987)

Chalke, Stephen, *Runs in the Memory: County Cricket in the 1950s* (Fairfield Books, 1998)

Clarke, John, *With England in Australia: The MCC Tour 1965–6* (Stanley Paul, 1966)

Clarke, John and Scovell, Brian, *Everything That's Cricket* (Stanley Paul, 1966)

Close, Brian, *The MCC Tour of West Indies, 1968* (Stanley Paul, 1968)

Close, Brian, *I Don't Bruise Easily* (MacDonald and James London, 1978)

Compton, Denis, *End of an Innings* (The Pavilion Library, 1986)

Corbett, Ted, Cricket on the Run (Stanley Paul, 1990)

Cowdrey, Christopher and Smith, Jonathan, *Good Enough?* (Pelham, 1985)

Cowdrey, Colin, *Time for Reflection* (Frederick Muller, 1961)

Cowdrey, Colin, *Tackle Cricket This Way* (Stanley Paul, 1964)

Cowdrey, Colin, *The Incomparable Game* (Hodder & Stoughton, 1970)

Cowdrey Colin, *MCC, The Autobiography of a Cricketer* (Hodder & Stoughton, 1976)

Denness, Mike, *I Declare* (Arthur Barker, 1977)

Dexter, Ted, *Ted Dexter Declares* (Sportsmans Book Club, 1966)

Dexter, Ted, *From Bradman to Boycott* (Queen Anne Press, 1981)

D'Oliveira, Basil, *The D'Oliveira Affair* (Collins, 1969)

D'Oliveira, Basil, *Time to Declare* (J. M. Dent, 1980)

Evans, Godfrey, *The Gloves are Off* (Hodder & Stoughton, 1960)

Favell, Les, *By Hook or by Cut* (Investigator Press, 1970)

Fingleton, Jack, *Four Chukkas to Australia* (Heinemann, 1960)

Fletcher, Keith, *Captain's Innings* (Stanley Paul, 1983)

Gibson, Alan, *The Cricket Captains of England* (Cassell London, 1979)

Graveney, Tom, *Tom Graveney on Cricket* (Frederick Muller Ltd, London, 1965)

Graveney, Tom, *Cricket over Forty* (Pelham Books, 1970)

Graveney, Tom, *The Heart of Cricket* (Arthur Barker Ltd, 1983)

Gregory, Kenneth (ed), *From Grace to Botham: Fifty Master Cricketers from The Times* (Times Books Ltd, 1989)

Greig, Tony, *My Story* (Stanley Paul, 1980)

Griffith, Charlie, *Chucked Around* (Pelham Books, 1970)

Haigh, Gideon, *The Summer Game* (Text Publishing, 1997)

Hawke, Neil, *Bowled Over* (Rigby, 1982)

Hill, Alan, *Les Ames* (Christopher Helm, 1990)

Hill, Alan, *Peter May* (André Deutsch, 1996)

Howat, Gerald, *Len Hutton: The Biography* (Mandarin, 1988)

Hutton, Len, *Fifty Years in Cricket* (Stanley Paul and Co, 1984)

Illingworth, Ray, *Yorkshire and Back* (Queen Anne Press, 1980)

Johnston, Brian, *It's a Funny Game* (W. H. Allen, 1978)

Johnson, Ian, *Cricket at the Crossroads* (Cassell and Co Ltd, London, 1957)

Knott, Alan, *Stumper's View* (Stanley Paul, 1972)

Knott, Alan, *It's Knott Cricket* (Macmillan, 1985)

Laker, Jim, *Spinning Round the World*, (Frederick Muller Ltd, 1957)

Laker, Jim, *Over to Me*, (Frederick Muller Ltd, 1960)

Lee, Alan, *Lord Ted: The Dexter Enigma* (Gollancz/Witherby, 1995)

Lewis, Tony, *A Summer of Cricket* (Pelham Books, 1975)

Lindwall Ray, *The Challenging Tests* (Pelham Books, 1961)

McGlew, Jackie, *Cricket for South Africa* (Hodder & Stoughton, 1961)

Mackay, Ken, *Slasher Opens Up* (Pelham Books, 1964)

Mackay, Ken, *Quest for the Ashes* (Pelham Books, 1966)

McLean, Roy, *Pitch and Toss* (Howard Timmins Ltd, 1957)

Manley, Michael, *A History of West Indian Cricket* (André Deutsch, 1987)

Marquesee, Mike, *Anyone but England* (Verso, 1994)

Marshall, Michael, *Gentlemen and Players* (Grafton Books, 1987)

Martin-Jenkins, Christopher, *Assault on The Ashes* (MacDonald and Co, 1975)

Martin-Jenkins, Christopher, *Oxford World Cricketers: A Biographical Dictionary* (OUP, 1996)

May, Peter, *A Game Enjoyed* (Stanley Paul, 1985)

Meckiff, Ian, *Thrown Out* (Stanley Paul and Co, 1961)

Moore, Dudley, *The History of Kent Cricket* (Christopher Helm, 1988)

Mosey, Don, *Jim Laker: Portrait of a Legend* (MacDonald Queen Anne Press, 1989)

Murphy, Pat, *The Centurions* (J. M. Dent and Sons, 1983)

O'Neill, Norman, *Ins and Outs* (Pelham Books, 1969)

Pawson, Tony, *Runs and Catches* (Faber &Faber Ltd, 1980)

Peel, Mark, *England Expects: A Biography of Ken Barrington* (The Kingswood Press, 1992)

Peel, Mark, *Cricketing Falstaff: A Biography of Colin Milburn* (André Deutsch, 1998)

Pocock, Pat, *Percy* (Clifford Frost Publications, 1987)

Redpath, Ian, *Always Reddy* (Gary Sparke, 1976)

Roebuck, Peter, *Great Innings* (Guild Publishing, 1990)

Robinson, Ray, *The Wildest Tests* (Pelham Books, 1972)

Ross, Alan, *Australia 55* (Michael Joseph, 1955)

Ross, Alan, *Cape Summer* (Hamish Hamilton, London, 1957)

Ross, Alan, *Through the Caribbean* (Hamish Hamilton, London, 1960)

Sandford, Christopher, *Godfrey Evans* (Simon and Schuster, 1990)

Sandford, Christopher, *Tom Graveney* (H. F. and G. Witherby Ltd, 1992)

Sheppard, David, *Parson's Pitch* (Hodder & Stoughton, 1964)

Simpson, Bobby, *Captain's Story* (Stanley Paul, 1966)

Snow, John, *Cricket Rebel* (Hamlyn, 1976)

Sobers, Gary, *King Cricket* (Pelham Books, 1967)

Sobers, Gary, *20 Years at the Top* (Pan Books in association with Macmillan, 1988)

Statham, Brian, *Flying Bails* (Stanley Paul, 1961)

Statham, Brian, *A Spell at the Top* (Souvenir Press, 1969)

Stevenson, Mike, *Illi* (Midas Books, 1978)

Swanton, E. W., *West Indies Revisited* (William Heinemann Ltd, 1961)

Swanton, E. W., *Cricket from all Angles* (Michael Joseph, 1968)

Swanton, E. W., *Sort of a Cricket Person* (Collins, 1972)

Swanton, E. W., *Swanton in Australia: With MCC 1946–75* (Collins, 1975)

Swanton, E. W., *Follow On* (Collins, 1977)

Swanton, E. W., *Gubby Allen: Man of Cricket* (Hutchison/Stanley Paul, 1985)

Swanton, E. W. (George Plumptre ed), *The 1980s Observed* (Willow Books/Harper Collins, 1990)

Tennant, Ivo, *The Cowdreys: Portrait of a Cricket Family* (Simon and Schuster, 1990)

Tyson, Frank, *A Typhoon Called Tyson* (William Heinemann Ltd, 1960)

Underwood, Derek, *Beating the Bat* (Stanley Paul, 1975)

Waite, John, *Perchance to Bowl* (Nicholas Kaye, London, 1961)

Walker, Max, *Tangles* (Gary Sparke, 1976)

Walters, Doug, *Looking for Runs* (Pelham Books, 1971)

West, Peter, *Denis Compton: Cricketing Genius* (Stanley Paul, 1989)

Whitington, R. S., *Captains Outrageous: Cricket in the 1970s* (Hutchinson of Australia, 1972)

Wilde, Simon, *Letting Rip* (H. F. and G. Witherby, 1994)

Wilson, Don, *Mad Jack* (The Kingswood Press, 1992)

Wingfield Digby, Andrew, *A Loud Appeal* (Hodder & Stoughton, 1988)

Woolmer, Bob, *An Autobiography* (Arthur Barker Ltd, 1984)

Wright, Graeme, *Betrayal: The Struggle for Cricket's Soul* (H. F. and G. Witherby, 1993)

Index